A Dangerous Mind

A Dangerous Mind

The Ideas and Influence of Delbert L. Wiens

Edited by W. Marshall Johnston
and Daniel J. Crosby

Artwork by
Josiah Muster

WIPF & STOCK · Eugene, Oregon

A DANGEROUS MIND
The Ideas and Influence of Delbert L. Wiens

Copyright © 2015 Wipf and Stock Publishers. All rights reserved. Except for brief quotations in critical publications or reviews, no part of this book may be reproduced in any manner without prior written permission from the publisher. Write: Permissions, Wipf and Stock Publishers, 199 W. 8th Ave., Suite 3, Eugene, OR 97401.

Wipf & Stock
An Imprint of Wipf and Stock Publishers
199 W. 8th Ave., Suite 3
Eugene, OR 97401

www.wipfandstock.com

ISBN 13: 978-1-4982-0395-1

Manufactured in the U.S.A.   5/21/2015

For Delbert, and Marj

Contents

Contributors | ix

Section 1: Front Papers

1. Introduction to the Festschrift: A *Liber Amicorum* | 17
   W. Marshall Johnston

2. Hope for *Halig*: An Intellectual (and Semi-Classical) Biography of Delbert L. Wiens | 26
   W. Marshall Johnston

3. "New Wineskins for Old Wine": A Fifty-Year Retrospective | 36
   Paul Toews

Section 2: Memoirs

4. Delbert Wiens: A Sage Among Us | 63
   Peter Klassen

5. A Living Braid of Social Justice | 70
   Faith Nickel Adams

6. Delbert Wiens: A Memoir | 79
   Richard Wiebe

7. Triangles, Lines, and Radical Signs: Human Transcendence in Classical, Modern, and Christian Worldviews | 84
   Silas Langley

8. Failing Forward | 97
   Devon H. Wiens

9. "Village to the City": A Grammar for "New Wineskins for Old Wine" | 104
   Greg A. Camp

Section 3: Essays

10 Pagans and Galatians: Reading Galatians 5:12 | 117
W. Marshall Johnston

11 A Dangerous Mind and Dangerous Times: The Rain Miracle of Marcus Aurelius and the Second-Century Church | 129
Richard Rawls

12 "Arrows Fletched from Our Own Wings": The Early Church Fathers and the "Delphi of the Mind" | 150
Daniel J. Crosby

13 From the Pueblo to the City | 164
Salvador Diaz

14 On Building the Kingdom: A Heresy in the Fresno Pacific Idea | 172
Peter Smith

Section 4: Delbert's Work

15 The Mennonite Syndrome | 195

16 Bowel Rumblings or Bone Roaring or Something | 208

17 The Sermon I Won't Preach Tomorrow (So Please Read It Today) | 238

18 My Saga: "In" and "Out" | 247

Appendices

A Bibliography of Delbert L. Wiens' Work | 265

Delbert, So Far: A Chronology | 268

Contributors

W. Marshall Johnston grew up and was educated through his undergraduate years and secondary credentialing in the Deep South. He attended graduate school at Bryn Mawr College, in Philadelphia, where he met his wife, Pam, also a classicist. They moved to Fresno in the late nineties to work at California State University, Fresno. Fresno Pacific displayed many of their educational ideals, and they moved across town as positions became available. They are Episcopalians, but many involved in this volume, Delbert, Richard, and Paul especially, made them feel that they were a part of the Anabaptist community. Marshall and Pam both teach classics and ancient history in the School of Humanities, Religion, and Social Sciences.

Daniel J. Crosby was born, raised, and educated in the Central Valley. He attended Fresno Pacific University for both undergraduate and graduate studies in classics and was an active member in the community by way of his involvement in the Alpha Chi National Honor Society and the foundation of Phi Alpha Theta, the first disciplinary honor society at FPU, music, drama, and intercollegiate athletics. Although raised in the Four Square Church, he now attends a "non-denominational" church. Currently, he is serving as adjunct professor of history and classics at Fresno Pacific, as well as a diving coach at the high school and club level locally.

Josiah Muster is a working designer and artist in traditional media from Clovis, California. He is a senior at Fresno Pacific University, currently pursuing his double major in graphic design and studio art, as well as a minor in art history. Josiah hopes to build the name of Muster Creations into a larger design and illustration company that will always seek to glorify God in the artwork that is completed. Family, friends, art, and education are what govern his schedule, but God is what ties them all together.

Paul Toews for over forty years taught history at Fresno Pacific University and was a colleague of Delbert for more than twenty-five years. In addition to teaching he was the director of the Center for Mennonite Brethren Studies and executive director of the Mennonite Brethren Historical Commission. He is the author and editor of numerous books, including *Mennonites in American Society, 1930–1970: Modernity and the Persistence of Religious Community* (1996).

Peter Klassen was born in Crowfoot, Alberta, and completed high school in Abbotsford, British Columbia. Upon graduation, he was awarded a Royal Institution Scholarship to the University of British Columbia, where he received his BA with a major in history and English. He then enrolled at the University of Southern California and received his PhD in history in 1962, and in that year he began teaching history at Fresno Pacific. Then, from 1966 to 2011, he served successively at California State University, Fresno, as professor of history, dean of the School of Social Sciences, and also part-time director of International Programs. His publications include *The Economics of Anabaptism* and *Mennonites in Early Modern Poland and Prussia*. He has given invited lectures at the universities of Muenster, Leipzig, Amsterdam, Harvard, Taipei, Shanghai and others. He first met Delbert while doing research at the University of Chicago, and was impressed by his global perspective, readiness to challenge traditional views, impressive intellect, and unflappable determination. He is married to Nancy Cooprider Klassen, and they have three sons, who have given them a total of seven delightful grandchildren.

Faith and Doug Adams live in Topeka, Kansas, where they retired as career educators. Their adult sons are Trevor and Justin, who is married to Kari. Their grandsons are Jaxson (5) and Joel (1). Faith's hobbies include indoor horticulture, cooking, and attending estate sales. Doug is active in several community clubs. Table conversations revolve around current events; the status of their canine, Powerball; and home improvements. The Adams' goal is to "age gracefully."

Richard Wiebe attended Fresno Pacific College as an undergraduate from 1970 to 1974. He was a philosophy minor and cultural history major. He studied at University of Chicago Divinity School between 1974 and 1976. He was associate professor of philosophy at Fresno Pacific from 1977 to 2014. He has done significant research in Navajo philosophy and culture and has served for decades on the Citizens Advisory Committee for the

Yosemite Area Regional Transportation System. He is also a founding board member of Restore Hetch Hetchy and a lifetime member of the Sierra Club.

Silas Langley's love of philosophy, theology, and history has its root in his contact with Delbert Wiens. Silas took Delbert's ancient civilizations course as a freshman at Fresno Pacific University in 1989, saw his chalk drawings, and was hooked. After graduating from FPU with an intellectual history major in 1993, Silas got a master's degree in theology at Duke Divinity School. He then earned a PhD in philosophy at Fordham University, specializing in the philosophy of religion and medieval philosophy. He has since taught as an adjunct in philosophy, history, and theology at various universities, including Fresno Pacific University; California State University, Fresno; the University of Portland; and Portland State University. He has just published a book through Wipf and Stock titled *Death, Resurrection, and Transporter Beams: An Introduction to Five Christian Views on Life after Death*. He currently lives with his wife, Rhonda, and two kids in Fresno, California.

Devon H. Wiens was born in Shafter, California, but grew up in Wichita, Kansas, where he graduated from Friends University. He received his ThM from Fuller Theological Seminary in 1963. His PhD is in New Testament and the early church from USC in 1963. His minor field was in classics and Greek history. He began teaching in biblical and religious studies at Huntington College in Indiana, and he came to Fresno Pacific College in 1971, retiring from full-time teaching in 2002. He and Delbert taught general education humanities courses together and were jokingly referred to as the "Wiens brothers" despite their lack of an immediate blood relationship. Among his scholarly activities are two National Endowment for the Humanities summer seminars: 1988 on the Jewish exile in the sixth century BCE, and 1999 on the relationship between the Jews and Christians in the late Hellenistic period. He has written on numerous subjects including one in the magisterial *Aufstieg und Niedergang der Romische Welt*.

Greg A. Camp is professor of biblical and religious studies at Fresno Pacific University. He holds a BA in philosophy and biblical and religious studies from FPU where he studied under Delbert, an MDiv from Mennonite Brethren Biblical Seminary, and a PhD in New Testament from University of Sheffield. Graduate studies initially led him to University of Iowa. The experiences at FPU and Iowa were part of a journey that brought different intellectual and cultural terrain. The decision to move back to Fresno for seminary was partially an attempt to integrate those areas of his life. He wrote a letter to Delbert asking for advice, remembering that Delbert had spoken on numerous occasions of his own journey out from and back into his community in Corn, Oklahoma. Delbert's response was pastoral and caring. Years later, as a retiring colleague cleaning out his office, Delbert gave Greg the letter that he had so long ago written. Greg's work in biblical studies tends to draw from the cultural and philosophical influences of Delbert and the literary and historical perspectives of Devon Wiens, Delbert's colleague for many years in the freshmen core program. It has been a privilege for Greg to be a work colleague with Delbert, a fellow parishioner, and a friend.

Richard S. Rawls earned his PhD and MA in ancient and medieval history from Emory University, his MDiv (emphases in church history and philosophical theology) from Princeton Theological Seminary, and a BA (double major in history and communication) at Fresno Pacific College. He further studied in Mannheim, Germany, at the Goethe-Institut. His advisor at FPC was Delbert Wiens, from whom he learned to question the relationship between religion and culture. For ten years, he taught at FPU in history, philosophy, and communication, cofounded the classics program, and was director of the Hiebert Library. He is currently professor of history at Georgia Gwinnett College in suburban Atlanta.

Salvador Diaz teaches history at Santa Rosa Junior College in Santa Rosa California. He was born in Mexico and lived there until the age of ten when his parents moved the family to California. He grew up working in dairies and farms in the California central valley while attending school whenever he could. He attended Cal State Fresno and received his BA in 2000. He then studied history at Princeton University and received an MA in history in 2004. He now lives in Santa Rosa with his wife, his children, and an angry guinea pig.

Peter Smith is assistant professor of peacemaking and conflict studies at Fresno Pacific University. Prior to joining the FPU faculty in 2011, he and his wife, Cheryl, and two sons lived in Zambia for several years where they did voluntary service in peace education through Mennonite Central Committee. Trained in theological ethics through the University of Wales doctoral studies, Peter's interests lie at the intersection of theology and peacemaking. His affiliation with the Anabaptist-Mennonite tradition began during his undergraduate education at Fresno Pacific and has been nurtured since then, along with other ecumenical flavors, in various venues around the world.

Delbert L. Wiens: You should read the book.

Section 1

Front Papers

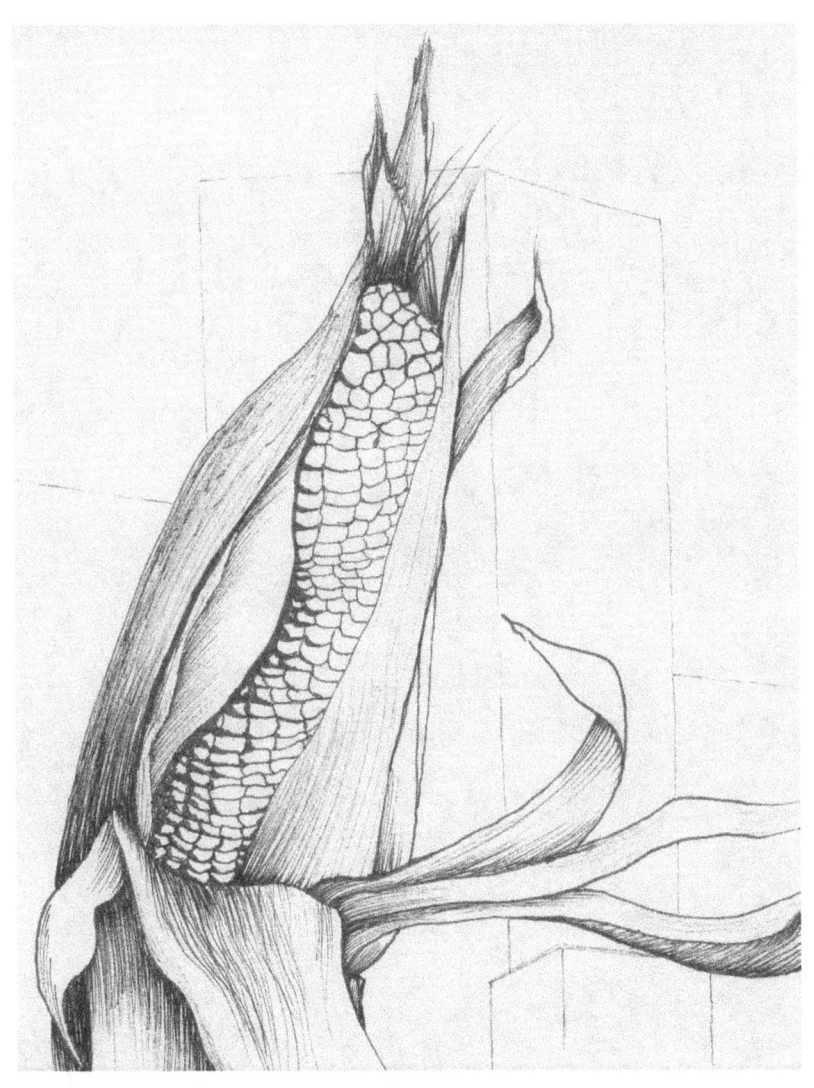

1

Introduction to the Festschrift
A Liber Amicorum

W. Marshall Johnston

The Project

WE ARE HONORED TO present this celebration volume to Dr. Delbert L. Wiens on the fiftieth anniversary of the publication of "New Wineskins for Old Wine" ("Wineskins"). Delbert Wiens has led an amazing life, from the tiniest of towns to the most important of universities;[1] from travel by scooter across Asia to decades in a small denominational institution. He has lived with curiosity, courage, humility, and generosity throughout these eighty-plus years, and he has been as hospitable to those of us who have arrived at Fresno Pacific University (FPU) in this millennium as he was to those with whom he worked for thirty years. A collaboration of a number of individuals who know and have been touched by Dr. Wiens and his work seemed a very valuable medium in which to thank him, and to work in community, living into a notion that he has always articulated and valued; indeed, many of us

---

1. Richard Wiebe enumerates in his "Memoir" some of the great scholars of the twentieth century with whom Delbert worked, *infra*.

would not have worked together as closely, or even perhaps have known each other at all, but for him.

How we address Dr. Delbert L. Wiens is a useful microcosm of who the man is, and how he has been shaped by his lifelong relationship to the Mennonite Brethren Community: he earned a PhD from the most august of institutions, so "Dr. Wiens" is more than merited; he has touched generations with his teaching and writing, so "Professor Wiens" rolls properly off the tongue; yet in conversation he is "Delbert" to everyone. It is true that this form of address is an outgrowth of the Mennonite Brethren egalitarianism that in part attracted me, and many others, to the institution, but it is often at least partly an affectation. For Delbert it summarizes his presence, almost as a one-name footballer, his view of equality and openness, and his belief in communitarianism. Because of this belief, there will be different forms of address in this volume as befits each contributor's view of the scholarly context—such a difference might appear uneven elsewhere, but Delbert would have it no other way. Devon Wiens herein and elsewhere has regularly used the adjective "Delbertian," an adjective we see in others' work in this volume. So dramatic is the evocation of that name in the community that when the excellent student Delbert Warkentin recently came to campus, I am sure he had to use all his good-natured reserve by the tenth time he had heard the name association!

Why *A Dangerous Mind*? Besides being a catchy title, this phrase was actually spoken in reference to Delbert by a pastor who felt that Delbert pushed the theological envelope too much. "You need to watch out for that Delbert Wiens, he has a dangerous mind."[2] Indeed, Delbert does challenge non-reflective traditionalism and failure to practice deep engagement of the meaning of our beliefs. A major message we want to convey in our celebration of Delbert is that it is not easy to be prophetic and, to the extent we do so herein, we hope we are firmly in the tradition of Delbert's generosity and forbearance, two virtues that allow kinder reception of difficult ideas without obstructing clear explication of them. When he presented his recent ideas on interpretation of Romans during two sessions of FPU's Council of Senior Professionals in the fall of 2013, after John E. Toews and I responded with some criticisms, he honored our contributions, and yet clearly articulated in a culminating comment why he believes that we must reenvision the meaning of the first and

---

2. Toews, "Man," 3.

second chapters of that letter. We heard at a senior professionals gathering a year later of coercion that had shaped movements among the Mennonite Brethren of the sixties: Delbert's witness, his dangerous mind, has been important both for the desirability of presenting challenging ideas and openness to conversation.

Paul Toews touches in this volume on how Delbert effectively applies sociological categories to understanding the Mennonite community, and indeed all communities struggling with modernity. I am fascinated by how he was in the first, or even anticipated the first, generation to realize that classics, biblical studies, philosophy, theology, history, and apologetics do not have to be treated as separate areas of inquiry. He, in classic "Delbertian" humility, insists that German higher criticism started that process, but real integration of the methods of the disciplines, and respect among their various perspectives, seems to be a more recent phenomenon. Thus, it is especially appropriate to honor Delbert with a volume that draws from across the disciplines. We present this Festschrift as a testament to the kind of community that Delbert has worked for his whole career: students, colleagues, and scholars thankful for his legacy—his ideas and influence.

We have included at the beginning of this volume brief personal biographies by each of the contributors. Their contributions are divided into four major sections. The first section material includes this introduction, an attempt to locate and understand Delbert intellectually, and a consideration by Paul Toews of the reception of his "Wineskins" and its signal epoch. Next there is a section of tributes, especially from his students. Essays dedicated to him follow, extending from inquiry into the beginning of the Christian era, through late antiquity and the Reformation to the religious realities of the present day. We are especially pleased to include, as a final section, four unpublished works of Delbert himself, representing his thinking over a period of more than four decades.

The Contributors and Their Contributions

I am humbled currently to occupy the faculty position in ancient history at FPU that Delbert Wiens passed to his student Richard Rawls. Delbert's "From the Village to the City" ("Village") provided a transformative moment for me as I read in the French countryside in the summer of 2010.[3] It

---

3. Wiens, "Village," 98–149.

is a pleasure to organize the very bright and fascinating people who have become part of this project. Delbert, his works, and the FPU colleagues I have come to know, have helped me to tease out the realities implied by my favorite quote of the great classicist Ronald Syme: "The primary task of an Ancient Historian is to notice what isn't there."[4] More importantly, I have learned from the Anabaptist worldview the importance of trying to understand the incarnation of Christ and the model he provides. It is certainly a bit presumptuous for an Episcopalian southerner of Scottish extraction to undertake this project, but I have been blessed by mentors in the Brethren tradition, and I believe in my ten years at FPU I have gotten a sense of the community and its values. Thus, while my involvement will always border a bit on the anthropological, my interest and affection for it are genuine.

I hope that I will remember to include all the various anniversaries that this Festschrift celebrates. The specific observance is that this fall will mark fifty years since he challenged the Mennonite Brethren and the larger Christian community with "Wineskins." It is also fifty years since Fresno Pacific's regional accreditation. The significance of that year is well documented by Paul Toews herein. This year is also the sixtieth since Delbert undertook his MCC service in Vietnam—he founded a project that thrives to this day. Appropriately, FPU will undertake its first semester in Vietnam in the fall of 2015.

There are also a number of more recent decennial (or near to it) anniversaries this year. The seventies saw his further attempts to articulate the reasons for the impasse he had explained in "Wineskins": "Village" and "Bowel Rumblings," which is included among Delbert's works in section 4. In the eighties, the broadened base at Fresno Pacific resulted in his rejection of easy answers to the meaning of the Academy through his "Sermon I Won't Preach Tomorrow," which is also included in section 4. In the nineties, there was a renewed version of the Fresno Pacific Idea, and *Mennonite Idealism and Higher Education*[5]—including Delbert's article called "Heresy of the Christian College."[6] This was the same period in which Delbert published *Stephen's Sermon*. It was in the nineties that FPU became a university, and ten years ago it divided into separate schools.

---

4. Mortimer Chambers, "Early Christian Martyrdom" (presentation at the first annual Graduate Student Symposium, California State University, Fresno, 2003).

5. A chronological review of Delbert's works is included in the appendices. Toews, *Mennonite Idealism*.

6. Wiens, "Christian College," 43–65.

INTRODUCTION TO THE FESTSCHRIFT

The contributors to this Festschrift for Delbert have shown in literary form the lasting contribution he has made to the community, whether it be locally in Fresno, California, or in the larger world. I wanted to take a moment here in the introductory comments to give an overview of the pieces herein. In a section of tributes to Delbert, the preeminent Fresno educator and historian Peter Klassen shows how he can be seen in the context of some of the great early Anabaptist reformers. Faith Nickel Adams was a student of Delbert's in the sixties at Tabor, and her "Braid" reveals that his mentoring, familiar from Fresno Pacific, was practiced equally effectively at Tabor.

Richard Wiebe was a student and colleague of Delbert, and he explicates how he thinks that Delbert's approach should be tempered by modern economic theory, namely Marxist theory. Delbert does address socioeconomic concerns in "Old Wine: Will It Sour" and "Bowel Rumblings," but it is likely that Richard had not heard or read the latter. Silas Langley treats Delbert's legendary images: these allegorical ways of thinking about our conceptions of reality made an impact on generations of students. Devon Wiens and Greg Camp reflect on the tremendous value of developing curriculum with Delbert. In a real sense, the center of Fresno Pacific's General Education and School of Education curriculum are still quite indebted to our honoree.

It is purely by chronology that my essay is located first among the essays. I was pleased that Delbert was interested in the subject of understanding the full ramifications of Paul's meaning in his dramatic statement at Galatians 5:12 when we discussed the subject. Daniel Crosby, the next contributor, is one of a group of very promising students who have come through FPU in the time since my wife and fellow classicist Pam and I arrived in the last decade. Folks like Dan, Brian DePalma, Brandon Cain, Sam Musgrave, Michaelynne Whitsitt, Anthony Fredette, Charlie Castanon, and many others have been influenced in their thinking and training in a community so deeply shaped by Delbert. Delbert and I thought we should include a participant who could represent that recent generation. Daniel is ideal because he was a highest-honors history major, one of only two multiple winners of the Outstanding Student of Classics and Ancient History Award, and wrote an extraordinary thesis in classics. His work as assistant editor of this volume has been invaluable—from his careful eye to his mastery of social media.[7] He has a

---

7. I hope as you read this we will still be regularly updating the *Dangerous Mind* Facebook page. You may review many of Delbert's works at Academia.edu thanks to

special interest in Greek religion and the history of the Delphic Oracle, so the intellectual history of the Christians' way of dealing with the Delphic Oracle was an excellent fit, and I think a first-rate addition to classical scholarship.

Richard Rawls has cut a wide swath in our community. He was a student of Delbert, and professor of history as well as director of the library. He has remained close to many members of our community since becoming a full professor at Georgia Gwinnett College. As one of the leading experts on Christian conversions in late antiquity, it is especially valuable to have his essay on the religious interpretations of the "Rain Miracle" and Christian engagement with pagan culture during the reign of Marcus Aurelius.

Pam and I taught at Fresno State before coming to FPU. We were blessed with a number of extraordinary students during our season there; several, including Nate, Curtis, Patrick, and Kristi, have gone on to be professors themselves. We were especially close to Sal and Sadie Diaz. Sal covered Pam's classes at Fresno State when she had to be out of town to help her mother, Rosie, and he also took on classes at FPU as the curriculum in history grew. He is now tenured at Santa Rosa College, and he and his extended family (as well as Sadie's) represent a story we must tell and one that he tells with his usual clarity and humor.

I have been honored to have multiple visits with Sal and his family in the last few years, and the "two worlds" in which they live have much to teach us, and much for comparison with the Anabaptist experience. Our FPU student body is now more than a third Roman Catholic, but within Roman Catholicism, the Mexican experience is quite akin to the biblical realities of strangers in the land. The tension within that experience is well expressed by Sal.[8] As a white man from the South, I have relied heavily on folks like Sal, Yun, Addison, and others of many ethnicities to help me see the diversity of experience in our community. And I especially thank God for Sal and Sadie's youngest, our godchild, Aleria.

Peter Smith examines the FPU Idea in an inquiry in the "Delbertian" tradition. At a time that has brought major challenges to Fresno Pacific, it is useful to ask whether we are articulating a genuinely ecumenical

Daniel.

8. Another very successful CSUF student from a Mexican family pointed out to me that the tensions between Roman Catholic and Protestant contingents were so great in his family that when his grandmother saw his uncle, a Protestant Evangelical, walking toward her house, she would cry, "Here comes the Devil!"

Christian path in the Idea, and turning to the Anabaptists to understand the answer to that question should be our first resort. In an era in which we are less likely to explicate the full context of our Christian walk, it may be that we are in special need of being reminded of, in Delbert's terms, the difference between "discipleship" and "sonship." After twenty years of the current form of the Idea, we are very pleased to have this admonition in our volume dedicated to Delbert. We will also include some of Delbert's insights into the value of previous generations' understanding of the Idea.[9] We refuse to trade our birthright as members of the FPU community for a mess of pottage. Devon Wiens and Richard Wiebe herein admonish us for how we may be failing in that task.

We have tied our contributions together with art inspired by Delbert's ideas and carried out by Josiah Muster. He is a senior graphic arts major at FPU, and has been deeply involved in work for the school while starting his own firm. As he read Festschrift material and met with Delbert and me, he showed stunning insight into out-of-the-box ways of thinking about worldviews, radical signs, and sermon topics. We hope that his illustrations, in order, "A Dangerous Mind," "Korn," "Radical," "Triangle Theory," and "On Water," will contribute to the coherence of the work for the reader. The cover illustration, "A Dangerous Mind," contains erased hints of some of Delbert's own sketches.

Acknowledgments

I was only able to put this volume together because of great help from many, especially Delbert, and Daniel Crosby. Otto Skutsch told the story of being Felix Jacoby's assistant, when Jacoby needed to spend the day working on the *Fragments of the Greek Historians*, and was unable to attend to his other responsibilities: "Skutsch, the ferry's not running."[10] Daniel has gracefully accepted the expected ferry stoppage many times! We are grateful to Wipf and Stock and particularly Matthew Wimer and Laura Poncy for seeing the value of this volume and for their patience in its preparation. Besides those named elsewhere or participating in this volume, we would especially like to thank Dalton Reimer for his assistance. Kevin Enns-Rempel and Paul Toews have been tireless in

---

9. "Hope for Halig" and section 4 (Delbert's unpublished material) will reveal the connection. I will also introduce Delbert's unpublished material in "Hope for Halig."

10. Skutsch, "Recollections," 387–408.

answering questions about Anabaptist history, and Gary Nachtigall's tour of Mennonite sites in Fresno County has been invaluable.

I am deeply indebted to FPU for providing a sabbatical in spring of 2013, during which the groundwork for this volume was laid. This has been a period of great intellectual ferment for me. My wife Pam and my advisor Corey Brennan have been the most significant figures in my formation, but only slightly behind them is being a part of the Anabaptist community at FPU that Delbert was so important in forming. I hope that the valuable distinctives of that community remain into the next generation.

Fresno, CA
January 15, 2015

Bibliography

Skutsch, Otto. "Recollections of Scholars I Have Known." *Harvard Studies in Classical Philology* 94 (1992) 387–408.
Toews, Paul. "A Man with a Dangerous Mind Retires from FPC." *Pacific Magazine* 10.2 (Summer 1996) 3.
———, ed. *Mennonite Idealism and Higher Education: The History of the Fresno Pacific College Idea.* Fresno: Center for Mennonite Brethren Studies, 1995.
Wiens, Delbert. "The 'Christian College' as Heresy." In *Mennonite Idealism and Higher Education: The History of the Fresno Pacific College Idea,* edited by Paul Toews, 43–65. Fresno: Center for Mennonite Brethren Studies, 1995.
———. "From the Village to the City: A Grammar for the Languages We Are." *Direction* 2.4 (October 1973–January 1974) 98–149.

2

Hope for *Halig*
An Intellectual (and Semi-Classical) Biography of Delbert L. Wiens

W. Marshall Johnston

What Is Biography?

DELBERT, SON H.R., RAISED in and returned to Korn, is notable for a varied life among the Mennonite Brethren dedicated to increased understanding between Christians. That is how a Roman biography of Delbert would begin. And while I have to realize that my engagement with ancient biography renders me an anachronism for the most part, it does apply in one significant way. For the Greeks and Romans, biography was not a "birth-to-death" genre, but communicated a life according to a theme illustrated by significant moments.[1] The key significant moment that leads to this Festschrift is this year's fiftieth anniversary of the publi-

---

1. At least I so argued in my dissertation, Johnston "Cornelius Nepos." Daniel Crosby has put together a chronology of Delbert's life and a chronological bibliography, found in the appendices, which provides the skeleton of what would comprise a more modern version of a biography, the life from birth to death. The ancient definition of biography would also require intricate lineage; I hope Delbert's and our comments will provide some context in that regard.

cation of "Wineskins," but I hope I will be able to illustrate Delbert's ideas and influence through several other significant moments and concepts as well.

I cannot edit a Festschrift entitled *A Dangerous Mind* without explaining a little of why the notion applies so well to Delbert,[2] or proving context for those who have not spent time lately with his writings or presentations. His ability to challenge orthodoxies is a nice model of what is at the heart of real education. He asks big questions and is willing to make prophetic statements, even as he generously provides space for response. I believe a perfect example of his clarity of admonition is found in his essay in the Paul Toews-edited *Mennonite Idealism and Higher Education*: why is "knowing a form of killing"?

> In the Humanities, . . . one destroys the composition as a whole and exchanges enjoyment of it for the always somewhat vicious pleasure of critiquing it. In the Social Sciences one performs the same operations on oneself and one's societies. In the Life Sciences, one literally kills the "specimen" to dismember it. The advanced quest for knowledge always involves separation and alienation. Thinking kills.[3]

Delbert has avoided such deathblows to contentious subjects, and vivisection of them, through allegory, allusion, and adumbration. Very often his thick descriptions and attempts to bring his reader fully into the realm of his thinking seem opaque (ask him about how he remembers the meaning of halibut: the sacred fish!), but advance the conversation by depth and openness. Indeed, I have had the pleasure of interaction with some of the brightest people in the Academy who were also Delbert's students, and they acknowledge moments at which his classes were left at sea—even if they were by the end of the session brought back at least in sight of shore. And they frequently have held on to valuable expressions that model Delbert's thought to the advantage of their own: the separation of the "central from the peripheral" is a regular discipline and value of the intellectual circle that has been touched by him.

Delbert's ability to see patterns to an intricate level, as perhaps is best witnessed in the Abraham, Joseph, Moses, and Temple sections of *Stephen's Sermon*, where he analyses the famous passage in Acts, really casts new light on the material—even if the framing (chiastic) pattern can

---

2. See, *supra*, the chapter "A *Liber Amicorum*" for the actual inception of the term.
3. Wiens, "Christian College," 43–65.

be somewhat forced. In recent work, he shows how a case for a new interpretation of Romans 1–2 can be made based on the ancient penchant for chiastic structure: he points out, as do I in "Pagans and Galatians" herein, that the pagan reception of the verses is the key to contextualizing them. One of my favorite quotes about *Stephen's Sermon* was from a colleague: "That book is like Delbert—complex, brilliant, and deeply idiosyncratic." I would, however, add that Delbert is correct that we are not attuned enough to look for chiastic structure and literal architecture carried out on multiple levels in ancient works. Darby Scott at Bryn Mawr showed how far we have to go in grasping that aspect of the classical world when he explained the full meaning of the shield of Aeneas in Vergil.[4] We should also be aware that such levels of thought and expression help to understand the way Delbert responds to interesting questions. Like me, he lives in the ancient and modern worlds simultaneously. He is likely to answer on a literal level, explicated through analogy, and then enlarged through allegory. One of my professors at the University of Georgia referred to a mutual acquaintance as a person of whom you should be careful about asking questions, because he just might answer them. That is Delbert.

Worlds in Collision

It is perhaps easy to over-psychologize Delbert's interpretation of the world. As he came from a background in which an old-world culture collided with the twentieth century, so does he see the classical ways of thinking colliding with the (then) new Christian beliefs; and so does he see how the modern and postmodern world must learn from the premodern one. But the fact that this developmental reality about his nurture and journey is true is no reason not to take what he is able to put into prose as an extremely valuable tool, an exemplary template or pattern, for helping our minds to unlock those philosophical truths. I regularly have noted that when I take students to events at which Delbert is present, his is often the only voice they will clearly remember; he has set in motion whole weeks of reflection.

Delbert is able to articulate associations, Paul and Stoicism for example, or commonalities among epochs of thought, a gift so well illuminated by Silas Langley and Devon Wiens herein, that make students and

---

4. Scott, "Problem of Ecphrasis," 301–8.

colleagues pause and really activate and use their knowledge. But it is the combination of concrete and abstract, the narrative and the metaphor, that have proved the deepest value in his thought: how do we explain the difference in the biblicism of our ancestors and our bibliolatry? It is by means of the metaphors that he has developed throughout his career. I have tried to include in this volume the progress of those metaphors, including the intermediate period at "Bowel Rumblings" when he was between metaphors. He began with the heralded moment for this volume, "New Wineskins for Old Wine," a metaphor that challenged the Mennonite Brethren community at an important crossroads, and was published the same year in which he gave the Tabor graduation address "Imitate Their Faith,"[5] formative to many—including Faith Nickel Adams in this volume. He has frequently used the Peter walking-on-water metaphor, the full meaning of which Dale Suderman at Tabor was the first to understand: Delbert is able to speak to those still in the boat and those who have ventured out from it. "From the Village to the City" and the levels of that metaphor inspired the cover of this volume, and, as Greg Camp's piece herein illuminates, gave a language for better understanding of our students' experience. In the nineties, the images he drew had a great deal to do with protective canopies, the linear and triangular human arrangements, and transcendence through the radical sign, which Silas Langley has nicely treated herein.

Delbert himself marks the significance of "Wineskins" (and the continuing struggle to complete the metaphor) in the journal *Direction*:

> Twenty-five years ago I made a first attempt to analyze and criticize the modern attitudes and practices we Mennonite Brethren had adopted by contrasting them with those of our grandfathers, I insisted that we had to learn how to reincarnate an older spirit and wisdom that was being lost. And so I titled it, "New Wineskins for Old Wine."
>
> On one level, that essay helped me to discover that we could let go of some of the "official pieties" that had become spiritually destructive. On a deeper level, that essay failed to chart a way to do what I called for. As one reviewer complained, I had not been clear about the "old wine" which I desired. Nor had I shown the cut and materials needed to construct new wineskins adequate for the old wine. That failure was symbolized in repeated

---

5. Wiens, "Imitate," 3–5, 21. This piece was published in the *Christian Leader*—it was given on his birthday, May 23, 1965, which is, thus, adopted as the ceremonial publication date of this volume.

comments to me about "your piece on old wineskins and new wine."[6]

About eight years later I tried again. In "From the Village to the City" I attempted to describe traditional Mennonite Brethren attitudes and ways of thinking, to show how they had changed, and to point to what they might become. In that piece I implied that Evangelical and Liberal forms of Christianity belonged to a transitional ethos [that] I labeled "town."[7]

Pastor Michael VandenEnden in his work at Canadian Mennonite University has seen how Delbert's works on understanding the Mennonite Brethren in the modern world have formed a triad ("Wineskins," "Village," and "Neither Liberal Nor Evangelical"). VandenEnden articulates this notion in his master's thesis.[8] His idea, and mine, is that Delbert has indeed succeeded in articulating his prophecy: he explains the problem, then addresses the divide, and finally provides a theological approach to its solution.[9]

The collision of cultures and worldviews that Delbert had experienced by the time he was thirty led him to need a shorthand way to express what it was like to return to teach at Corn Bible Academy in Oklahoma after graduate school at Yale. He found that folks he had known his entire youth were skeptical about him upon his return. Delbert has famously said that they only took him in as favor to H.R. He has lit upon a very useful simile: he is like "an anthropologist investigating a new tribe and finding it is his own"; this is a wonderful metaphor for a reality that still is very active in the world of Mennonite Brethren. Sam Panderla, the

---

6. At a Council for Senior Professionals meeting in the fall of 2014, when queried, he answered that he has worked for fifty years to be more specific about the referents. At that meeting he said the separation was form and substance. Wiens, "Paul on Human Error and Sin and on God's Fundamental Character" (presentation to the Council for Senior Professionals, Fresno Pacific University, fall 2014).

7. Wiens, "Mennonite Brethren," 39.

8. VandenEnden also highlights how this understanding must happen at a metaphorical level, most clearly articulated in Delbert's "Incarnation and Ideal," where he reasonably claims that the modernist "man the maker" metaphor results in a failure to stay true to the ancestral faith because the partial truth creates heresy. VandenEnden, "Toward Authoritative Tradition," 50.

9. Ediger, "Response," 64–66. Gerald Ediger points out that the solution Delbert provides can be quite off putting, but I would maintain that a prophetic statement may not be easy, or crowd pleasing; and that Delbert's generosity and openness allow it to be heard.

son of the great Mennonite Brethren Pastor MennoJoel Panderla, grew up in Shamshabad at Mennonite Brethren Centenary Bible College near Hyderabad, and went to school at Kodaikanal International School. He studied with us at FPU for three years in the graduate school to prepare himself to start a sports-based NGO, and then accompanied a group of students for a semester of study back to Andhra Pradesh. Having spent time at an ecumenical Christian college in a medium-sized American city that welcomed non-Christian students (FPU), Sam found the unworldliness and disconnection of the community in which he had grown up quite a shock: he too became a sympathetic anthropologist.[10]

How to deal with the collision of modern and premodern ways of thinking, as articulated by Delbert, has value for all groups in which both worldviews are active. He was intellectually alive to the divisive stances on evolution in the sixties and seventies, a point of contention mentioned in "Bowel Rumblings and Bone Roaring" and in Paul Toews' "Fifty-Year Retrospective" herein. On such questions, Delbert has told parables of children returning to their farms, or seminary students to debate with the elders in their towns, and tried to encapsulate how the two groups are likely to speak past each other. My sister Gage married into an Aramaic family of Syriac Christians, and has encountered several similar moments. One of them is most pronounced in its broader applicability.

Because her brother-in-law was giving a lecture in Turkey, my sister and her husband Jack decided to go to visit the eastern region of that country where there was a significant ancestral connection for Jack's family. It worked out because of various unexpected connections that they were even able to go visit the monastery near where Jack's mother had been born—it is called Mor Gabriel. The trip was amazing by all reports, and gave them a real sense of whence the family had emigrated. After that wondrous travel, they returned to the United States, and relatively soon, our two brilliant nephews Gabriel and Christian were born.

Now, what Gage and Jack had not known is that Mor Gabriel is famous as a pilgrimage site for women seeking to become pregnant. Among the Syriac community, the assumption was that they had gone to pray for success in having children, even though Gage and Jack had not known of that reason for visiting Mor Gabriel. The assumption seemed to be corroborated by their first child being named Gabriel, but as a matter in fact, Jack named his son after his favorite uncle. Thus, the same act

---

10. Sam stayed with Pam and me when he first came to Fresno. I remember how shocked he was that Mennonite Brethren in the United States watched films.

was twenty-first-century ethno-religious travel and premodern fertility intercession. Perhaps they are both right.

The questions, however, in whatever terms they are put or metaphors they are cast, get back to the issue of how we live a holy, healthy, and whole—*halig*—life. Thus, the title of this chapter is best expressed as "Hope for *Halig*." Delbert very much lives up to the Anabaptist idea of acting humbly with hope for community, whether that community is centered in a village, town, or city; or whether it is in the context of family, tribe, or nation. All he has ever said about the value of his parables, analogies, and metaphors is that he hopes he has helped a few people understand their faith or ask meaningful kinds of questions. Students and colleagues have pointed out that his ideas really are about reaching spiritual maturity: even if one's faith is not recognizable to certain friends and associates with premodern understandings, a pilgrim whose journey has left the village still must honor that more literal path.

Korn to Corn

Delbert, like many of us, associates the whole and healthy life with a functional community in which he grew up. For him, it is Corn, Oklahoma. A close reader of his material knows that it occasionally appears as Korn. Though the spelling of the name of the actual town was changed from Korn to Corn at the beginning of the twentieth century because of anti-German feeling, Delbert has admitted his usage is less chronologically driven. For him, Korn is the mythical setting of archetypes and allegories, and Corn is the town near his original home in Bessie, Oklahoma, in which Corn Bible Academy is located. Delbert has been driven throughout his life to see the world, and to organize his thoughts, through analogy, metaphor, and allegory. Perhaps it was his early association with the "premodern" generation of his older relatives that made him resistant to the over-intellectualization and analysis of the details of his relationships and pieties; yet he is still desirous of finding language through which to express the too-often unexamined realities.

Delbert spent time in Vietnam, learning how to minister in a very difficult strait, and creating the basic approach to Anabaptist service in that land; he often found the situation quite different from what he would have expected, and it was challenging in ways that he found hard to process. He travelled through South Asia after his service in Vietnam, almost as a way of decompressing from Vietnam experience, and upon his return realized a chance to study at Yale Divinity School. His work there, after spending those years in Asia, took him far away from his worldview developed in his youth in Oklahoma and early adulthood in California's Central Valley. One almost feels he is still processing the dissonances. Thus, for him theology is listening and conversation.

The ways that he helps those around him to engage in that conversation are quite outstanding even among the unusually close "tribe" of the Mennonite Brethren. He is very intentional about involving all interested in reading his latest thoughts; he has meetings for coffee and meals with people from throughout his life. Devon Wiens mentions Oscar the Fetal Pig, a preserved piglet that Delbert used to explain tribalism.[11] I still have that fetal pig (in airtight storage) in my office.

Delbert's works that are included in this volume show a range of his interests and periods of his writing during the over fifty years of productive intellectual inquiry. "Mennonite Syndrome" was delivered to fellow graduate students in the sixties, a kind of companion piece to "Old Wine: Will It Sour?" When accused of failure to define the old wine, he comments:

> I had discovered the almost forgotten ideals of *Gottesfurcht* and *Gelassenheit*. I have tried in my writing to develop the meaning of the old wine in terms of my discovery of a deeper shift in the how of our thinking that lay beneath the contents of what we were thinking.[12]

His "Bowel Rumblings and Bone Roaring (or Something)" is based on an idea taken from Isaiah to address the kind of prophetic insights Delbert had near the end of Arthur Wiebe's long and successful tenure as president of FPU.[13] "The Sermon I Won't Preach Tomorrow" shows continuing meditations on the plight of education in the modern context; he

---

11. Richard Rawls and I are two relatively intelligent academics, and Delbert spent a morning in the Carmel-like atmosphere of Fig Garden Village explaining how Oscar illustrates the concept to us. We had started to understand the idea by the end of the morning.

12. Wiens, "Corn to Fresno," 1.

13. It was during the fall semester of 2014 as the last pieces of this Festschrift were being put together that Arthur Wiebe passed into the Greater Life. Delbert's prophetic nature is also a useful admonition to those of us associated with the University: it was in that same semester the Pete Menjares, the first CCCU Hispanic president, unexpectedly resigned.

is prophetic even by his standards in regard to problems in the church and academy in the twenty-first century. He would further publish "The Christian College as Heresy" a decade later in Paul Toews' *Mennonite Idealism*.

I have included his "In and Out," a personal journey he shared with the Council of Senior Professionals at FPU last decade, as a way of showing how he understood his journey at that time. His thoughts about the lessons his "pilgrimage" therein (as it is rightly called in Anabaptist circles)[14] provides are similar to this day. In fact, he is writing a long treatment for his grandchildren that might be an excellent companion volume to *A Dangerous Mind*. I will certainly view it that way. Delbert himself provides a useful summary to the themes and subjects of his work over the years:

> When I look back over my life and thought, it seems to me that I have followed a more focused trajectory than I could ever have planned, and so I am deeply grateful that its meaning has increasingly become clear to me.[15]

A shortcoming of ancient biography is its virtual unconcern with the (always female) spouse of the subject. Because Delbert's wife Marjorie Gerbrandt Wiens worked as a groundbreaking physician in a completely different area of expertise from Delbert,[16] I want to place at a point of honor at the end of this chapter an encomium to her significance as his intellectual equal, provocateur, muse, fellow parent to their two children, and, frequently, his handler when he (and I, in conversations about this volume) got off on unnecessary tangents. It is for all of these reasons that Marj is one of two people to whom this Festschrift is dedicated.

---

14. "Pilgrimage" is what many of us still call the new faculty candidate presentation in which we are asked to provide an integrated narrative of our lives.

15. Wiens, "Corn to Fresno," 3.

16. Indeed her presentation to the Council of Senior Professionals was one of the most thought provoking yet offered, and probably would require a book-length treatment itself. *Marjorie Gerbrandt Wiens*, "Why a Physician? What Is a Calling?" (presentation to the Council of Senior Professionals, Fresno Pacific University, February 25, 2014).

Bibliography

Ediger, Gerald. "Response to Delbert L. Wiens." *Direction* 20 (Spring 1991) 64–66.
Johnston, W. Marshall. "Cornelius Nepos: The Historian and His Tradition." PhD diss., Bryn Mawr College, 2003.
Scott, R. T. "The Problem of Ecphrasis." In *Ultra terminum vagari: Scritti in onore di Carl Nylander*, edited by Börje Magnusson et al., 301–8. Rome: Edizioni Quasar, 1997.
VandenEnden, Michael. "Toward an Authoritative Missional Tradition: D. H. Williams in Dialogue with Recent Mennonite Brethren Ecclesiology." MA thesis, Canadian Mennonite University, 2011.
Wiens, Delbert. "The 'Christian College' as Heresy." In *Mennonite Idealism and Higher Education: The History of the Fresno Pacific College Idea*, edited by Paul Toews, 43–65. Fresno: Center for Mennonite Brethren Studies, 1995.
———. "From Corn to Fresno: My Search for a Usable Past." https://www.academia.edu/10151066/From_Corn_to_Fresno_My_Search_for_a_Usable_Past.
———. "Imitate Their Faith." *Christian Leader*, June 8, 1965.
———. "Mennonite Brethren: Neither Liberal Nor Evangelical." *Direction* 20.1 (Spring 1991) 38–63.

3

"New Wineskins for Old Wine"
A Fifty-Year Retrospective

Paul Toews

THE OCTOBER 12, 1965, issue of *The Christian Leader* (*Leader*) contained a twenty-eight-page insert titled "New Wineskins for Old Wine." The *Leader*, a denominational publication of the United States Mennonite Brethren Conference (USMBC), was distributed to every Mennonite Brethren (MB) household. Delbert Wiens, the author, wrote the piece during the summer of 1965 as he transitioned from a teaching position at Tabor College (an MB undergraduate college in Hillsboro, Kansas) to PhD studies in the cultures of the ancient Mediterranean world at the University of Chicago. The publication turned Wiens into an instant celebrity in this small denominational community. Wiens, ever since, has been an intellectual gadfly for the MB. In the years since 1965, he has written extensively, published often in MB periodicals, but subsequent articles and books have not generated the kind of interest as "Wineskins." The paper remains his signature publication.

The immediate context for writing "Wineskins" was three years of teaching at Tabor College and a year prior at Corn Bible Academy (a small MB high school) in Corn, Oklahoma. Into the 1960s, both of these institutions were largely populated by MB young people. In addition to living in these small communities, Wiens actively participated in the life of the Corn MB Church and the Ebenfeld MB Church, a country church near Hillsboro. "Wineskins" addressed the contradictions of the MB story. He had spent the past four years with the young who often struggled to understand their religious inheritance. Always a counselor to reflective, inquisitive and frequently rebellious youth, Wiens no doubt felt a special interest in exploring issues that might help them sort through what could seem like a bewildering religious culture. The young, less invested in the dominant ways, are frequently more able to see the limitations and hypocrisy involved in their maintenance.

The first twenty years of Wiens' biography paralleled the experience of those students. He grew up in Bessie, Oklahoma, an outback Mennonite settlement west of the Corn, Oklahoma, Mennonite community and in Corn itself. At age fifteen, the family moved to Reedley, California, where his father became principal of a small MB secondary school. By age thirty-four when he wrote "Wineskins," Wiens' personal biography included life in several domains. After two years as a student at Tabor, he finished a BA degree at Fresno State, a California state regional university. From there he went to do alternative military conscription service with Mennonite Central Committee (MCC). In 1954, MCC sent him to Vietnam ostensibly to work with refugees following the defeat of the French and the regroupment of the population between what became South and North Vietnam. In Vietnam this village boy mixed it up with high Vietnamese governmental officials, with the now defeated remnants of the French aristocracy, and with agency representatives of many global relief and development agencies. It was a heady three-year stint. After a long motorcycle trip from Vietnam across Asia up through the Middle East and Europe, he went to Yale Divinity School for the next three years. During all of those years, he wrestled with the meaning of MB religious expressions and expectations like the students he subsequently taught.

The publication of "Wineskins" might be thought of as bringing the insights of Yale to the small MB world. It seemed to be a very good time to bring the flowering of university insight for 1965 can be described as a good year in the history of MB intellectualism, in fact maybe a kind of "coming of age" year. In the spring of 1965, both Tabor College and Pacific College (now Fresno Pacific University) received regional accreditation as four-year baccalaureate institutions. The USMBC, meeting in Dallas, Oregon, in late fall 1965, authorized a separate charter for the MB Biblical Seminary (MBBS), which had begun in 1955, in Fresno, California, and encouraged this institution also to pursue accreditation.¹ MB, since its emergence as a separate denomination in 1860, had long relied on lay ministers. The widespread utilization of seminary-trained ministers began only after World War II. Within twenty years of the movement to the professionalized ministry the credentialing by national associations had become important.

The gaining of accreditation suggests a certain coming of age for the MB intellectual tradition. The quest by Tabor, begun in 1908 as a liberal arts college, had been long and difficult. Pacific College, begun in 1943 as a Bible institute, in the late 1950s added a junior college program and received approval by the Western Accrediting Association simultaneous with graduating its first baccalaureate class.²

If this achievement of accreditation is not sufficient to suggest 1965 as the coming of age of an MB intellectual tradition there are other developments that buttress this notion. The *Leader* of February 2, 1965, announced the formation of the MB Historical Society of the Midwest. The purpose of the society was "to collect information, promote research and encourage publication of resource materials in the area of Mennonite Brethren history." A month later the MB Historical Society of the West Coast held its inaugural meeting. The need for historical analysis, as typified by the formation of these entities, represents a certain degree of intellectual self-consciousness.³

The first issue of the *Journal of Church and Society* was published in 1965. The journal began under joint sponsorship from the MBBS, Tabor College, and Pacific College. Peter Klassen, professor of history at Fresno, was the initial editor with Wesley Prieb, dean at Tabor, and John B. Toews, president of the MBBS, as associate editors. The name itself was intriguing—*Church and Society*—something that Mennonites historically held to be separate realms. Their two-kingdom theology—the kingdom of this world and the kingdom of God—suggested a measure of separation between the two. The new journal, however, was established to articulate the need for engagement, not for distance. The first editorial made clear that the *Journal of Church and Society* "addresses itself to the challenge

---

1. "Tabor College Receives," 10–11; "Pacific College Awarded," 10. See *Minutes and Reports*, 43–55, for a discussion of the seminary.

2. On the history of Tabor College, see Goertzen, et al., *Tabor College*. For the history of Fresno Pacific University, see Toews, *Mennonite Idealism*. For the history of Mennonite Brethren Biblical Seminary, see Klassen, *Seminary Story*.

3. "Mennonite Brethren Historical Society," 21; Toews, "Peter Klassen," 1–4.

of bringing Christianity and the world into meaningful encounter. If the church is indeed to be the church, then confrontation with the issues of our time is imperative." This was the call for a different mentality than that of withdrawal.[4]

The 1965 commencement speakers at the two colleges drew from the citadels of American academe. J. Lawrence Burkholder of Harvard University was the speaker at Tabor College. At Pacific College, Ernie Boyer, then of the University of California, Santa Barbara, but already president-elect of the State University of New York (SUNY) system, graced the ceremony. The invocation of these two names needs admission that both had Mennonite connections. Burkholder in a few years would become president of Goshen College, a Mennonite institution in Indiana, and Boyer had grown up in the Brethren in Christ denomination, a group that worked closely with Mennonites in various ways.

So it would seem that 1965 was a propitious moment for the appearance of "Wineskins"—an extended critique of almost everything in the MB churchly world—theology, practices, structure of authority, denominational emphases and alliances. Orlando Harms, the courageous editor of the *Leader*, in the issue that announced that "Wineskins" was forthcoming, assumed it would generate controversy: "You may boil at some things and agree wholeheartedly with others. We believe, however, that what it says needs to be said at this juncture of the history of the Mennonite Brethren Church."[5] The editorial accompanying the insert noted that it was time to face the many changes that had taken place in the one hundred year history of the denomination. Those changes needed to be faced "squarely and honestly."[6] By publishing it, Harms obviously felt that the MB could handle such a critique.

"Wineskins" was divided into two parts: "The Bottling and Aging of Wine" and "Old Wine Is Better." Internal to each section were subthemes with references to many aspects of the MB tradition. Several respondents noted the perils of a short summary not being able to reveal the rich metaphorical allusions, poetic language, and subtle interrelationships of the kind of cultural analysis that the booklet entailed. The world is a complicated place, religious experiences and religious communities operate on multiple levels, and Wiens, so conscious of the complexity and

---

4. "Editorial," 2.
5. Harms, "Special Edition," 2.
6. Harms, "Special Insert," 2.

interrelatedness of everything, sought to weave many of them into the analysis. In many ways, it is a piece that is to be read and savored; it is an intellectual feast with an uncommon abundance.

As Wiens told the story the initiators of the MB tradition, in their self-understanding, came to a climactic religious experience, a personal encounter with God. This involved an inner struggle, a personal crisis. They experienced the morphology of conversion: guilt, repentance, peace, and assurance. They reformed old habits, congealed new beliefs, and built a new religious community. They were adults who, as a sign of their newfound religious faith, were re-baptized and, in so doing, rejected their earlier baptism. They were schismatics; they left the larger Russian Mennonite Church with the fervor and denunciations of the "old" church that is frequently common to schismatics.

The founding generation of MB paid for the articulation of this new faith. The political and religious structure of Russian Mennonite society, in which the MB emerged as a distinctive entity, vigorously sought to undo the new movement and if not, at least to corral and limit its influence. The elites used harassment and even imprisonment in seeking to thwart its expansion.[7]

Given the antagonisms, it was natural that a certain over-againstness emerged among the Brethren. That expressed itself in rigidifying markers of separation: the necessity of experiencing the same morphology of conversion, guilt, repentance, and release, identifying certain social practices as acceptable and others as unacceptable. These discriminations sometimes included behaviors that were intrinsically harmless. Children growing up in Christian homes often had little that needed reformation. They had little in their past that could prompt the dramatic conversion experience and change of direction. Conversion for adults surely meant something different from the inculcation of a young child in the ways of faith. The dream of every faith community is to pass on the understandings that shaped it. That the MB wanted to pass on the faith was natural, and yet problems emerged within one or two generations. The morphology of conversion, appropriate for adults, could be injurious and psychologically damaging when foisted on children as normative and even necessary. Wiens, as counselor to troubled MB youth, surely heard the lament and anguish of young adults pressured into what for them was an inauthentic morphology. Experience, shaped by adult conversions, had

---

7. See Toews, *History*; Toews, *Perilous Journey*; Dyck, "1525 Revisited," 55–77.

not developed an adequate concept of Christian nurture, and yet the ineffable needed some kind of external validation. Often that became a set of "dos and don'ts." These behavioral discriminations became important boundary markers. In a relatively homogeneous Mennonite village in Russia, those markers had cultural cachet.

With time that homogeneous culture was lost through sociological, religious, and migratory change. From location in the hinterlands of Ukraine, where the MB began as a separate denomination, being members of a similar social class and sharing a common worldview they moved to social, geographic, and economic differentiation. Inevitably, religious outlooks also changed. The behavioral discriminations transferred to new communities in North America often without reflective judgment as to the degree to which the beliefs were bound up with old or preexisting cultural containers. St. Paul understood that "we have this treasure in earthly vessels."[8] Distinguishing the treasure from the vessel is often difficult, and perhaps particularly so for immigrant groups needing to negotiate differing cultural realities.

The essential containers (the wineskins) that were to preserve the wine from going bad were a system of community authority and the scriptures. Wiens argued that in the early generations a community consensus was shaped by the "wise" people of the community who could understand and articulate the consensus. The concept of "brotherhood"—I apologize for the gender exclusion in the term—meant that dialogue, sometimes even extended dialogue, was utilized until consensus was reached on important issues. An article of faith was that a community, engaged in the process of careful discernment, would reach appropriate conclusions. In the "brotherhood," the wise people who understood the rhythms and ethos of the community could articulate the consensus that then became binding.

As the lay leaders gave way to a new professionalized and trained ministry, oftentimes by people who came from outside the community, these leaders did not fully understand the community consensus. Wiens was not the first to find the transition to the professionalized clerical class troubling. It was a common theme in MB discourse beginning in the late 1940s and extending into the 1960s. The new clerical class coming with training in non-MB seminaries often brought expectations that were associated with the office of minister or pastor. The notion of authority

---

8. 2 Cor 4:7 KJV.

vested in a position ran counter to the earlier shared and consensual modes of authority and governance.

Biblicism, long an honored badge of identity for MB, also changed over time. For generations they insisted that the Scriptures and the Scriptures alone were the authoritative source, as Wiens put it, "for thought and action."[9] The origins of the MB can be traced in part to home gatherings for Bible study, and if you had asked the leaders of the movement in 1860 by what authority they separated from other Mennonites, they would have pointed to the Bible. Wiens argued that while earlier generations "used the scriptures, we defend them."[10] A smart epigram, but also revelatory. For the generations that had ultimate faith in the validity of the Scriptures, they need not find consistency. If things were unclear, so be it. The post-higher-criticism generation, especially as affected by fundamentalism and evangelicalism, were more concerned about proving the Bible's veracity than using it. The correct doctrine of inspiration became the litmus test, not the practical application of its teaching. Wiens wrote that the pleas in conference periodicals for a "return to the Scriptures . . . seem as concerned that we venerate them as that we use them."[11] Decisions increasingly were made on the basis of other considerations. A resort to systematized doctrinal beliefs was often rooted in imported modern categories of thought.

The departures in the traditions of authority, community consensus, and understanding the Scriptures were part of a larger shift in worldviews. MB, like virtually all people, became unwittingly imprinted by a modern worldview. Worldviews were the *a priori* factor that shaped understandings. The premodern and modern determined the nature of discourse. Each could reveal truths and heresies. What was required was a discerning stance that relativized the truth claims of both.[12]

Many incongruities now marked the small world of the MB as it stood between differing worldviews. Practices that once gave vitality now stultified. The question was how to address the incongruities. One alternative was to maintain the same forms and practices and insist that they were meaningful even when it was clear they were not. One could pretend to turn the clock back and return to the simplicities of an earlier

9. Wiens, "Wineskins," 15.
10. Ibid.
11. Ibid., 16.
12. Wiens addressed these shifts of worldview in subsequent writings. See Wiens, "Village," 98–149, and "Mennonite Brethren," 38–63.

era. That alternative would belie the "New Wineskins" part of the title. Another alternative was to borrow the forms that seemed to give vitality to other groups. Thriving evangelical groups would be the natural folks to emulate; however, that alternative would be to imbibe new wine and, thus, belie the "Old Wine" part of the title.

Wiens' alternative seemed to be neither. Where to find the "New Wineskins for Old Wine"? In common MB parlor conversation, Wiens has often been described as an incurable romantic who called for a return to an idyllic past that realists call mythical, but "Wineskins" was not a call to return, rather a call to construct a coherent present as some in the past had done. He wrote:

> Grounding ourselves in the past we must learn to do in our own way for our own time what our grandfathers achieved in their time. . . . What was essential for our fathers were not the specific forms and answers which were given. What was essential was their experience with God and the honest commitment by all members of the brotherhood to search out the mind of Christ through prayer and Bible study and a common waiting for the spirit of God to move in the church.[13]

Mennonite Brethren identity is largely rooted in notions of renewal and revitalization, so Wiens was doing what others before him had done: appeal to a tradition that, when properly understood and reappropriated, could shape the future.

The editor's fear that some would "boil" at some issues was largely unfounded. The letters that came to the editor, at least those published in the *Leader* as well as those that came to Wiens, were overwhelmingly positive.[14] The issue of the *Leader* following the publication of "Wineskins" contained two letters. George Nachtigall, a Buhler, Kansas, banker, commended Wiens for "his rare courage in saying what needs to be said." Esther Vogt, a Hillsboro novelist, observed that her English prayer group in the Hillsboro MB Church voted to use it for their winter Bible study

---

13. Wiens, "Wineskins," 24.

14. A total of thirty-four response letters from MB constituents were published in the *Leader* between the November 9, 1965, and June 7, 1966, issues. Thirty were affirmative, three express some disquiet, and one was very critical. Additional letters that came directly to Wiens are in the Delbert Wiens papers, Box 1, "New Wineskins for Old Wine": Responses, 1965-1967 and 1967-1992 files, Center for Mennonite Brethren Studies, Fresno, California. How many letters came to Orlando Harms, editor of the *Leader* and were not published is unknown. His papers remain in the possession of the family and were not available for this study.

sessions. She was sure that "these discussions [would] help [them] to face honestly what the Mennonite Brethren church [was] saying to [them]."[15]

The subsequent affirmations came from many quarters: John R. Dyck of St. Paul, Minnesota, wrote, "It is the most significant writing I have ever read coming from an M. B. source. It has been useful in giving me insights about myself, my relation to God, the church and the community."[16] Wilhelm and Frieda Kaethler, leaders in the MB Church of Paraguay, wrote that the author "said and explained many things that needed to be said. . . . We need a frank evaluation of ourselves, of our practices, our taboos and motives."[17] Dale Suderman writing from Wichita, Kansas, who had been a student of Wiens at Tabor, thought that perhaps the "article at times understates the problem facing the Mennonite Brethren conference" but still was "a vast improvement over much of the vague and meaningless trivia we as young people are often asked to endure." For Suderman it was "a ray of hope in what to me is a dark picture."[18] Numerous letters echoed these themes: appreciation for the courage to say what needed to be said, affirmation that the analysis rang true to personal experiences, and evocation of considerable discussion in varying churchly forums.[19]

For some young academics working outside MB institutions or communities, the embrace was strong. R. J. Froese, a student at the University of British Columbia, thought that it was "the most significant, searching and constructive study of the Mennonite Brethren church made in the 20th century."[20] Robert Enns, a student at the University of California, Santa Barbara, wrote that "*Wineskins* provided an uncommon amount of insight into what we had long felt" and the fact that it was said in the *Leader* "was a source of some kind of courage when it was sorely needed."[21] James Schellenberg, teaching sociology at Western Michigan University, had been a student at Tabor and a fellow resident with Wiens in a Tabor dormitory. Since leaving Tabor in 1951, he had not had close

15. Nachtigall and Vogt, "What Readers Say," 2, 14.
16. Dyck, "What Readers Say," 19.
17. Kaethler and Kaethler, "What Readers Say," 13.
18. Suderman, "What Readers Say," 25.
19. See, e.g., Neuman, "What Readers Say," 25; Flaming, "What Readers Say," 21; Seibel, "What Readers Say," 24; Schmidt, "What Readers Say," 9.
20. Froese, "What Readers Say," 21.
21. Enns to Wiens, September 28, 1966, Wiens Papers, Box 1, "New Wineskins for Old Wine": responses 1965–1966 file, CMBS-F.

contact with the MB Church. He left Tabor "thoroughly convinced" that one could not make a "critical analysis of dominant M.B. ideology and practices" that was "intelligent, honest and sympathetic." He commended Wiens for doing exactly that and for doing it with so much "grace."[22]

A goodly number of letters to the *Leader* were from persons in other denominations who felt the study was just as applicable to their denomination as to the MB. From a sister Mennonite denomination, the General Conference Mennonites, came requests for copies from their central administrative offices and from several ministers.[23] Pastors and denominational leaders of the "Old" Mennonite Church also requested copies.[24] Requests also came from other denominations and agencies: Richard P. Vouge, of Conservative Baptist Association affiliation, read and felt that "we have much in common." Eugene Nida, a translator with the American Bible Society, wrote to Wiens, "I was impressed with the careful and insightful manner in which you analyzed the development of the Mennonite Brethren movement."[25] For a stretch of time it was required reading in missionary anthropology classes taught by Charles Kraft at Fuller Seminary. Six months following publication, Orlando Harms, editor of the *Leader*, wrote that about 2500 copies had been sold to other Mennonite groups and other denominations. He wrote: "The exclusive reactions we have received from those who have studied the essays are that 'this speaks to us' regardless of denomination."[26]

Three letters expressing disquiet and one very critical were published in the *Leader*. Dale Warkentin, pastor of the Ulysses MB Church, in the December 7, 1965, issue, wrote the most critical response.[27] He did not think it could be called "A Study of the Mennonite Brethren Church," the subtitle of the piece, since it was "personal opinion more than an adequate knowledge . . . based on careful investigation." He found "too many misrepresentations, over generalizations, misconceptions and mistaken suggestions for it to be given the status and authority of a

---

22. Schellenberg to Wiens, December 31, 1966, Wiens Papers, Box 1, "New Wineskins for Old Wine": responses 1965–1966 file, CMBS-F.

23. See Unrau, "What Readers Say," 25; Esau, "What Readers Say," 20; Janzen, "What Readers Say," 20.

24. Cutrell, "What Readers Say," 12; Bishop, "What Readers Say," 20.

25. See letters in Wiens Papers, Box 1, "New Wineskins for Old Wine": responses 1965–1967 file, CMBS-F.

26. Harms, "More about Wineskins," 2.

27. Warkentin, "What Readers Say," 2, 21.

'study.'" He thought Wiens' generalizations came from experience in a "few large Mennonite Brethren settlements" and the educational institutions. It ignored many who were "on the progressive frontiers and cutting edge . . . in many other churches." What particularly seemed to offend Warkentin was that Wiens had some doubts about a new program, the Decade of Enlargement, which had been a matter of discussion for some years and was officially launched in the fall of 1965 as a USMBC initiative. The aim of the program was to double denominational membership in the next decade through a program of aggressive evangelism. Wiens feared that the program would only reinforce the conversionist emphasis of MB theology and was reductionist in understanding growth primarily in numerical terms. Furthermore, it was a ready-made example of technic, of a bag of strategies and organizational principles that Wiens thought too often had become a substitute for real encounters with God. In 1965, the MB were still disproportionately a rural folk, and given the reality of rural America slowly depopulating, Wiens thought the ambition to double in a decade placed an undue expectation on city congregations which in the 1960s were relatively young.

Warkentin's other chief concern was that Wiens seemed to be advocating a kind of antinomianism. Wiens' call for groups of Christians to seek the "guidance of the Holy Spirit and similar experiences with God" could easily develop less reliance on the authority of the Scriptures and more on groups of Christians as interpreters. For Warkentin, when pitting the guidance of the Spirit against the objectivity of the Scriptures the latter was to be preeminent.

The other critical letters were brief and less analytical. One thought the church needed a more positive analysis; the second felt that the study cast an unnecessary "shadow on all our young people" and that Wiens "strained at gnats to ridicule the belief of the conservative elements."[28] William Siemens thought "*New Wineskins* . . . [was] a heaping teaspoonful of warmed-over Barthianism" that contained a "watering-down of regeneration to a subjective decision to be a disciple."[29]

The most substantive response in the *Leader* came from Jacob Loewen, "A Personal Reaction to 'New Wineskins for Old Wine,'" in the April 26, 1966, issue.[30] Loewen, formerly a colleague with Wiens at Ta-

---

28. See Jantzen, "What Readers Say," 21; Gross, "What Readers Say," 2, 15.
29. See Siemens, "What Readers Say," 2, 20.
30. See Loewen, "Personal Reaction," 4–6.

bor, was now in South America as a translator with the American Bible Society. Loewen, after a sympathetic summary, noted that in such a wide-ranging study one could quibble about many assertions. Perhaps Wiens had overstated his case. If so, it was because the denomination had "been so smug about our biblicism and our orthodoxy, that only a very pointed barb could actually stir us to action."

What troubled Loewen more was the lack of response. The favorable response suggested an "absence of those who were smitten by the prophet's message." He wondered, "Have we become so complacent that we can even agree to these severe indictments and still not repent?"

A more extended analysis of "Wineskins" appeared in the *Mennonite Brethren Herald* (*Herald*), the Canadian MB conference periodical. Harold Jantz, editor, wrote in the October 29, 1965, issue that "*New Wineskins* . . . has already elicited a great deal of discussion. To some it is the beginning of a new day, for others it is the 'event that will split our conference down the middle.'"[31]

The April 15, 1966 issue of the *Herald* carried responses by three Canadian MB leaders, and the April 29, 1966, issue reprinted the Jacob Loewen piece that first appeared in the *Leader*. Victor Adrian, member of the faculty at MB Bible College, long an advocate of the role that pietism played in shaping the Brethren, was drawn to Wiens' call for "authentic faith, for a genuine brotherhood and for an imaginative expression of Christian faith." This plea for rethinking theology and practice that would be appropriate for "our time and place" and the call for Christian maturity should not be ignored. Peter Penner, professor at Mount Allison University, was grateful that Wiens called for a new theology of Christian nurture and forcefully raised the problem of behavioral legalism that was culturally bounded. Penner also embraced Wiens' critique of chasing after evangelical alliances when Mennonite alliances offered "more wholesome partnerships."

Herbert Brandt, minister at the Killarney Park Church, Vancouver, British Columbia, and the only MB pastor to respond in either the *Leader* or *Herald* was both appreciative and concerned. He applauded the insightfulness: "I do not intend to dispute the fact that what has been said needed to be said," and yet he feared that "unless we know what to do

---

31. Jantz, "Wineskins," 3.

with an evaluation, it will create havoc. Its concepts can far too easily run rampant and become the master instead of the tool."[32]

The three responses in the *Herald* were undoubtedly solicited. That Wiens wrote a searing analysis and the absence of unsolicited responses from conference officials, professors at the denominational schools, or pastors drew the interest of the editors of both the *Leader* and *Herald*. Jantz, editor of the *Herald*, in his first comments about "Wineskins" in the October 29, 1965, issue replayed the comment of one pastor who wrote, "I am surprised that the article had to come from a layman. Why didn't it come from the seminary, Bible college, Bible schools or even one of our pastors?"[33] Harms, six months following the publication of "Wineskins," wrote that "one of our basic reasons for bringing *Wineskins* to the entire readership was to get us to face the indictments therein and either to refute them or to repent.... What has bothered me most... is that there has been almost total silence on the part of the ministers and leaders of the brotherhood."[34] Several months later, a small item in the *Herald* carried the news of an "official decision on the West Coast not to respond in print to the Delbert Wiens paper."[35]

That note about the West Coast leaders making an official decision not to respond piqued the interest of Harms. He subsequently wrote to Wiens that he had noticed the item in the *Herald* regarding this "so-called 'official' decision," investigated the allegation, and was not able to find any evidence of such an official position, but added, "It seems that our ministering brethren were determined not to respond."[36] Whether the decision not to respond was official or unofficial is unclear. What Jantz later did report was that Rueben Baerg, faculty member of the MBBS, stated that a West Coast committee was formed to respond to Delbert but that it eventually decided "that the best way to let the whole furor raised by the essay die would be to say nothing. And so nothing was said."[37]

---

32. See Adrian, "Where Do We Go?," 4–6; Penner, "Application," 6–7; Brandt, "What Does 'New Wineskins' Say?," 8–9.

33. Jantz, "Wineskins," 3.

34. Harms, "More about Wineskins," 2.

35. See "You Should Know That," 12.

36. Harms to Wiens, September 13, 1966, Wiens Papers, Box 1, "New Wineskins for Old Wine": responses 1965–1967 file, CMBS-F.

37. See Jantz to Warkentin, September 12, 1966, Mennonite Brethren Herald Archives, Center for Mennonite Brethren Studies-Winnipeg.

So why did those leaders who objected to Wiens not publicly express themselves. They would have done so had there been an egregious departure from normative MB theological understandings. Perhaps some of the clerics and denominational leaders did not fully understand "Wineskins." It did traffic in sociological and historical analysis that may have been unfamiliar to the clerics who comprised most of the denominational hierarchy. Wiens' critique struck harder at ineffectual church practices than at theological convictions. Perhaps some realized they were deeply implicated in the change of leadership that had put on the shelf the older, lay leadership and were too compromised to respond.[38] Perhaps they instinctively knew, as Baerg had suggested, that it would fade away before a response was required. "Wineskins" was strong on analysis, but weak in proposing concrete actions. In the realm of the ethereal, it is easy to make the case for the necessity of change. In the congregational trenches, constricted imaginations often mitigate against change. So minus programmatic directives it would have only short shelf life.

And yet more seems to be at stake. The general absence of responses from people in positions of leadership for this call for renewal does invite further analysis. Renewal and revitalization are almost sacred themes in MB history. Here was a strong call for renewal, and yet the church hierarchy and the intellectual class were muted in their response? Did they disagree on the need for renewal, or did other considerations prevail? The answer perhaps, unwittingly, lies in an October 31, 1965, letter written by John A. Toews. Toews, at the time president of MB Bible College in Winnipeg, Manitoba, wrote to Wiens, not to one of the periodicals: "This is just a simple and sincere word of appreciation for your articles or essays in 'New Wineskins for Old Wine.' It is providential . . . that the Lord would use you as a so-called 'lay-brother' to speak to us on some of the crucial issues facing our brotherhood today." One can surmise that the reason J. A. Toews wrote personally rather than for publication is contained in subsequent lines of the letter: "If it had been a member of one of our theological faculties, or an ordained minister of one of our larger churches, it would have been much easier to label the school or the individual, and thus dismiss the subject."[39]

The hesitancy of Toews to engage in public is even curious, for he wrote to H. R. Wiens, Delbert's father, "May I just add a personal note.

---

38. Wiens, interview by author, Fresno, CA, December 10, 2013.

39. Toews to Wiens, October 31, 1965, Wiens Papers, Box 1, "New Wineskins for Old Wine": responses 1965–67 file, CMBS-F.

We really appreciate the articles of your son Delbert in the insert of the *C. Leader*. I believe he speaks to our Brotherhood with a 'prophetic voice' and he deserves a very careful and sympathetic hearing. After I read that treatise on the M.B. church, I said to a friend of mine: This gives me hope for the future of our church! God grant us more such brethren, who will not fear to speak out, and give us the truth in the spirit of love and deep concern."[40]

Toews' letter holds at least a partial answer to why the academic and clerical class was largely silent, and why the denominational impact of "Wineskins" was limited. In a world of restricted theological thinking, labels, particularly pejorative ones, are easily utilized to categorize, to shunt aside, and even to dismiss. "They are not in our camp," so we pay no heed to their words.

Timing may also have limited responses. If 1965 seems like a good year for this critique, there were also headwinds, particularly for the academic class. Almost simultaneous to the publication of "Wineskins" a seminar on creation and evolution was held at Tabor College with participants also from Pacific College and the MBBS. There were multiple originating points for the seminar that grew out of differing positions within the academic class and denominational leaders on questions relative to the creation/evolution issue. In October 1964, the General Conference Board of Missions sent a letter to the General Conference Board of Reference and Counsel that expressed concern about the "educational program of our conference schools."[41] It identified a set of ethical, moral, and doctrinal issues. First up for discussion was the charge that "the theory of evolution as a possible and alternative view in the place of the creationist (Biblical) view is quite acceptable in certain departments within the educational program of our conference schools." Other concerns were suspicions of "a neo-orthodox subjective view of the doctrine of inspiration," and standards on moral and ethical issues "to the extent of impugning our conference position on separation and worldliness."[42]

40. Quoted in a letter Delbert's mother, Barbara Wiens wrote to him on November 2, 1965. See Wiens Papers, Box 1, "New Wineskins for Old Wine": responses 1965–67 file, CMBS-F.

41. The General Conference was a binational conference consisting of the Canadian and American national conferences. It also had a Board of Reference and Counsel.

42. See the letter from P. R. Lange, chairman of the Board of Missions, to Frank C. Peters, chairman of the General Conference Board of Reference and Council. Lange to Peters, October 2, 1964, "Minutes of the General Conference Board of Reference and Counsel," January 15–16, 1965, CMBS-F.

The General Conference Board of Reference and Counsel responded to the wide-ranging concerns with request that Sol Loewen, professor of biology at Tabor College, write a paper on "Theistic Evolution" and Frank C. Peters, chairman of the General Conference and professor at MB Bible College in Winnipeg, write one on "Ethical Relativism." Both were to be submitted to the *Leader* and *Herald*. If completed, neither was published in either periodical.[43]

The Board of Reference and Counsel of the United States Conference echoed the position. Minutes of meetings in late August 1965 note a "concern over the lack of confidence in our faculty" in the denominational schools. The solution was to draw up a "unified doctrinal statement" that should be used by the schools. The specific trigger issue was theistic evolution: "In view of the current problem concerning the question of theistic evolution, this statement shall include an amplification of the point on the creation of man."[44]

The Southern District Conference, the regional conference in which Tabor was geographically located, established a working group together with the presidents of Tabor, Pacific, and the MBBS to stage a seminar on the creation/evolution issue. It convened on October 21 and 22, 1965. Program participants included scientists Daniel Isaak, professor of biology at Pacific; Solomon Loewen and Clarence Harms, professors of biology at Tabor; and theologians John B. Toews, president of the MBBS, and George W. Peters, formerly president of Pacific Bible Institute and dean of the MBBS during the 1950s.[45] Harms' paper, "A Perspective on Creation," was subsequently published in the *Journal of Church and Society*.[46] He identified five alternative positions: literal-day creation and fixity of species, catastrophism and fixity of species, progressive creation and fixity of species, threshold evolution, and monophyletic evolution. He concluded his review of the alternatives with a question and reply. "'What are the live alternatives?' For me as a Christian biologist, there are

---

43. See "Minutes of the General Conference Board of Reference and Counsel," January 15–16, 1965, CMBS-F.

44. See "Minutes of the US Board of Reference and Counsel," August 23–25, 1965, US Conference Archives, II:C:1, File 2, Center for Mennonite Brethren Studies-Hillsboro.

45. See "Proceedings of the Creation Seminar held at Tabor College, October 21 and 22, 1965," CMBS-H.

46. Harms, "Perspective," 3–21.

only two: Threshold Evolution and Monophyletic Evolution."[47] He was embracing a position commonly known as "theistic evolution." It was a position that provided room for evolutionary change and the formation of new subspecies and species that "takes place orderly and is creative activity of God himself upon which the affirmation, 'It is good' can be applied properly."[48] It was a position that did not pit creation and evolution against each other.

Following the seminar, George W. Peters wrote an extended letter to various conference leaders including Edward J. Peters, chairman of the USMBC Board of Education; Toews, president of the seminary; and Roy Just, president of Tabor. He pled for "holding on to the absolutes of biblical creationism," a position that in his understanding could not accept theistic evolution. Abandoning biblical creationism would open the door for other dangers: "It is my firm conviction that if we lose first creationism in relation to matter, life and man (man as a duality in unity) in biology, we have opened the door for evolutionism in social sciences and in religion. We are thus lost in relativism."[49]

Beyond rejecting the position articulated by Harms, Peters also wanted restraint in what was said in conference schools. He noted that there was a "passionate plea for academic freedom. It was emphasized that freedom is a virtue." Academics were asking for freedom to speak, but pastors were not to criticize the schools publicly. "Should not the classroom be at least as cautious and restrained in reflecting negatively upon positions held and cherished by the conference as the pastors are requested to be in relation to the school. Are the schools to reform and reconstitute the conference or is the conference to guide the schools that it has established and is maintaining? Who has the priority? Are we losing our moral perspective in clamoring for academic freedom?"[50]

Almost immediately following the seminar at Tabor, the USMBC, meeting in Dallas, Oregon, dealt with statements on creation/evolution and the inspiration of the Scriptures, issues on which there was certainly

---

47. Ibid., 10.

48. Ibid., 10–11.

49. See G. W. Peters to E. J. Peters, Wieke [sic], John Ratzlaff, Roy Just, and Toews, J. B. Toews Papers, CMBS-F.

50. Ibid. A follow-up conference on creation and evolution sponsored by the Board of Reference and Counsel of USMBC was held at Tabor in November 1966. This time the speakers were only theologians: David Ewert of MB Bible College and John C. Wenger.

some room for divergent opinions and the kind of issues that could encourage the academic class to keep their opinions to themselves.

Creation/evolution and the question of how to understand the inspiration of the Scriptures were then, as today, what are often termed hot-button issues. The slightest deviance from commonly accepted formulations could seem like heresy. Almost immediately after publication of "Wineskins," one young minister, Marvin Schmidt of the Minneapolis MB Church, wrote to Wiens that the forthcoming USMB conference would be "enlightening to say the least and maybe a kind of showdown." He no doubt concluded that "Wineskins" and the Tabor seminar would emerge as conflicting issues. There was "a need to do some real thinking and fast or be swept down the stream of mediocrity." He mused, "Perhaps we have already been 'washed out.'" He had not intended to attend the conference but now recognized that "[he could not] sit idly by and let things go down the river." He went "hoping and praying that schism [might] be avoided." His comments paralleled those of Harold Jantz who wrote that some thought "Wineskins" would "split our conference down the middle."[51]

Under the guidance of the USMBC Board of Reference and Counsel a resolution on creation/evolution was passed:

> We believe and hold that the events recorded and people named in the Genesis account of creation are history; that the creation of man was unique, in that he was created in the image of God; that he was created by a special act of God, both biologically and spiritually, and not from any previously existing organic forms of life.[52]

The other contentious issue in the conference proceedings on confessional issues was what some regarded as the insufficiency of the article on the inspiration of the scriptures. The USMBC Board of Reference and Counsel responded by noting that divergent understandings in the evangelical world on the meaning of inspiration were not simply "superficial differences of opinion, but a profound and subtle divergence of theological rootage and principles of biblical interpretation." Whether

---

51. Schmidt to Wiens, October 23, 1965, Wiens Papers, Box 1, "New Wineskins for Old Wine": responses 1965–1967 file, CMBS-F; Jantz, "New Wineskins," 3.

52. *Minutes and Reports*, 17–18.

this discussion referenced Wiens is not noted. It certainly parallels the concern expressed in the dissenting letter by Dale Warkentin.[53]

Both of these issues, creation/evolution and the inspiration of the Scriptures, were part of a larger confessional conversation. The multiplication of abridged confessional statements by schools and churches argued for the need of a standardized version. So the abridged version created by the USMBC Board of Reference and Counsel was introduced. To it was added the amended article on creation/evolution. This need for standardization was coupled by a request from the Lincoln Glen MB Church, in San Jose, California, that all ministers, conference workers, officers, and teachers in conference schools and graduates of the seminary "be required to accept the Confession of Faith of the General Conference with special emphasis and amplification being given to the acceptance of the Inspired Scriptures, and acceptance of the biblical account of creation in contrast to the various theories of evolution." This resolution was accepted with the exemption that the question of assent by seminary students be referred to the MBBS president and faculty.[54]

The weight and role of "Wineskins" in these conference deliberations are not entirely clear. If, as the editors of the respective denominational periodicals thought, it had generated discussion in many quarters, then it surely was part of the backdrop for these conference discussions.

The larger question of whether this powerful call for renewal had denominational consequence is also difficult to discern. The many response letters certainly suggest that individuals better understood their own religious culture. Practices that were supposedly rooted in scriptural understandings often turned out to be cultural markers. Understandings of the morphology of conversion through the social sciences could demystify the sublime and ineffable. It facilitated understandings as to the way in which the denomination had changed. It renewed hope that open, honest conversations about denominational shortcomings could be addressed.

Ideas can have consequences, but oftentimes it is difficult to see how they affect denominations. Did "Wineskins" reshape the MB? Did it achieve what I think was Wiens' central concern: attention to the development of spiritual maturity? Did it broaden the conversionist preoccupation of the MB toward nurture and growth? Such questions are not

---

53. Ibid., 19.
54. Ibid., 11, 15–20.

readily answered. However, evidence of corporate change is hard to find. The reason it is difficult to find any denominational impact is in part because of Wiens' writing style. The piece is not linear, the allusions are numerous, the meanings sometime elusive. It was certainly informed by social-science understandings. Some of the clergy were no doubt shaped by an orthodox rationalism that could ignore a critique grounded in historicism where everything emerged out of a specific context. "Wineskins" by invoking change implicitly challenged disembodied systems of thought. "Wineskins" was not didactic. It did not lay out an agenda that conference bureaucrats could implement. It was a call to reflection, integrated thinking, and vital encounters with the Divine.

The impact of pieces like "Wineskins" depends at least in part on how it appeals to those with the power to shape the denominational dialogue. In the case of the USMBC, the disproportionate energy of the years subsequent to the publication of "Wineskins" went into the Decade of Enlargement program. Every issue of the *Leader* in the year following had encouragement for activism in this program. Letters to the editor suggested that "Wineskins" was of interest. Official denominational preoccupation was elsewhere. With no track record of significant growth beyond biological reproduction during most of the denomination's history there was, in fact, no basis for even dreaming about doubling in a decade. Wiens was correct in "Wineskins" to question it. The decade concluded with an 8.6 percent growth, not the one hundred percent for which the planners hoped. It was a program rooted in illusion well beyond reasonable expectation.[55] Trying to understand and work out the implications of "Wineskins" might have produced more authentic growth than this misconceived program.

1965 may seem like a year when United States MB intellectuals came of age, and yet 1965 may also be a revelatory moment for helping us to understand the emasculation of the academic class in MB circles. Silence in the face of the opportunity that "Wineskins" presented is best understood as hesitancy of the intellectual class to speak forthrightly. With calls for confessional conformity, bounded conference formulations on critical questions like creation/evolution, and restrictive expressions about academic freedom, one can understand the hesitancy of MB academics to engage in a vigorous public discussion. The silence is an episode in the larger history of the marginalization of MB academics.

55. The percentage of growth is from tabulations made from consulting the yearbooks of the national conference and the regional or district conferences.

The US Conference Board of Reference and Counsel in less than a year following "Wineskins" spent a session identifying what it termed "major concerns of the USA brotherhood." Among them were "the widening chasm between church and school."[56]

Delbert Wiens' own career for the past fifty years is a prime example of that marginalization. During the half-century since its publication Wiens has been a kind of public intellectual among the MB. He has advanced degrees from the finest universities of the land. In the world of academic discourse, professional peers become the evaluators of one's work. Wiens long ago eschewed those conventions and instead wished to function more in the tradition of a public intellectual; he has addressed broad social and religious issues. Even as he reveres the integration of life and thought of earlier generations, so he has sought to address serious issues in a learned tradition that was accessible to the MB of his generation.

Wiens has a commitment to his church community. He has not written for the scholarly world, but rather for the churchly community. Within that community, he has functioned like an intellectual should: tracking down mythologies, unmasking partial understandings that have been elevated to cardinal truth, and seeing beyond the conventions and simplicities that blind us to deeper and larger truths. He has been not only critical of select issues, but also of our larger metaphysical worldviews. He had the courage to take on our entire belief system, not to denigrate, but to enlarge. He has been willing to challenge the assumptions that denominations tend to develop. In challenging obsolete assumptions, he created space for new ones to emerge. For MB (and others) who repeated simple litanies filled with half-truths, his mind has indeed been dangerous. Often times people who work for denominational institutions feel the necessity to become spin doctors for denominational positions; they feel the need to become apologists for denominational understandings. Not Wiens. He has not played the non-partisan role, the non-ideological role, but has been an advocate. He has done it in his gentle way, with humility, with tolerance, and always accompanied by a self-deprecating sense of his own profound insights.

Generations of troubled students at Corn Bible Academy, Tabor College, and Fresno Pacific University found their way to Wiens' office. For close to twenty-five years, I occupied an office next to his at Fresno Pacific. I know something of the traffic into his office. The brightest

---

56. See "Minutes of Board of Reference and Counsel, USMBC, August 9 and 10, 1966," US Conference Archives, I:C:1, file 2, CMBS-H.

students gravitated into his orbit. With him they could express their most profound doubts and skepticism, and he helped them find their way to a religious understanding appropriate to their station in life. Unfortunately, his denominational community has not often turned to him to address issues of critical importance. It is the lesser for not having engaged one of its most creative and devoted minds.

Bibliography

Adrian, Victor. "Where Do We Go From Here." *Mennonite Brethren Herald*, April 15, 1966.
Bishop, Marcus. "What Readers Say." *Christian Leader*, January 4, 1966.
Brandt, Herbert. "What Does 'New Wineskins for Old Wine' Say about Conversion?" *Mennonite Brethren Herald*, April 15, 1966.
Cutrell, Ben. "What Readers Say." *Christian Leader*, January 18, 1966.
Dyck, C. J. "1525 Revisited: A Comparison of Anabaptist and Mennonite Brethren Origins." In *Pilgrims and Strangers: Essays in Mennonite Brethren History*, edited by Paul Toews, 55–77. Fresno: Center for Mennonite Brethren Studies, 1977.
Dyck, John R. "What Readers Say." *Christian Leader*, November 9, 1965.
"Editorial: Invitation to Involvement." *Journal of Church and Society* 1, no. 1 (Spring 1965) 2.
Esau, John A. "What Readers Say." *Christian Leader*, October 26, 1965.
Flaming, Jeanette. "What Readers Say." *Christian Leader*, December 7, 1965.
Froese, R. J. "What Readers Say." *Christian Leader*, April 12, 1966.
Goertzen, Peggy, et al. *Tabor College: A Century of Transformation, 1908–2008*. Hillsboro, KS: Center for Mennonite Brethren Studies, 2008.
Gross, Mrs. Duane. "What Readers Say." *Christian Leader*, June 7, 1966.
Harms, Clarence. "A Perspective on Creation." *Journal of Church and Society* 2, no. 2 (Fall 1966) 3–21.
Harms, Orlando. "More about Wineskins." *Christian Leader*, April 16, 1966.
———. "Special Edition Next Issue." *Christian Leader*, September 28, 1965.
———. "Special Insert Issue." *Christian Leader*, October 12, 1965.
Jantz, Harold. "New Wineskins for Old Wine." *Mennonite Brethren Herald*, October 29, 1965.
Jantzen, G. H. "What Readers Say." *Christian Leader*, December 7, 1965.
Janzen, Lester E. "What Readers Say." *Christian Leader*, January 4, 1966.
Kaethler, Wilhelm, and Frieda Wilhelm. "What Readers Say." *Christian Leader*, May 10, 1966.
Klassen, A. J., ed. *The Seminary Story: Twenty Years of Education in Ministry, 1955–1975*. Fresno: Mennonite Brethren Biblical Seminary, 1975.
Loewen, Jacob. "A Personal Reaction to 'New Wineskins for Old Wine.'" *Christian Leader*, April 26, 1966.
"Mennonite Brethren Historical Society." *Christian Leader*, February 2, 1965.
Minutes and Reports of the Eighth Convention of Mennonite Brethren Churches of the United States, October 30–November 1, 1965. Hillsboro, KS: Mennonite Brethren Publishing House, 1965.
Nachtigall, George. "What Readers Say." *Christian Leader*, October 26, 1965.
Neuman, Robert. "What Readers Say." *Christian Leader*, November 23, 1965.
"Pacific College Awarded Western Accreditation." *Christian Leader*, May 25, 1965.
Penner, Peter. "An Application of 'New Wineskins for Old Wine to the Canadian MB Church Scene." *Mennonite Brethren Herald*, April 15, 1966.
Schmidt, P. A. "What Readers Say." *Christian Leader*, February 15, 1966.
Seibel, Ervin E. "What Readers Say." *Christian Leader*, February 1, 1966.
Siemens, William. "What Readers Say." *Christian Leader*, December 21, 1965.
Suderman, Dale. "What Readers Say." *Christian Leader*, November 23, 1965.

"Tabor College Receives North Central Accreditation." *Christian Leader*, April 13, 1965.

Toews, John A. *A History of the Mennonite Brethren Church: Pilgrims and Pioneers.* Fresno: Board of Christian Literature, General Conference of Mennonite Brethren Churches, 1975.

Toews, John B. *Perilous Journey: The Mennonite Brethren in Russia, 1860–1910.* Winnipeg: Kindred, 1988.

Toews, Paul, ed. *Mennonite Idealism and Higher Education: The Story of the Fresno Pacific College Idea.* Fresno: Center for Mennonite Brethren Studies, 1995.

———. "Peter Klassen: Mediating the Past to Shape the Future." *California Mennonite Historical Society Bulletin*, Fall 2009.

Unrau, William G. "What Readers Say." *Christian Leader*, November 23, 1965.

Vogt, Esther L. "What Readers Say." *Christian Leader*, October 26, 1965.

Warkentin, Dale. "What Readers Say." *Christian Leader*, December 7, 1965.

Wiens, Delbert. "From the Village to the City: A Grammar for the Languages We Are." *Direction* 2, no. 4 (October 1973) 98–149.

———. "Mennonite Brethren: Neither Liberal Nor Evangelical." *Direction* 20, no. 1 (Spring 1991) 38–63.

———. "New Wineskins for Old Wine: A Study of the Mennonite Brethren Church." Insert in the *Christian Leader*, October 12, 1965.

"You Should Know That." *Mennonite Brethren Herald*, July 8, 1966.

Section 2

Memoirs

4

Delbert Wiens
A Sage Among Us

Peter Klassen

For those fortunate enough to have studied under Professor Wiens, or to have made his acquaintance in a variety of settings, the image of a sage comes readily to mind. Since Delbert specialized in ancient history and philosophy, Raphael's painting "The School of Athens" seems an appropriate allusion. I think most of us can readily remember scenes where we see Delbert holding forth as others listen in rapt attention.

Delbert clearly enjoyed the classroom; students who raised serious questions could expect a detailed, highly informative response. The professor assumed the student really wanted to know, and so the resulting reply was lengthy, highly informative and usually well beyond anything the inquirer had expected. It was very evident that the scene reflected a situation where wisdom and insight were readily available to anyone with the temerity to inquire. There was never a flip answer, no suggestion that the question was foolish or reflected ignorance. Rather, the professor took students and questions seriously and gave the inquirer a full measure of knowledge needed to understand the issue raised.

Those who have known Delbert for an extended period have gained respect for his patience and breadth of knowledge. Clearly, he holds the view that anyone raising a serious issue deserves an answer that indicates respect for the inquirer by giving a response that provides both a setting and an interpretation of the question. His breadth of learning and analysis has not been for those who lack patience or want short responses. However, I suspect some onlookers would echo the sentiments in lines from Oliver Goldsmith's "The Deserted Village" where the reader is reminded of observers who "came to scoff remained to pray."[1]

History is replete with instances where serious questions were asked but received only cursory responses. I doubt that many ever had that experience with Professor Wiens. Most of us can recall instances where the situation was more reminiscent of a scene described in the Gospel of Luke where we read that "it will be given to you: good measure, pressed down, shaken together and running over. . . ."[2]

Those of us who have pondered Delbert's analyses of the development of Mennonite thought and practice, as depicted in the provocative studies such as "Wineskins," his later "Village," as well as subsequent analyses of the impact of the quest for finding a balance between *Gottesfurcht* (fear or reverence of God) and *Gelassenheit* (confident yieldedness to God), have come to respect his ability to examine and explain trends and factors in the shaping of a faith tradition.

Sometimes I have thought that the Delbertian response and analytical technique is somewhat reminiscent of interrogation sessions in early modern times, when Anabaptists were interrogated on matters of faith and practice. In many instances, they were ordered to recant or face death, although under some rulers, such as Phillip of Hesse, they were given permission to explain their beliefs. Fortunately, we have a number of accounts where Anabaptists in Phillip's territories were able to present lengthy explanations of their beliefs, so that, unlike many other contemporary rulers, he refused to condemn Anabaptists to death. Sometimes these interrogations would extend over many days; one can almost imagine Delbert in such a situation. I am confident that if such a drama had been presented, Delbert would not have been the one to be worn out by weeks, even months, of debate.

The sixteenth and seventeenth centuries were replete with religious controversy and persecution. In some instances, formal debates were held; on other occasions, dissenters were simply invited to present their

---

1. Goldsmith, "Deserted Village," 624.
2. Luke 6:38 NKJV.

points of view. Persons not conforming to the "official" truths of faith risked incurring heavy penalties. In a striking exception among the larger countries, Poland provided a remarkable degree of toleration. At a time when Germany was torn by religious strife, such as the Thirty Years' War, France was expelling Protestants, and England was burning bishops and later imprisoning nonconformists such as John Bunyan, Poland offered a haven of toleration. At the same time, some champions of the "old order" apparently wanted to determine just what kinds of "heresy" were being tolerated in the Polish kingdom. In 1678, at the direction of Polish King John Sobieski, an investigation was conducted into the teachings and practices of Mennonites in the Danzig area. Accordingly, Stanisław Sarnowski, bishop of the region that included Danzig, attired in his episcopal robes and attended by lawyers and theologians of the Catholic Church, conducted an investigation of the Frisian and Flemish Mennonite churches in Danzig.[3]

Handwritten accounts of the sessions attended by the ministers of the Mennonite churches are abbreviated but, nonetheless, reflect the basic tenor of the interrogations. Van Duhren of the Frisian church appeared first and, since the question of Arianism had arisen, the first query dealt with the Trinity. Van Duhren emphatically asserted that Mennonites believed that Christ was a member of the trinity, truly divine and truly human. Another question raised an issue that reflected a view of some Lutheran leaders, such as Luther's comment that the pope was the antichrist. To the query whether Mennonites also regarded the pope as antichrist, the minutes record that Van Duhren responded in "the strongest negative." When he was asked about baptizing infants to free them from the condemnation of original sin, he responded that he did not believe infants were born already condemned by original sin.

The interrogation continued for several days, and each congregation was invited to respond to a series of questions. When Van Duhren's sessions were finished, Elder Georg Hansen appeared on behalf of the Flemish Mennonite congregation. In preparation for this interrogation, Hansen had written his "*Confession oder kurzes, Einfältiges Glaubensbekenntnis der Mennoniten in Preussen.*"[4] He too was subjected to a series of

---

3. A fascinating account of the meeting between the bishop and his supporters, confronting Mennonite leaders Hendrik van Duhren and Georg Hansen, is found in the *Bibliotheka Polskiej Akademia Nauk w Gdańsku* (*BPANG*), MS. 973. See also Plett, "Georg Hansen."

4. *BPANG*, MS. 694.497; Plett, "Georg Hansen," 221.

questions. When he was asked about the Mennonite refusal to bear arms, he suggested that the old adage of "an eye for an eye" had been superseded by Christ's command to love one's enemies, and so he rejected participation in war. When he was asked about his view of the pope, he cryptically responded that he was prepared to give the pope all of the honor that God had given him. One can almost imagine the Jesuit scholar, who was in attendance at the session, wondering just what that response meant, or perhaps smiling at casuistry worthy of his own order.

The question of baptism provided the opportunity for stimulating dialogue. When the interrogator argued that infants should be baptized, lest they die and be condemned, Hansen replied that a newborn infant had done neither good nor evil, and, since Hansen rejected the dogma of original sin, infants should not be regarded as already in need of baptism. Instead, the child should be given proper training and instruction, and then be invited to be baptized. Hansen said he had no desire to denigrate Catholic baptism, but his belief was that baptism should be a response to someone's faith and obedience to Christ.

The question of baptism became a thorny issue when the Jesuit challenged Hansen on the practice of rebaptism of those who had been baptized as infants. Where was there a scriptural warrant for such a practice? Hansen responded that the book of Acts records how those who had been baptized by John were later baptized, as Acts puts it, "into Jesus." Evidently the bishop and his entourage were satisfied with the responses, and Hansen stated that the churches had been freed "from suspicion." At the same time, some of the interrogators suggested the Mennonite leaders might strengthen their good relations by making a financial contribution to the construction of a tower for a Catholic church. The Mennonites gathered the funds and helped build the tower. Apparently local Lutherans, by then a strong force in the city, felt they deserved equal treatment and, not surprisingly, Mennonites contributed 300 fl. toward the building of a Lutheran church as well. Apparently, money could be a powerful palliative. In any event, Hansen and his colleagues held that strengthening good relations with other religious bodies was well worth a modest financial contribution. Then, as now, constructive diplomacy, buttressed by financial considerations, could build bridges of understanding.

It might also be noted that building bridges of understanding and good will was by no means restricted to church issues. Just a few years after the sessions with the bishop in Danzig, King John III issued a statement praising Mennonites for their many generous contributions to economic prosperity and agricultural development in the Vistula Delta, reaffirming their "rights, privileges and practices." In view of the record established by numerous Mennonite communities, the king warned that no "restriction of their rights or the free exercise of their religion" would be tolerated.[5] Clearly, Mennonites had firmly asserted their beliefs, and had effectively answered their critics.

Since the king chose to issue a statement supporting the Mennonites, it might be noted that this was by no means unique. King John III's position reflected one taken by King Władisław in 1642 when he pointed out that Mennonites had been invited to come to Poland:

> We are well aware of the manner in which the ancestors of the Mennonite inhabitants of the Marienburg islands *(Werder)*, both large and small, were invited here with the knowledge and by the will of the gracious King Sigismund Augustus, to areas that were barren, swampy and unusable places in those islands. With great effort and at very high cost, they made these lands fertile and very productive. They cleared out the brush, and, in order to drain the water from these flooded and marshy lands, they built windmills and constructed dams . . .[6]

At the same time, it should be remembered that Mennonites in Poland continued to face criticism both from political authorities as well as from Catholic and Lutheran church leaders. When, for example in 1779, a young woman who had been baptized as an infant expressed a desire to join the Orlofferfelde Mennonite church, Pastor Heinrich Donner and other church leaders declared their readiness to accept her, but the question of baptism would need to be clarified. Donner insisted she would need to be baptized upon her profession of faith. Meanwhile, some of Donner's associates suggested that she be accepted upon her profession of faith alone, since her rebaptism might arouse sharp criticism from both Catholic and Lutheran leaders. To baptize her might conjure up images of Mennonites as rebaptizers, and might revive some of the charges brought against them during the Reformation. Now that Mennonites enjoyed relative freedom, both in religious and in economic matters, one should not resurrect images of the harsh events of the sixteenth century. Donner, however, asserted that church policy and belief could not be accommodated to the wishes of those who did not agree with

---

5. Plett, "Georg Hansen," 364.
6. *Archivum Państwowe Gdańsku (APG)*, 358/132.

Mennonite practice. Accordingly, he insisted that this young woman be fully instructed in Mennonite belief and then be baptized and welcomed into the church. To help assuage fears of fellow ministers, Donner invited some non-Mennonite community leaders and personal friends to come and witness the ceremony. They did attend and the critics of Donner were largely silenced. His view had prevailed; he had been exonerated. Courage and openness had carried the day, and Donner had not simply adapted practice to the whims of the moment.[7]

Donner also worked to achieve broad doctrinal unity in the large Mennonite community. He entered into dialog with Mennonites in the Netherlands to establish a measure of unity and uniformity in confessional statements and doctrinal practices. He was also a leader in championing the concept of equality before the law. Together with another Mennonite leader, he led a move to gain greater religious equality before the law, and to free Mennonites from having to pay a special tax, solely because of their faith.[8] His legacy includes a collection of historical documents, sermons, and numerous notations about his positive relations with other church leaders, both Protestant and Catholic.

The times of persons like Hansen and Donner called for persons of courage, vision, knowledge, diplomacy, and tact. Our honoree, I am confident, would have felt very much at home in that setting. When a probing analytical question is asked, we have come to expect a thoughtful, enlightening response, and we have not been disappointed.

---

7. See the account in *APG*, 358/301. Donner's handwritten account of this event and many other experiences that demonstrate his strong leadership begins simply, "Anno 1774 on the twentieth of September, I began to write this book, recounting noteworthy events that occurred since I began to serve this congregation."

8. *APG*, sig. 836/1, 12-13.

Bibliography

Archivum Państwowe Gdańsku. 358/132, 358/301, 836/1.
Bibliotheka Polskiej Akademii Nauk w Gdańsku. MS. 497, 694, 973.
Goldsmith, Oliver. "The Deserted Village." In *The College Survey of English Literature*, edited by Alexander M. Witherspoon, 624. New York: Harcourt, Brace, 1952.
Plett, Harvey. "Georg Hansen and the Danzig Flemish Mennonite Church: A Study in Continuity." PhD diss., University of Manitoba, 1991.

5

A Living Braid of Social Justice

Faith Nickel Adams

As a girl and young woman, I never learned to crochet, knit, or sew, yet I retain my liking for and interest in fabrics. Indeed, I do love the braid, despite the epistolary injunction against "braided hair."[1] One needs only to visit the *Republique du Congo*, as I did between 1965 and 1967, to delight in the glorious array of braids. At that point, I began to separate what is cultural and what essential in terms of hermeneutics. I relate to the braid. It has a beginning, and it has an end.

Professional scholarship finds its focus through a separation of what is central from that which is peripheral, proceeding in an evidential trajectory to a well-argued conclusion. Despite the unorthodox nature of the metaphor of the braid, its use is necessary to my reflections here. The metaphor of the braid does not lend itself to a central strand or to a peripheral strand. Each strand is essential to the hank that will become aesthetic or useful.

I have entitled my reflection "A Living Braid," as there is not just one strand. Rather, there are many instances, traditionally and historically, in which a group of persons encounters a teacher or mentor in authentic contemporaneity who instructs and exposes them to larger-than-life, emulable figures—in my case, the life, epoch, and works of *a* person. My

---

1. 1 Tim 2:9 RSV.

braid, then, may be said to have three strands: the class of 1965 at Tabor College; Mr. Delbert Wiens, long since a scholar, writer, and teacher at the postdoctoral level; and the historical personage of Dietrich Bonhoeffer.

As I set out to characterize my colleagues and myself, I would caution the reader that I am working from memories nearly fifty years in age. I would be loath to misstate, understate, or overstate "the facts," but I will attempt to recount those memories so far as I can remember them. Where I am venturing into speculation, I have tried to indicate so.

I recall our class of 1965 as fun loving, high-spirited, and rambunctious. The two required courses, into which we all as freshmen were enrolled, were English and Life and Times of Jesus Christ. Freshman English featured the supplemental instruction and guidance of Tabor seniors who were teaching assistants. The Life and Times of Jesus Christ was taught by the Rev. Marvin Hein and was convened in what served as both chapel and auditorium at 7:30 a.m.! (The early start time served morning people well; it was otherwise for night owls.) Mr. Hein, however, kept us all awake. He anticipated PowerPoint with his humorous yet astute slideshows from Charles Schultz' *Peanuts*. No one, ever after, picked up that comic strip wearing the old lenses. A freshman elective to which students flocked was the Monday night practice for Dr. Paul Wohlgemuth's presentation of the Christmas section of Handel's *Messiah*. The practices were a social occasion, an opportunity to sing without audition, and a legitimate chance to let off steam.

The larger spiritual and social fabric into which freshmen were "braided" was chapel. We had amazing moments such as the live lecture of John Griffin, author of *Black Like Me*, whose dermatological experiment resulted in his graphic narrative. I for one will never forget administrative use of chapel as a disciplinary measure out of which grew confession and restitution. My own parents had always taught me that "the church is a closed garden," and so it still seemed between 1961 and 1965. Our famous Wittenberg Door, paradoxically, allowed a freedom of expression that we cherished. Dorm life and dorm councils offered sounding boards that were at times terse, at others hilarious. To be serenaded beneath one's third-floor window was a treat, with young men vocalizing in *Plaut Deetsch*: "Du best meene zunsheene, / Du best meene zunsheene." Indeed, students who were local residents of Hillsboro were not left out of the mix; they mingled well at chapel, socials, and retreats. Of course, we envied them their joyrides and sorties to Marion, Peabody, and Wichita. We dorm-bound were stuck with an evening malt at the Dude and discussions about coursework.

The phrase that comes to mind in characterizing our class is unity in variety. If one were to avail oneself of it, Tabor held something for everybody. In a more speculative mode, the class of 1965 had several one-of-a-kind types. There were students who had dropped out of high school yet enrolled as freshmen anyway. There were students who "CLEP'd in" or "AP'd in"—enrolled with advanced standing. Always there were students with independent studies and directed reading projects. There were students who graduated early, and students who transferred out of Tabor. We were by no means monolithic.

With the influence of the senior teaching assistants and several seniors in formal individualized studies as protégés of faculty, there was a lot in the air. There was an upward draft in the academic atmosphere. Inevitably, a number of freshmen liked to hang out with older students. (I am tempted to draw upon the work of family systems analyst Murray Bowen and will put the following under speculation.) It seems we had a number of "parentified" members as well as some "special" ones, i.e., leaders, eldest siblings, youngest siblings, and only siblings.[2]

A magnetic class that attracted some of these was English 101A. By *A*, it is not meant that members earned *A*s, but rather that requirements for critical reading and thinking as expressed in oral discourse and composition were higher. Heightened discussion, debate, and disputation were encouraged. We had great *esprit de corps*. Meanwhile, our instructor, the restrained and understated Mr. John Heidebrecht, tempered us. I call the class of 1965 a "strand" in my "braid." Undoubtedly, upon the fiftieth anniversary of the class in 2015, an appointed secretary will compile a directory featuring marriages, professions, offspring, and necrology. A braid has a beginning, and it has an end.[3]

---

2. The concept of "the special child" is a household concept among psychologists and social workers operating within the Murray Bowen Family Analysis and Therapy System.

3. Where are we now? Perhaps we should revisit Menno Simons' view on law, court, and attorneys. In early 1980, I was pleased to visit Mr. Jim Nikkel (class of 1964) as he discussed his decision to make international law his specialty. May we have more like Jim! Meanwhile, we have become aware of the position of the honoree of this Festschrift. Dr. Delbert Wiens has long held that ordination is an admirable calling; however, he has said, the Christian community needs more laypersons who are biblically educated.

My proposal, an analogy, is not unique, profound, or complicated. Just as it is

Braiding on, I consider the unique ways in which Dr. Delbert Wiens interacted with and influenced us. Here, I make my *entrée* with a salient point: fellowship over food decreases barriers. Having scootered, sampled, sipped, and supped his way through much of Asia, Europe, and the States, Dr. Wiens was to become an *habitué* of Tabor's student cafeteria and, later, our new Student Union. Teaching took place not only in the classroom; it was ubiquitous. I have a distinct memory of an all-school retreat that was to kick off my sophomore year. I had been assigned to the food committee and was scrambling to get the condiments situated on a blanket on the grass. Dr. Wiens asked quietly, "Are you in charge here, Faith?" "Apparently not," I sighed. As dusk descended upon my friends and me, we realized that the retreat would be what we made it. No planning for activities or program had been announced, so I grabbed my baritone ukulele, and we sang an after-dinner, sit-down hootenanny. In an aside, I told myself, "Well, perhaps I was in charge, a little bit."[4]

Besides what I call *a ministry of presence*, one cannot help asking what constitutes good teaching, and who is a good teacher. Dr. Wiens played cognitive hardball. His classes in ancient, medieval, and modern philosophy challenged us to ask the hard questions, postulate answers, and act upon our convictions with vigor. Our professor's skills in framing questions, especially from secular, Socratic philosophy, were considerable. We found ourselves in positions to tolerate ambiguity, although sometimes we "wigged out." Persevering students marched right into Dr. Wiens' Honors Seminar in their eighth semester. I was a piker; I did not take the dare. As I write, I am assaying to repay that debt. Invariably, in surveying the pre-feminist era, anyone interested in cultural change would want to know what comprised the education of young women at Tabor. Although Dr. Wiens was not my advisor, he was on hand to ensure that academic challenge was available to the intellectually curious female. He was a feminist ahead of the emerging feminist era.

---

possible that we do not need more ordained pastors to congregations—we need more laity who are knowledgeable in biblical truths and principles—so also it is possible that we do not need more attorneys, but more citizens who can wield social justice through legal knowledge and skill.

4. The following is a list of names of Dr. Wiens' colleagues who also adroitly and noninvasively occupied student spaces to good effect: Miss Anna Bergen, Mr. Ken Esau, Rev. Marvin Hein, Mr. John Heidebrecht, Dr. Dean Kliewer, Dr. J. A. Loewen, Mrs. Malinda Penner Nikkel, Dr. Delmar Reimer, Mrs. Grace Utting, Mrs. Kaethke Warkentin, Dr. Orlando Wiebe, Dr. Vernon R. Wiebe.

In what follows, my "second strand" meets my "third strand." In the fall of 1964, Tabor's devotional committee chose *The Cost of Discipleship*, by Dietrich Bonhoeffer, for campus-wide reading, study, and discussion. What, then, was going on in our heads? We hailed from communities termed *die Stille im Lande*. As wannabe pacifists, could we justify the use of violence in the service of deterring violence, as in Bonhoeffer's decision to join a plot to assassinate Hitler? With no prior studies in either patristics or martyrology, we were disturbed with questions about genocide and social justice. Could one or should one open oneself to the negotiation of social justice with one's own martyrdom? Could one not? Two central tenets from *The Cost of Discipleship* were "costly grace" and "cheap grace."[5] At what price does social justice come? This period of our senior year may be constructed by what I term *the theater of the mind*. (I, for one, was reared by parents who verbalized and enacted practical Christianity. For them, after the singing, testifying, and praising were over, their admiration went to the person who quietly and consistently worked at improving the human lot. Dad and Mom were Book-of-James people.) Meanwhile, away from home, we read Bonhoeffer through lenses of utility and came up with nothing. Axiology, of which utility is a branch, forced us into the study of values. For Machiavelli, whom Hitler emulated, utility was all. From Theatre of the Absurd and other art colored by nihilism, we heard the typical voice of Addie Bundren: "People to whom sin is just a matter of words, to them salvation is just words too."[6] What of the utility of our own lives? Our forebears had reared us with a work ethic that emphasized service to others. Where did service to others fit into the *ethos* and mind of our decade?

In the midst of this tumultuous *theater of the mind*, arrived some actual, graphic theater. Then-Miss Malinda Penner, professor of English, drama, and speech, was a primary member of the devotional committee. With energy and insight, Miss Penner directed the visionary drama of Elizabeth Berryhill, *The Cup of Trembling*. Berryhill is abundantly versed in biblical material that lends itself to dramatization. Further, her extensive research into the life, works, and times of Bonhoeffer makes for credibility. One could say she succeeds as a dramatist because she combines historicity and immediacy. Berryhill effectively conveys the extent of the efforts of the West to rid the world of Hitler. The plot was not simply that of a lone Lutheran pastor,

---

5. Bonhoeffer, *Cost*, 45.
6. Faulkner, *As I Lay Dying*, 176.

rather it was organized and intercontinental. Bonhoeffer was an exemplar for the courage and faith in Christ that drove him to action. He was also known for his compassion and kindness to others in their suffering.

The last scene of the second act of *The Cup of Trembling* features one of the famed Suffering Servant passages that some have identified as a characterization of Jesus Christ in the context of the canon of the Old Covenant as transmitted into New Testament Christology.[7] (My own central metaphor suits the dramatist's use of the biblical phrase "like an antelope in a net."[8]) At any rate, this trammeled Suffering Servant is far beyond what can simply be dramatized, as it is theologically rich with doctrines of judgment, punishment, atonement, redemption, reconciliation, and theodicy. Berryhill's dramatic devices include a stage name for her central figure and a number of features of Reader's Theatre, even chancel drama. Her devices are classic although not necessarily akin to Greek Theatre: her main character's behaviors in this scene's climax include mute screaming, random pacing, befuddlement, exasperation, and uncontrollable shaking of hands;[9] in its denouement, there is affirmation, surrender, and joy.[10] One can almost hear Martin Luther's foregrounding: "*Hier stehe ich; ich kann nicht anders.*"

With these dual think pieces, text and drama, (later) Dr. Wiens and Miss Penner had packed a "double whammy." Further, from Miss Penner, our class received a short course that would prepare us to address anti-Semitism as an inflammatory concern revealed in Jewish literature, film, and stage in years to come.[11]

Four prongs of social consciousness honed our moral awareness in the sixties. Each of the four was emotionally charged and galvanizing. Each also had one or more upshots. The War in Vietnam increased our awareness of the world outside of our nation and of third-world countries. The upshot of this awareness was multiplex. For one, our friends felt the summons of the Peace Corps. Second, the Civil Rights movement

---

7. Isa 51:17–23 RSV.

8. Isa 51:20 RSV. See also the boy Isaac in Gen 22:9 and Eur. *IA*. The net as an organizing metaphor in Aesch. *Ag.*

In *Face of the Deep*, Charles B. Hanna paves the way for a Jungian progression from Taurus, to Aries, to Pisces.

9. Berryhill, *Cup*, 78–80.

10. Ibid., 82–90.

11. E.g., *The Borgias*, *The Boy with the Striped Pajamas*, *The Devil's Arithmetic*, *The Diary of Anne Frank*, *The Fiddler on the Roof*, and *The Pianist*.

prompted a sweeping glance around campus that revealed the faces of foreign students. An upshot of this awareness would, in time, yield to the formation of Tabor's School of Social Work and School of Nursing. Third, the emergence of feminism nudged female students to question our role in church and community, and whether our careers should revolve around the higher education of our husbands. Fourth, in assessing one's human potential, how far could therapy take a young person? What about affect? Did the way I felt about a moral issue dictate how I would behave in responding to it? The human potential movement was the domain of psychology, ontology, and aesthetics, yet it left an aching void. We wanted to go beyond theory.

Ours were confusing, exhilarating days. The class of 1965 had cut its teeth in the throes of change and reality long before television invented "reality shows." Our final words from Dr. Wiens comprised his address at our baccalaureate. It was a succinct summation of his time with us. Customarily, we expected to say good-bye at ceremonies on this weekend. However, Dr. Wiens' text exhorted us to "remember [our] leaders."[12] The eleventh chapter of Hebrews was replete with heroes and martyrs who had fought for social justice: "These all died in faith."[13] Some were martyrs, and some were not, but all were heroes. We should "imitate their faith."[14] If logic serves, one can imitate only that which one has remembered and, in imitating, one memorializes. Our baccalaureate and our commencement were our "beginning," our "imitating," our "following."

With my final strand, I "braid-in" Dietrich Bonhoeffer as he expresses himself in his poem "Who Am I?"[15] Despite acute sensory deprivation, this man on death row is nonetheless capable of formulating sensuous imagery. He does not accuse God of abandoning him. Yes, he feels isolated, missing loved ones while making friends of his warders.[16] He is in step with the psychology and art of the times, which, I think, tolerate, even embrace, what I call the *inexactitude of the self*.[17] As one examines the modern science of criminal justice, one encounters studies in "solitary" and other confinement. In "Who Am I?" Bonhoeffer

---

12. Heb 13:7 RSV.
13. Heb 11:13 RSV.
14. Heb 13:7 RSV.; cf. "whose faith follow," KJV.
15. Bonhoeffer, *Cost*, 18–20.
16. Ibid., 19.

17. See Berryhill, *Cup*. There is a visceral nature to the physical response typical in incarceration.

reflects some feelings that anticipate constructed "dementia," e.g., "like a beaten army fleeing in disorder."[18] This same feeling is also stated poetically in the Old Covenant: inevitably, "the silver cord [will] be loosed."[19] The synapses will snap. Most importantly, Bonhoeffer's was a process of mutual knowing: "Whoever I am, Thou knowest, O God, I am [T]hine!"[20] Bonhoeffer was able to praise his God as a God who knew humans. Can we, who are committed to social justice, do less?

What is the function of a braid? How does it operate? Primarily, the braid can be aesthetic, a thing of beauty. It can also be a lasso, securing a stray calf. It can be the definitive hemp that extends the white life preserver on the sea. In tropical villages, gnarled tendrils reach out to form bridges that sway in the wind yet still permit passage. And powerful cords bind the lumber upon which rests the city of Venice. Is the braid of social justice that I have been developing also the noose by which Bonhoeffer was summarily hanged? As grisly as it was, it was obviously somebody's sick notion of social justice. What, we ask, is beautiful about the hank of rope by which Bonhoeffer died? To say it is a mystery of martyrdom is unsatisfying; Bonheoffer "received not the promise."[21] His attitude toward his "days of misfortune" was one of acceptance.[22] He knew whose he was. Could we believe, as he did, that there is One who braids the braids, controls the cords, flings the nets? I believe this is the Bonhoeffer, the man who "died in faith," whom we should "imitate."[23] It is not the person who "scores"; it is not important that our exemplar score. I close with perhaps an odd, peripheral fragment from *Letters and Papers from Prison*:

> Guilt and freedom, not the humility
> of putting the blame on oneself, but the
> alternative of knowing that one is not the
> only cause of what has happened.[24]

We do not always "win,"[25] but in Christ, we can "always [say] Yes."[26]

18. Bonhoeffer, *Cost*, 19.
19. Eccl 12:6 KJV.
20. Bonhoeffer, *Cost*, 20.
21. Heb 11:39 KJV.
22. Bonhoeffer, *Cost*, 20.
23. Heb 11:13 RSV.
24. Bonhoeffer, *Letters and Papers*, 332.
25. Bonhoeffer, *Cost*, 19.
26. 2 Cor 1:19 RSV; Berryhill, *Cup*, 87.

Bibliography

Berryhill, Elizabeth. *The Cup of Trembling*. Greenwich: Seabury, 1959.
Bonhoeffer, Dietrich. *The Cost of Discipleship*. New York: Macmillan, 1963.
———. *Letters and Papers from Prison*. Edited by Eberhard Bethge. New York: Touchstone, 1971.
Faulkner, William. *As I Lay Dying*. New York: Vintage, 1990.
Hanna, Charles B. *Face of the Deep*. Philadelphia: Westminster, 1967.

6

Delbert Wiens
A Memoir

Richard Wiebe

DELBERT WIENS WAS MY philosophy and cultural history professor at Fresno Pacific College from 1970 to 1974. I took a philosophy minor and a cultural history major, the first custom major in that field, under him. I took Introduction to Philosophy, Modern Philosophy, Philosophy of History, Ethics, Logic, Philosophy of Religion and the independent study Ancient Philosophy of Education from him. He had earned an MDiv from Yale Divinity School and a PhD from the Cultural History Committee at the University of Chicago. His thesis advisor was Robert Grant, classics professor in the University of Chicago Divinity School. His dissertation was on the "General Education of Musonius Rufus." Rufus proposed an egalitarian liberal arts education for men *and* women.

Delbert wrote two seminal papers. "Wineskins" was published as an insert in the *Christian Leader* in 1965. He then published "Village" in the early 1970s. He came to Fresno Pacific College in 1969 having just completed his PhD. My father recruited and hired him despite his "controversial" reputation. After all, he was the eldest son of Rev. H. R. Wiens, the respected Mennonite Brethren (MB) pastor of the Reedley MB Church.

Delbert's two essays were widely read and provoked fierce debate. In actuality they were mild, reformist documents, classic studies in the functionalist school of the sociology of religion founded by American sociologist Talcott Parsons. Coupled with sociolinguistic analysis, Delbert's functionalist sociology of religion was a conservative, appreciative analysis of the MB Church. It was anything but radical, especially for being written during the 1960s. That his essays were controversial indicates the hyper-conservative character of North American MB. Delbert's major failure was to ignore the impact of economic class membership in his analysis. He eschewed anything that looked like a Marxist or neo-Marxist interpretation.

Marx had argued a number of salient points. (1) Religion, as the "sigh of the oppressed creature," the "opium of the people," meant, literally and at face value, that religion was a coping system of belief that allowed one to live a healthy life (Nietzsche's active, not reactive, will-to-power or will-to-life) in oppressive circumstances. Anabaptist-Mennonites suffered imprisonment, torture, and death for rejecting any official, government-subsidized state church. Together with their pacifism, this made them *personae non gratae* in Europe. They were martyred by Roman Catholic, Anglican, Lutheran, and Calvinist state churches. They eventually left Switzerland, Holland, and Germany and went to Poland and then Russia at the invitation of Catherine the Great. Settling in the Ukraine, Russia's premier wheat-growing region, the Mennonites flourished for two hundred years, from 1700 to 1900. They became *kulacks*, wealthy peasants. After the Bolshevik Revolution of 1917, their farms were collectivized and they were caught in the Civil War between the Reds and the Czarist Whites. They sided with the Whites, briefly established self-defense militias, later recognized as a huge mistake, and fled to Canada, the United States, and South America.

Marx argued that if the oppressive pain were abolished, the need for religion as a drug (opium) to mitigate the pain would diminish. Religion was not the issue or problem. The pain, exploitation of the working class, was the problem. Religious critique led inexorably to economic and political critique. Marx and Engels only wrote ninety pages on religion in twenty volumes of collected writings, and these were all early pieces. They quickly left off writing about religion and moved on to fry bigger fish, culminating in Marx' *Das Kapital*—a classic analysis focusing on Adam Smith's *Wealth of Nations*, David Ricardo's capitalist economics, and Thomas Malthus' population thinking. Marx argued that religion "covered-up" the real, substantial economic and political basis for human society and intellectual constructs.

(2) Marx did not argue for a "deterministic" view of class consciousness grounded in economic class. Marx used the German word *bestimmt* ("conditioned") to characterize the formative influence of class on consciousness. He held it was possible, and indeed actual in that a portion of the bourgeoisie defected to the petite-bourgeoisie and the proletariat in the French Revolution. He is crystal clear on *bestimmt* and the possibility of freeing oneself from a crude economic or political class-consciousness. Marx never argued for a crude base partaking in superstructural determinism with no free will. He called that a "heresy" and termed it "economism."

To ignore conditions, in the opposite extreme, was to articulate the "heresy" of "voluntarism," the idea that a person is totally free of all circumstances and can do anything they desire. Our first language, our family, our nation, and our residence are all *for us*. They condition us "always already" (Ricoeur) in the first instance. We do not choose our initial circumstances. But once educated, linguistically competent, and of age, we can move, learn other languages, leave home, marry, and learn many other things in a lifelong dialect of ever new initial conditions and creative additions. Just as the Irishman James Joyce learned English as a second language, once competent to write in English, redefined the nature and character of the modern English novel. He took initial conditions ("determinism") and used artistic creativity ("freedom") to rewrite the English novel genre. *Portrait of the Artist as a Young Man*, *Ulysses*, and the impenetrable *Finnegan's Wake* were the result. With Marcel Proust, *A la recherché du temps perdu* (*In Search of Lost Time*), they are the high priests of literary modernism. Joyce and Proust are explained by Marx' "conditioning" (*bestimmt*).

(3) Marx argued that the base (economic) conditioned (*bestimmt*) the superstructure (arts, politics, intellectual ideas, and consciousness in general). This was a dialectical relationship where, in the first instance, one is born into unchosen circumstances. These shape one's initial consciousness. But later, one can dialectically engage those circumstances, rise above or apart from them, and create new circumstances that, in turn, lead to more creative dialectical responses, etc., through history. Dialectical materialism is the "engine" of human history. It is materialism because we *begin* with concrete circumstances, empirically verifiable. It is dialectic because we are *not* "stuck" with those circumstances endlessly

and in a rote manner condemned to simply repeat them. Marx' name for the "history of dialectical materialism" through the trajectory of time is "historical dialectics," the history of dialectics.

This excursus into Marx is the basis for a critique of Delbert's two essays, "Wineskins" and "Village." Both are, as I said, examples of functionalist sociology of religion. They are conservative, appreciative, reformist, pious examinations of MB religious tradition. As such, they fail to engage the real underlying basis that conditions MB ideology. They rely on horizontal breadth, staying on surface phenomena like language, demographics, family, tradition, and history. They do not dig vertically in-depth. There is no Foucauldian "archaeology" at work in these essays. They opt for biblical metaphor ("Wineskins") or sociolinguistics ("Village"). Demographics—village, town, city or the rural, the community, the urban—dominate and are the hermeneutical key. Delbert ignores economic class membership.

Mennonite Brethren are overwhelmingly middle middle class. They are typically not wage-earning working class. They are family farmers, small, independent business owners, and professionals (teachers, pastors, doctors, lawyers, and dentists). They are Marx' petite-bourgeoisie, the French notion of "shopkeepers." The petite-bourgeoisie aspire to be members of the bourgeoisie. They want to move up to the proverbial "upper East side and own a piece of the pie" (*The Jeffersons* television program). Grasping after wealth and power is the petite-bourgeoisie way. Some Mennonite Brethren have succeeded. Today, the Tea Party dominates the Republican Party in Kern, Kings, Tulare, Fresno, and Madera Counties. As petite bourgeoisie in the San Joaquin Valley, the MB have been infected by the Tea Party virus. In a rush to be "acceptable" they "sold their birthright," their Anabaptist-Mennonite heritage. They have become, "self-haters," in order to "belong."

Delbert glosses over the economic realities that condition (*bestimmt*) consciousness. Instead of the village, town, and city, it is the working class, the petite-bourgeoisie middle class, and the upper-class bourgeoisie that inform the MB ideology. Wineskins and wine are surface phenomena. It is archaeological, empirical depth that calls the shots. By ignoring economics, Delbert misses the point. He fails to reveal and examine the empirical dynamic that conditions and "chooses" theology and ideology. Sociolinguistic forms arise from their economic foundation or ground. He has created a "safe," "false consciousness" about MB consciousness.

I will credit Delbert with getting me into graduate school. As an alumnus of the University of Chicago Divinity School, he was a key reference. I studied at Chicago from 1974 to 1976. My professors were James Gustafson (Delbert's Yale Divinity School professor) and Alvin Pritcher in ethics, David Tracy, SJ, and Langdon Gilkey, in systemic theology, Martin E. Marty in American religious history, Bernard MacGinn and Brian Gervich (Cambridge University) in historical theology, Norman Perrin in New Testament, and Paul Ricoeur in philosophy (from the University of Paris X, Nanterre). Ricoeur was a rare scholar, conversant in analytical British-American philosophy *and* continental philosophy (existentialism and phenomenology). He was also comfortable with linguistics, the philosophy of science, and the philosophy of language. He coined the term "hermeneutics of suspicion" to describe Marx, Nietzsche, and Freud. This predates "deconstruction" by thirty years. Jacques Derrida, Jean-Francois Lyotard, and Michel Foucault were his colleagues and friends.

Delbert taught via the "*explication de texte*," close readings of the primary texts. He was the model for my own pedagogical style. Instead of topical, dualistic textbooks or anthropology "snippets," I use only primary texts, complete and in English translation in my courses. Thereby, the student builds up a "library" of texts that they have mastered in-depth. It is better to do a few things *well* than to do many things *superficially*. This is also part of Delbert's legacy. It was in his classes I first read Augustine, Aquinas, Socrates/Plato, Aristotle, Descartes, Hume, Kant, Mill, Nietzsche, Heidegger, Ayers, and Gilkey. He was the "Chicago great books" model before I went to Chicago. (Robert Hutchins, made president of the University of Chicago at the age of twenty-nine, abolished football—Chicago had been the collegiate national champion in the 1930s—created the great books program, and made the University of Chicago into a global university of the first rank.) I have Delbert to thank for having been educated there.

I owe Delbert my heady education at the University of Chicago Divinity School. But his legacy must be ambiguous: excellent pedagogy, ironic self-deprecating humor, learned scholarship, flawed analysis of the MB, creative construction of independent studies (along with Dalton Reimer), and a custom-crafted major in cultural history. I never could convince him to take Marx seriously. Thanks, Delbert, for a first-rate education, provocative essays, and introducing me to the University of Chicago Divinity School!

7

Triangles, Lines, and Radical Signs
Human Transcendence in Classical, Modern, and Christian Worldviews

Silas Langley

Professor Delbert Wiens is known for his chalkboard drawings. In the classroom, circles, triangles, lines, and radical signs flowed directly from his mind, through his chalk, and onto the board. Perhaps no students were more enthralled by them than I.

No Festschrift to Delbert is complete without at least a nod to his drawings, which the artist of this volume, Josiah Muster, has also interpreted in his own artistic style.[1] So I aim to give more than a nod. I will use Delbert's triangles, lines, and radical signs as symbols of three different understandings of transcendence.

Delbert is also known for his skill in describing worldviews—be they "village," "town," and "city," or premodern, modern, and postmodern. True to Delbert's spirit, I will connect the three understandings of transcendence with three larger worldviews, one premodern, one modern, and one Christian.

Finally, Delbert is known for promoting the creation of communities in the city. Again, true to Delbert's spirit, I will conclude by reflecting

---

1. See Josiah's drawing "Radical," *supra*. –DJC.

on the implications of the triangle, the line, and the radical sign for the possibilities of achieving transcendence in community.

Transcendence comes from the Latin words *trans* and *scandere*. *Trans* means "across," "beyond," or "through." *Scandere* means "to climb" or "to ascend." Transcendence, thus, means going beyond, but beyond what and to where? *Merriam-Webster* defines "transcendent" as "extending or lying beyond the limits of ordinary experience."[2] How then do triangles, lines, and radical signs represent different ways of going beyond the ordinary to reach the extraordinary?

The Triangle

The triangle represents a common premodern vision of the world that early Christian thinkers knew well. It consists of a single point at the top with one line drawn diagonally downward to the left and the other drawn diagonally downward to the right. Delbert uses the triangle to represent top-down polities, or ways of organizing and understanding society in which power flowed downward from an all-controlling top. He often drew a circle around the triangle's top to represent that power.

Delbert's prime example was ancient Egypt. The pharaoh was its top. Power flowed downward from him and into all of Egypt, shaping the identities of all living beings and their interrelationships. The pharaoh made the Nile flow and the plants grow. As a result, Egypt was considered eternal and unchanging. "Their polity and ethos were supposed to exist only in an eternal present tense in which the pharaoh is understood to be father of all and god of all."[3] Egypt itself was like the pyramids that its early pharaohs built—an eternal, unchanging, stable triangle. These pyramids seemed to emanate from their peaks like rays from the sun. So too Egypt seemed to emanate from its peak, the pharaoh.

The triangle also represents various Greco-Roman philosophical and religious systems and their visions of transcendence. I will consider two: Gnosticism and Neoplatonism. Gnosticism is diverse but in addition to its focus on accessing the secret knowledge it does tend toward the following worldview. An eternal distant God lies at the top. Various beings emanate from God like water from a fountain, some becoming more distant from God than others. The more distant, or lower ones,

---

2. *Webster's Ninth New Collegiate Dictionary*, s.v. "transcendent."
3. Wiens, *Stephen's Sermon*, 24.

do not know God. They create the material world, which is evil. Our souls and bodies are part of that world, but our true selves are sparks of the divine, or parts of God, that fell from God and became trapped in physical bodies. At death, these selves escape from their bodily prisons and ascend through the levels of the various beings that emanated from God and finally reunite with God. Some of these intermediary beings try to block their ascent. Fortunately, a messenger comes from God to give secret knowledge that will help them get past the intermediary beings.

Neoplatonism also posits an eternal distant God. All reality emanates from that God, forming a hierarchy of beings extended from those closest to God to those furthest from God. God is no more lessened by these emanations than the sun is lessened by its rays. A creature's degree of being, goodness, and unity depends on how high it is on the hierarchy. Matter, which is the farthest emanation from God, is nonbeing. As such, it is evil.

God is absolutely simple, with no inner distinctions or divisions of any kind—much like the undivided point at the top of a pyramid. Mind is immediately below God. In thinking about the forms, or the ideal patterns according to which all things are structured, mind introduces distinctions and differences into the world. Below mind is the higher soul that is above matter. Below it is the world-soul, or the soul of the material-world. Below it is the material world. The material world is itself good because it is an emanation from God, even though the matter of which it consists is evil.

Our souls emanate from the world-soul and have higher and lower parts. The higher parts belong more to the level of mind. The lower parts are connected to our bodies. Belonging to higher levels, our higher souls strive to reach those higher levels. They do this by concentrating on gaining knowledge of the forms and eschewing all material and bodily things. They then rise from that level to attain a mystic union with God, to what Plotinus calls the "flight of the Alone to the Alone."[4] Some interpret this union as a union in which all distinction is erased, in which the soul becomes identical to God in much the same way that *Atman* is identical to *Brahman* in the Indian philosophy of *Advaita Vedanta*.[5] Others interpret this union as retaining the ontological distinction between God and

---

4. Plotinus, *Enn.* 6.9.11, trans. Louth.
5. See Rist, *Plotinus*, 228–29.

self.[6] They view the union as more like the union of two points when one is placed directly on top of the other. There is no noticeable distinction between them. Yet it still exists. In either case, unity with God is achieved by putting aside those characteristics that distinguish one from God.

Gnosticism and Neoplatonism differ over the goodness of the material world and the nature of our ultimate union with the One, but their understandings of transcendence are essentially the same, as is shown in the following shared beliefs:

1. There is one principal being, God, at the top that is beyond and far removed from matter, space, and time.
2. There are intermediary beings that emanate from God, are responsible for the existence of the material world, and stand between that world and God.
3. Reality consists of a hierarchy of levels stretching from God at the top through the intermediary beings, with the great diversity of the material world at the bottom. It, thus, stretches from a unitary point to greater and greater plurality as one proceeds down the hierarchy. It thus resembles a pyramid.
4. Matter is evil.
5. We rightly belong at a higher level, but are imprisoned in our material bodies.
6. We reach the higher level by disentangling ourselves from our bodies and all material things. This disentanglement involves denying bodily pleasures and seeking purely intellectual knowledge. It involves turning inward and thereby moving upward.
7. We move up the hierarchy as solitary individuals, not as communities.
8. Our ultimate goal is union with God, or the One. Such union means becoming like the One, thus erasing noticeable distinctions between the self and the One. It may also mean giving up being a distinct individual or self.
9. Reality is ahistorical. It does not develop or progress. It is as changeless as Egypt and her pyramids. Movement up the hierarchy occurs by escaping from time, not by moving forward in it.

---

6. See Rist, *Plotinus*, 227, and O'Meara, *Plotinus*, 106.

For both, transcendence involves moving up the hierarchy, the pyramid, the triangle. It is an escape from the bottom—from embodiment, matter, space, time, history, and individuality. We transcend all that distinguishes us as separate individuals. Yet transcendence is a solitary and internal affair. Its goal is akin to a point uniting with a point.

The Line

Lines divide. They cut off one side of the line from the other. They can also make a box, which separates an inside from an outside. When applied to reality, lines cut off different parts of reality from each other or divide reality into isolated self-contained boxes.

While the triangle represents one major player in the premodern world, the line lies at the heart of most modern worldviews.[7] It does so in two different ways. One way is dualistic, using the line to separate the spiritual immaterial realm from the familiar material realm in which we live. The other way is atomistic. It denies the spiritual realm altogether and uses the line to box in the different parts of the material realm into isolated self-contained units.

The first way is a halfway house between ancient pyramidal and modern atomistic worldviews. As in pyramidal views, transcendence means turning inward to move upward. We are immaterial souls, not material bodies. We belong in the transcendent spiritual realm. As with the triangle, we eschew sense perception and all interaction with the material world. Instead, we think, like Descartes, only about the ideas in our minds, or we pray and meditate, meeting God within our minds and hearts. Transcendence is escape from embodiment.

Unlike pyramidal views, however, modern dualism carves up both the material and the spiritual. It reduces the former to atoms. It reduces the latter to distinct souls or minds and their distinct ideas. It does not allow for larger unities, whether with the One or with others. Transcendence is escape from body and earth, but not from separate selfhood.

Atomism, on the other hand, allows no escape at all. Reality is reduced to interchangeable atomic parts. Everything can be explained in terms of atoms and the laws of physics and chemistry that govern their

---

7. There are, of course, exceptions. Hegelianism is one. In some ways, however, it is more a pre-postmodern worldview than a paradigmatic modern one. It also, in some ways, resembles the radical sign.

movements and interactions. Wholes are merely the sums of their parts. Nothing is spiritual. Nothing is mysterious.

As bodies are reduced to atoms, so too are societies reduced to individuals. The whole society's behavior can be fully explained in terms of the individual behaviors of its members, just as a bag of marbles can be explained solely in terms of the individual marbles that make it up. Societies are nothing more than collections of individuals who agree to come together for mutual benefit.

Individual persons, in turn, are reduced to the atoms that make up their bodies. Each person can be fully explained in terms of her atoms and the laws of physics and chemistry that govern her movements and actions. There is no immaterial mind, no consciousness, and no free will. There is nothing inward or upward to which to turn, nor is there a will with which to turn inward or upward.

Atomism denies transcendence altogether. There is no going "beyond" because there is nothing "beyond." One cannot cross or climb, because there is nothing across or above. There are no larger unities of any kind. There can be no union of all persons in the One. There can be no union of all times in an eternal present. One cannot find transcendence through identifying with a cause or a movement, as some modern thinkers have inconsistently sought to do, because causes and movements are nothing more than collections of individuals. These individuals are, in turn, nothing more than collections of atoms.

Some moderns hope for a kind of horizontal transcendence through transcending one's self-interest or transcending one's previous value systems.[8] Although you cannot become *one* with another, you can still help that other. If you cannot reach another world, then aim to better this one. If you cannot access transcendent values, you can still go beyond your current ones. One wonders though whether such moves count as a form of transcendence, especially if one also believes that we are entirely determined by our atoms.

Others, such as some existentialist philosophers, at least as they are commonly interpreted, accept atomistic individualism and the meaninglessness of our purely material world, but refuse to reduce us to our atoms. Through our free will, we can create our own meaning in life and thereby achieve self-transcendence. Even so, we remain isolated individuals.

---

8. See Ruschmann, "Transcending Towards Transcendence," 428–31. Ruschmann cites Abraham Maslow as advocating "horizontal transcendence." See Maslow, "Various Meanings of Transcendence," 66.

The Radical Sign

I first encountered Delbert's drawings when I took the core course "Literature of the Ancient World" as a student at Fresno Pacific in the fall of 1989. One drawing stood out more than all the others. If I remember correctly, it was Delbert's co-teacher, Devon Wiens, who introduced it. He drew a radical sign on the board and said that it was the theme of the course. Delbert also embraced the sign as shown repeatedly in his chalkboard drawings.

The radical sign is a mathematical symbol that consists of a horizontal line, followed by a *v* whose right riser extends higher than its left, and ending with a second horizontal line that is higher than the first.[9] The sign represents both literal and metaphorical death and resurrection. It represents Jesus' literal death and resurrection and the metaphorical deaths and resurrections that we as individuals and communities undergo throughout our lives and histories. The sign represents dying to something of the old, but then rising to something new that reclaims what was good in the old. It represents moving to a higher level that takes with it much of the lower one. It represents transcendence.

Gnostics and Platonists also die to the old and rise to the new. They die to body, time, space, and self, and rise to a nonmaterial and nontemporal existence. But their dying and rising is more like the shedding of a skin than the dying and rising of a body.

The radical sign's shape shows its difference from the triangle. Its end point is diagonal, not straight up. This is important because it represents a historical progression, a movement through time. It moves *forward* to something new. It is not the restoration of a "true self" to the higher reality from which it fell. The radical sign is also rooted in the *historical* event of Jesus' death and resurrection. The radical sign is a sign in time, not a sign moving up to a point beyond it.

There is also a horizontal line on both sides of the *v*. That line represents earth, time, space, body, matter, and individuality. The radical sign restores all of that, but now at a higher level. Transcendence is a lifting up of the lower level, not an escape from it.

Both the radical sign and Christianity are rooted in the idea of resurrection. Jesus' bodily resurrection showed the real possibility of a

---

9. In mathematics the symbol is used to indicate the square root of a particular value. See Josiah Muster's "Radical" *supra*. Silas Langley prefers the first stroke of the symbol to be horizontal rather than ascending. –DJC.

non-escapist transcendence. Jesus' earthly and material *body* rose. It also rose in *this* world—on *this* earth and in *this* time. Jesus did not escape from this world but rose up *in* it. He remained a creature of time and space—of *this* time and *this* space—but his body did not rise as it was before. It was transformed and glorified, no longer capable of corruption and death. The resurrected Jesus ate and drank as before, but could also now walk through walls. His *body* had *transcended*, but in time and on earth.

Dying and rising is a biblical *leitmotif*, which, of course, is why it was also a *leitmotif* of "Literature of the Ancient World": wilderness to promised land, exile to restoration, baptismal dunking to baptismal rising, and our coming deaths to our future bodily resurrections.[10] The pattern shapes our Christian lives "as we are being transformed . . . from one degree of glory to another."[11]

Full transcendence awaits the future resurrection, but there is partial transcendence here and now. Here are some of the various ways to describe such transcendence:

1. Transcendence involves sharing in God's life. We in our bodily and earthly lives become caught up in the life of love shared between the persons of the Trinity.
2. Heaven intersects our earthly embodied lives. These lives are taken into God's realm where his will is done. At the same time, God's realm gains a foothold on earth so that his will is done on earth as it is in heaven.
3. Our earthly embodied lives are healed so that they can thrive.
4. God's presence and God's spiritual blessings become mediated in and through our earthly embodied lives. We experience God and God's gifts through face-to-face fellowship, nature, art, and the sacraments. Transcendence is communal, ecological, cultural, and sacramental.
5. The future reality of the new heaven and the new earth become present in our earthly embodied lives here and now, if only temporarily and in part.

---

10. Literature of the Ancient World was the name of the first class that I took from Delbert Wiens at Fresno Pacific College.

11. 2 Cor 3:18 NRSV.

6. Our earthly embodied lives are glorified as they more greatly reflect God's glory.

Transcendence is, thus, both a meeting with heaven and a foretaste of the future when heaven and earth become forever interlocked.

If we do not die to body, space, time, and self, then to what do we die? We die to the perversions and corruptions of the horizontal line—to all that makes the line lower on the left. We die to lust, but rise bodily. We die to materialism, but rise materially. We die to slothfulness and busyness, but rise in time. We die to individualism, but rise as individuals. We die to selfishness, but rise as selves. We die to "nature red in tooth and claw,"[12] but rise as earthly animals.

Community as Transcendence

Delbert also taught me why we need community and how we lack it. I have come to believe, as a devotee of the radical sign, that transcendence comes through community.

The triangle thinks so too. In uniting with the One, we also unite with others who have united with the One, but the resulting community is no longer a community of individuals, since it was achieved by transcending individuality. The result is a comm-unity without the *comm*, to use a folk etymology—a oneness that removes the *other* altogether so that there is no longer an *other with* which to be one. This community is also disembodied, existing on a spiritual, invisible plane that transcends earth, body, place, and time. It is a union of minds but not of bodies.

The line denies both community and transcendence. Modern society is a society of the line—a society that divides our lives into separate boxes. I remember Delbert making this point by drawing such boxes on a chalkboard. These boxes represented distinct spaces where distinct functions are performed with distinct sets of persons. They rarely overlap. There is a spiritual function: church at 9 a.m. Sunday with church members. There is a physical function: gym at 7 a.m. on weekdays with gym members. There is an economic function: workplace at 8 a.m. on weekdays with coworkers. There is an educational function: university at 6 p.m. on Monday with other students. There is a recreational function: golf course at 9 a.m. on Saturday with other golfers. There is a familial function: home at all other times with a spouse and kids. Some

---

12. Tennyson, "In Memoriam A.H.H.," canto LVI.

separation is healthy, but the degree and severity of the separation in modern life renders daily, face-to-face community nearly impossible and the transcendence that comes through it.

The line, according to the radical sign, is akin to death. It dis-integrates by dividing up the parts. Death is dis-integration. An organic body becomes a corpse when the cells and organs no longer function together as an integrated whole. Resurrection reintegrates the parts, as the cells again begin to function together as parts of a living body.

The radical sign resurrects the places, functions, persons, and times of our lives. It reintegrates them into an organic whole, forming what Delbert calls "concrete community." By "concrete," Delbert means "grown together," combining the prefix *con*, which means "with," and the verb *crescere*, which means "to come to be," "to grow," or "to thrive." The living human body is a concrete entity because its parts, its organs and cells, function together as parts of a complex whole that is greater than the sum of those parts. Likewise, a concrete community is a community in which its parts function together as parts of a larger whole that is greater than their sum. The parts include the community's members and also the natural and artificial features of the place that they share. The functions of life, whether worship, work, exercise, education, or play, are woven together with the same people, in the same places, and at the same times.

The participants of a concrete community attain a sense of real and profound unity with each other and their shared place through participating in a whole that is greater than their sum. The community as a whole has its own *Geist*, or *spirit*. It is, as Delbert puts it, a "real presence" that gives to the community its essence—its unique personality and culture. It is its "local culture," to borrow a term from Wendell Berry.[13] That *spirit* in turn shapes the participants of the community.

Concrete community, therefore, delivers unity and spirituality, two of the transcendent goods that the triangle seeks. Yet unlike the triangle, it delivers them in and through a fully embodied face-to-face existence in time and space.

Delbert looks back to his hometown of Corn, Oklahoma, as an example of concrete community, but he also points forward to the possibility of restoring concrete community in the city, by forming "a village in the city."[14] Delbert inspired me with that vision by introducing me to the

---

13. See Berry, *What Are People For?*, 153–69.
14. Wiens, "Village," 147.

concept of cohousing. Cohousing is a form of intentional neighborhood in which individually owned homes are deliberately clustered around a central courtyard and residents co-own both a common house and common outdoor spaces. It resembles condominiums in some respects but is radically different from them in that it is structured to encourage an active community life in which residents make decisions by consensus. Cohousing is not an elusive, utopian dream. I lived in one in Portland, Oregon, for six years. In it, I experienced a sense of unity and spirit that modern life lacks. I experienced transcendence.

Cohousing involves a shared life, centered on care for one another and a shared place. Family, education, exercise, work, and play are all woven together: Friday night game playing in the common house, followed by yoga the next morning, and then work on the common grounds—all with the same people in the same shared place. This shared life allows these activities to bleed into each other as members discuss the previous night's game as they do yard work, or as they discuss last week's yoga while they play games. They learn from each other about how to care for each other and how to care for the land. Thanks to the Internet, some are also able to work from the common house, thus interweaving another function into the community's life. These activities become part of a seamless rhythm in time, rather than the fragmented time to which we are accustomed. It would be easy to also infuse religion into this rhythm through weekly or even daily prayer and worship together.

Cohousing offers a form of unity that preserves individuality. It balances a shared place with the privacy of one's own home. Decisions are made by consensus, which gives every individual an equal voice. Cohousing also offers a form of spirituality that is fully embodied in the materiality of earth and yet counteracts the materialism of wanting to own more. It encourages sharing some possessions rather than privately owning them. It involves a deliberate choice to live in smaller homes. The community has its own *Geist*, and one feels its presence while picking blueberries from the community's blueberry bushes or spontaneously chatting with neighbors as they pass by your front porch.

Cohousing is not perfect. The economics of our age make cohousing less available to lower income persons, although many cohousing communities actively seek creative ways to make it available to some. There are unresolved tensions and disagreements. Should cats be allowed outside though they might kill the birds? Should money from the community's budget be used to fund the hot tub though some believe we should not have one? Such tension is also a means for transcendence. It makes possible reconciliation, which is itself a resurrection of relationships. The point is not that concrete community is perfect. The point is that it makes possible a transcendence that is otherwise inaccessible to us in our modern lives.

My experience in cohousing is a testimony that Delbert's drawings of triangles, lines, and radical signs are more than instructional aids. They also transcend themselves in pointing to what was, what is, and what may be.

Bibliography

Berry, Wendell. *What Are People For?* New York: North Point, 1990.

Louth, Andrew. *The Origins of the Christian Mystical Tradition from Plato to Denys.* New York: Oxford University Press, 1981.

Maslow, Abraham. "Various Meanings of Transcendence." *Journal of Transpersonal Psychology* 1 (1969) 56–66.

O'Meara, Dominic. *Plotinus: An Introduction to the Enneads.* Oxford: Clarendon, 1993.

Rist, John. *Plotinus: The Road to Reality.* Cambridge: Cambridge University Press, 1967.

Ruschmann, Eckart. "Transcending Towards Transcendence." *Implicit Religion* 14 (2011) 421–32.

Tennyson, Alfred. "In Memoriam A.H.H." Literature Network. http://www.online-literature.com/tennyson/718.

Wiens, Delbert. *From the Village to the City: A Grammar for the Languages That We Are.* Reprinted by offset from the October 1973–January 1974 issue of *Direction*.

Wiens, Delbert. *Stephen's Sermon and the Structure of Luke-Acts.* North Richland Hills, TX: Scott, 1998.

8

Failing Forward

Devon H. Wiens

THE TITLE STEMS FROM a College Hour address delivered by Delbert years ago at FPC, in his inimitable, humorous and self-deprecating style, in which he depicted his "successes" as a continuum of fits, pitfalls, stops and (re)starts. To this writer's way of thinking, it was an exquisite insight into the pattern of his life-course as a whole.

My initial meeting with Delbert took place, fittingly enough, in light of that opening paragraph, in his broom closet-like office, off the west side of the breezeway of Sattler Hall, consequent upon my trip to Fresno, to be presented as a candidate for the position of a professor in the Biblical Studies division. I have never forgotten my first and very positive impressions of that engaging, impishly broad grin and the Socratic-like, inviting, and merry twinkle of his optics.

I had not personally met him prior to that encounter—I had heard stories of his notable achievements—in spite of the fact that our lives were to become inextricably linked for years in the future. As *Fortuna* had it, I had already met Majorie Gerbrandt, his spouse-to-be, her parents, sister, and brother, who were missionaries to the Kiowa and Commanche tribal groups of Southern Oklahoma (west of the city of Lawton) when I lived there in my early teens. For that summer my family lived close to the Gerbrandts in the mission home occupied by the Herman Neufelds, while my father was assisting in the construction of a school building for the children of these Native Americans, located down the graveled road, in Indiahoma. Little did I know of the accomplishments, already of some notoriety among the knowledgeable cadre of Mennonite Brethren, lurking behind his welcoming demeanor and facial expressions at the time of our first meeting.

Over the next few years (of the early 1970s) my knowledge and admiration for him were enhanced, in the main, by two major recurring experiences. First, he had a readiness to accept me, as a relatively rookie professor with just four years of experience elsewhere who was attempting to overcome the "Future Shock," described by Alvin Toffler, in his work by that name. After all, I found myself in a strange, new world, quite alien to my first four years of collegiate teaching in Hoosierland in a relatively bucolic setting. Now I had come to California in the aftermath of the sixties Berkeley scene and the concomitant emergence of the Jesus People in that same geographical nexus. During that time of personal upheaval, Delbert was willing to offer guidance, encouragement, and, later, invitation to write some articles in the journal *Direction*, of which he was on the editorial staff.

Second, he had a charming sagacity that informed faculty and small-group meetings. His comments in those settings ranged from the rarity of the genuine New (if, at times, virtually imponderable), to the valuable Old (if, at times, unorthodox and "heretical," all the while recalling from church history that Yahweh used heretics, such as the second-century CE Marcion, as well as the Modalists, to grow his *ecclesia*!). I ought to add a caveat, namely, that Delbert's heresy was, by contrast with these ancient sorts, quite moderate and within the (outer) bounds of what is defined as normative Christianity. However, during this maelstrom of ideas exuding from him, he gently forced me and others to consider and embrace creative alternatives and a heretofore-unthinkable (speaking for myself) future.

The late seventies and early eighties proved to be a time of much closer association with Delbert. It was a challenging, initially a personally timorous, but, ultimately, immensely rewarding period of co-involvement. The first step involved strategizing and then planning an interdisciplinary series of yearlong courses, to be required of all freshmen. Was this an instance of derring-do, in view of the reality that exceptionally few US colleges/universities were offering such an ambitious curriculum, slated for entering students? Harvard was perhaps an exception to the exceptionally few, but its cross-curriculum was more theme oriented, offering students choice of a thematic course, among several such. Obviously, the hoary and much heralded history of the Core curriculum at the great University of Chicago, the provenance of Delbert's PhD, ought not be overlooked. This history should, but will not, given the parameters with which I am working, be recounted here.

Nonetheless, intrepidly we pressed onward. The challenge of inventing a course covering a long spectrum of Western history and thought, to be viewed simultaneously from the perspectives of several curricular disciplines, lay before us. A series of explorative sessions at a cabin in the Sierras took place under the capable, creative, and indefatigable leadership of then-academic dean Dr. Dalton Reimer, a communication expert. This planning group included Fresno Pacific College's master dreamer and schematicist, namely, Dr. Delbert Wiens, and a few more quiescent folk, such as myself.

I wish to insert, parenthetically, that this creative time period in the history of Pacific College, also included a lengthy process of writing and rewriting of the Fresno Pacific Idea by a group of several faculty, again with the capable leadership of Dalton. This Idea has most unfortunately, by now become largely ignored or undercut.[1]

After a series of tentative probes and repeatedly revamped outlines of content, clarity about the budding course began to surface. Consideration was given as to which departments of FPC's curriculum would be emphasized, and to what extent this could, realistically speaking, eventuate. Finally, the choice of instructional faculty for this errand into the wilderness was made. Lots were cast (prayerfully, of course, as in Acts!) and fell, logically enough, upon Delbert, and, perhaps not so logically, upon the writer of this piece. Finally, it was decided that, under Dalton's supervision, this audacious experiment would be launched in the fall quarter of the 1979–1980 academic year.

The edgy beginnings were marked, speaking at least for myself, by some anxiety, sleep deprivation, and prodigious amounts of (re)research into the material to be covered, especially that involving the ancient Near East, Homeric Hellas, and later, the Greece of the playwrights, the historians, and the classical philosophers. As providence would have it, we were blessed by the fact that the charter class of that quarter consisted of some one hundred students who met with us in the rather dismal domain of Marpeck room 6 and included a dozen or more rather extraordinary

---

1. See Peter Smith's contribution herein for more prophetic commentary on the FPU Idea. –WMJ.

students, who later went on to the finest graduate schools and, subsequently, on to laudable careers and achievements. This group got it and waxed enthusiastic(ally) about the series. There was another sizeable group, who gave the teachers the benefit of the doubt about such unorthodox course content and angle of vision from the standpoint of their high school experience whether Christian or secular. Then, there were some that seemed to have little clue as to what was happening and required considerable individual attention, dependent upon their willingness to engage privately with the teachers and assistants.

A generous apportionment of angst ensued, resulting both from the extensive reading of both primary and secondary sources for the ancient Near East (Mesopotamia and Egypt, principally), Greece, and long textual units of the Old Testament, together with periodic, demanding exams, comprised of essays as well as objective items. The consternation included students, some parents, and, candidly, other professors. This reaction, in turn, prompted calls to the college, which administrators (and teachers) attempted to mediate in the effort to explain and, frankly, to justify course rationale, content, and reading material. In time, the storm subsided, though intermittently, waves of dissent kept forming and cresting.

There was a serious and honest attempt to make of this experiment an inter-curricular series of courses with the art, literature, philosophy, science, religion, and social theory of any given historical epoch viewed as inextricably connected. Instructional responsibility was divvied up between the two original faculty members, depending on their special areas of familiarity.

A word about the selection of course titles is probably in order. Realpolitik required that titles be catchy and memorable, but, by the same token, faithful to actual content. (Perhaps an inserted word at this point is important. The fact is that a few years later, attributable to both internal and external pressures of various sorts, a titular evolution ensued, which was accompanied, unfortunately, by a lessening of required enrollment in the courses and resulted in a "survival-of-the-fittest" atmosphere among the students for the year's duration.)

The acronymic titles were as follows: (1) WOPAK, the World of Patriarch and King, covered the Ancient Near Eastern, Homeric Greek, and Old Testament stories and was offered in the fall quarter; (2) WOSAM, the World of Sage and Messiah, was concerned with post-Homeric and Hellenistic-Greek history and thought, Republican Rome's (e.g., Virgil's

Fourth Eclogue) anticipations of a new order, and the New Testament Gospels' evangel of the Anointed One, Jesus the Christ, all of which was covered in the winter quarter; and (3) WOPAE, the World of Priest and Emperor, dealt with varied New Testament works the Acts of the Apostles, selected Epistles/Letters, and some early Christian apostolic fathers, martyrs, and heretics, up to and including St. Augustine's life and his *Confessions*, and the history, thought, leadership, and institutions of imperial Rome. This class was offered in the spring quarter. (The title served as a most appropriate designation for the joy of *denouement* and the "Rites of Spring!")

I wish to describe the relationship that existed between the "Wiens boys" (as they notoriously came to be known) in and out of the classroom. Each always attended the other's class presentations. We composed and evaluated exams in collaboration, usually in the quietness of Delbert and Marjorie's home on College Avenue. We agonized long and hard over the determination and recording of final course grades, determined not to cave in to the nationwide inflation of grades, nor to refrain from overly high expectations, keeping in mind, with *sympathia*, that these students were not in graduate school, but in their first year of college.

Climactically, it is now appropriate to acknowledge my long-standing indebtedness, as a fellow student, not merely a co-teacher, to Delbert's hoary *chokhmah*, his exemplary patience with students, and his stimulating lectures, which were replete with illustrative stories and came to be transmitted from one year's class to the next year's incoming group.

I offer a few instances of such memorable wisdom. Living in fame are Oscar the fetal pig, the constant use of the radical sign to illustrate corporate and personal plateauing, falling and (re)rising, along with personal accounts of Delbert's study at Yale under H. Richard Niebuhr and with Paul Ricoeur at the University of Chicago (Paul Ricoeur, as Delbert regaled us, arrived on campus each day in his own limo, driven by his own driver), both of whom exercised a lasting, self-confessed, and formative influence on him. His postdoctoral experiences included an extended, self-guided motorcycle tour of big parts of India; his assignment as MCC director in Vietnam, during those turbulent war years.

Achievement relating more to the structure of these Core courses included his earnest and, to my way of thinking, largely effective *apologia* of the use of the term *myth* for both nonbiblical and biblical materials; his side glances at Socrates' companions in Plato's *Republic* as somewhat representative of various modern mind-sets; his view of Plato's "Allegory of the Care" as prototypical of the evolution of all students from observing only forms or the shadows of the real, the good, or the ideas, to a gradual, painstaking turning to the light and knowledge of the ideas themselves as the archetype of all ancient and modern educational attempts. His demonstration, while guiding us through Augustine's *Confessions*, that the story of the boyhood theft of pears was hardly a detached story about those early years alone, but also depicted Augustine's pre-conversion experience in the garden, during his pre-Ambrosian years, when he was enslaved to lust and to false and incomplete solutions to his personal and sinful dilemma, such as those emanating from Manichaeism and aberrational types of Christianity.

I salute also, more fully, the use of the radical sign, as profoundly symbolic of Israel's story as cyclically depicted in the book of Judges; then in the founding of kingship, which aped the ways of the surrounding *goyim*; the collapse of the northern kingdom of Israel at the hands of the (Nazi-like) Assyrians; the fall of Jerusalem to Nebuchadrezzar and the Babylonians; the long-prophesied exile; and, ultimately, the reconciliation of at least a portion of the exiles with Yahweh, issuing in the return of some of them to Jerusalem, and their scaled-down reconstitution; eventually, aided by Yahweh's *mashiach*, the Persian Cyrus, according to Second Isaiah, back in Jerusalem. The same symbolized, in ultimate fashion, Jesus' own life, particularly in his early successes in gaining a following in the "Galilean Spring" (so Ernst Renan), then the ongoing misunderstanding of him by his own disciples (especially portrayed in Mark's gospel) and the hostile rejection of him by, among others, a number of his own followers, the Jewish authorities (wrongly dubbed "the Jews," implying the people as a whole, in the Johannine gospel) and, of course, the Roman powers, climaxing in his crucifixion, but not of his end, because we conclude with his bodily resurrection from actual death and the appearances to his followers.

The same may be said to signify the pattern of our own personal and corporate journeys on the Way (using biblical language), sometime moving, with joyous alacrity toward the destination, but then suffering a reversal, constituting a fall or exile or a casting into the pit. Eventually, whether sooner or later, this results in repentance and deliverance, in Yahweh's pulling out of the pit, and there is a return to restoration and fellowship with Jesus our risen Lord and Savior. All in all, this cycle constitutes our own version of "Failing Forward."

What a high and lofty honor for this writer to have been closely associated for all these years with this great teacher, and, more importantly, a noble and decent human being, brilliantly reflecting the *imago Dei*! In the psalmists' (and Handelese) terms, *allelujah*!

9

"Village to the City"
A Grammar for "New Wineskins for Old Wine"

Greg A. Camp

IN 1973, A SECOND significant writing by Delbert Wiens made its appearance in *Direction*, the Mennonite Brethren academic journal. *Direction* had a smaller readership than *Christian Leader*, wherein his first work, "New Wineskins for Old Wine," appeared. It is this second writing, "From the Village to the City: A Grammar for Languages We Are," that fleshed out and put structure to the insights of "Wineskins." A "dangerous mind" is not only one that challenges existing structures and advocates for change; a dangerous mind also enables one to see existing, all-too-familiar, realities in a new light. This can unsettle "the way things are" by putting them into broader frameworks that can be shown to change over time. This is what Delbert brought to the Mennonite Brethren experience and gave voice to for many ethno-religious groups. Delbert not only helped to relativize deep cultural and theological experiences, but he provided a way to comprehend shifts between and unity within each cultural moment. This chapter is devoted to the way that "Village" serves as a fulcrum in my graduate course, Values in School and Society, for education students. I am deeply grateful for the years of friendship with Delbert and all that I learned from him, starting with my first undergraduate course with him and continuing to the present. His sensitivity to broad cultural trends in ancient and contemporary life has deeply influenced my work with biblical and philosophical texts.

The course description for Values in School and Society reads, in part:

> This course focuses on a cultural, historical, philosophical, and/or social analysis of schools and schooling as a basis for developing an understanding of the educator's role as a change agent and as a basis for personal and professional decision-making.

The course has two major sections with "Village" connecting them. The first section is an examination of influential readings in the philosophy of education, including writings from Plato, Aristotle, Confucius, Augustine, Locke, Mill, Spencer, Dewey, and others. These writings touch on wide-ranging issues, including curriculum, pedagogy, teacher training, the nature of learning, and educational purposes. The second half of the course examines various international systems of education, particularly focusing on factors that influence change. In order to bring a degree of coherence to all the readings, an analytical framework is applied to each. The framework includes three main components that push and pull against each other: ideology, political economy, and schools. Schools include the institutions we experience every day in terms of curriculum, staffing, facilities, funding, policies, and every other aspect that contributes to institutional existence. Political economy refers to the broad social and cultural forces of a society, particularly focusing on politics and economics. Educational institutions are recipients of changes in political economies, but they are also forces that contribute to positive and negative changes in political economies. Ideology is the term used to describe four aspects of a philosophy of education: the aim, or purpose, of education, views of the learning process, views of the learning, and the view of what constitutes knowledge. The first part of the course, which deals with various philosophical writings, focuses most heavily on understanding various ideological perspectives. Each source is historically contextualized in limited ways. Analysis of schools is limited to the writer's views of curriculum. The second half of the course examines tensions and changes in international systems of education brought about by shifts in schools, ideologies, and political economies. The challenge is putting the two halves of the course together into a coherent whole so that students see how ideological views are embodied in school systems in varying political economies, how schools are both recipients and agents of change in ideology and political economy, and how political economies shape and are shaped by educational ideologies and schools.

"Village" provides a model or a grammar of how cultural patterns cohere and what happens to various factors as change inevitably ensues. A grammar is a set of rules that govern language usage. These are usually informal, but build up over time and become viewed as "the way things are." Grammars are also fluid, perhaps more akin to the movement of a glacier than a waterfall, but fluid nonetheless. Three stages of modern cultural life and their grammars are posited: Village, Town, and City. Each stage has its own internal coherence, but each also entails features that lead to its instability and transformation to a different stage by participants of the culture. Delbert gave voice to the ethno-religious Mennonite Brethren experience as it was going through significant changes in the 1960s and 1970s. His description continues to ring true to the dynamics that many teachers face in their classrooms. In the following pages, I will attempt to translate Village, Town, and City into an analytical framework. The following diagram sets out what I will be describing.

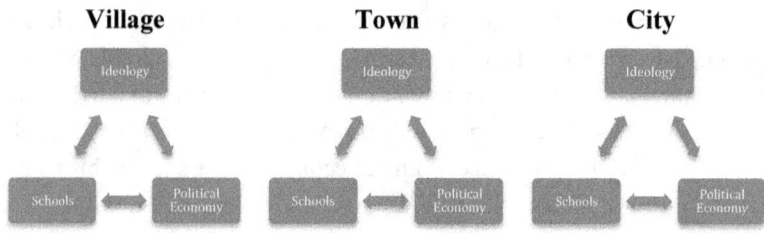

Village

The village political economy is based on agriculture in a geographical boundary set. The small population base of the village means that it usually shares common ethno-religious and linguistic boundaries. The strength of the village is its group cohesiveness and tie to the vitalistic forces of nature. Work is frequently shared among humans and between humans and animals. There are communal celebrations marking significant moments in individual and corporate existence. Religion is often the center of village life. There is little differentiation between various spheres of life. The village continues to function well when its members accept the social structure and the limitations placed on it by natural cycles. The village faces crisis when it becomes oppressive to members, when it no longer allows for the vitality of individual members, or when it presses beyond the limits of nature.

The aim of education in the village is to learn to fit in. Humans must fit into the rhythms and cycles of nature, which provides primary metaphors such as maturity. Just as agriculture aims to produce mature fruit, so village culture aims to produce mature people. Maturity is the mark of one who has appropriately learned the lessons of life and of cultural expectations, i.e., one who adequately fits into adult culture and contributes to its reproduction. The sage is the model of one who embodies "how life works." The sage has knowledge of what works in a given time, place, and situation.

Learning happens by multi-generational trial and error experiences. The individual learns by participating in cultural processes and by heeding the advice of the elders. Learning happens by observation and imitation of others and of the rhythms of nature. Learning has its shortcomings when one is not self-reflective and assumes that the way things are in one place is the way they are everywhere. Change and deviation from routine may present less of an opportunity for learning than a danger to the stability of the group.

Everyone is a learner in the village and the process of learning never ceases. Children learn by absorbing culture. Adults continue to learn by experiential, analogical, and allegorical interpretation of nature and religious texts. Each person must experience the cycle of life and, therefore, is always a learner.

The primary form of knowledge in the village comes from cultural systems, mores, ways of the ancestors, and what works. This is as true of life cycles and relationships as it is of baking bread or farming. Knowledge is often embodied in proverbs or other wise sayings. Sages know when and where to apply appropriate knowledge.

Schools did not need to replicate the broad cultural learning that happened everywhere in the village. Every village interacts with a broader world. Other parts of the world, including other villages, have their own languages, cultures and grammars. Schools in the village allow the opportunity to learn about these other people, places, and things, but is often limited to knowledge of immediately useful skills, such as reading and writing in the language of the dominant culture, or rudimentary skills in math and science. More "advanced" education is not always seen as useful or desirable.

Town

The town is not merely a larger version of the village, though population growth may spur the shift from village to town. A major aspect that causes shift is the belief that nature needs to be made to serve humans. The town allows for and promotes specialization that leads to the subjugation of nature to human will. This is a matter of degree rather than an absolute value, since the village also includes lesser degrees of specialization. The political economy of the town relies upon greater specialization and therefore leads to fragmentation of the various components of life. Isolated, specialized tasks create quantitative efficiencies. Machine power is produced and harnessed. The strength of tools and the repetition of machines are dominant metaphors for the town. Business lies at the center of town life, sometimes literally in the form of Main Street, and usually as an organizing principle for life. The town has geographically separated specializations, and lives are more separated from regions of economic productivity. Economic productivity and specialization allows for and demands greater mobility. Families are less likely to live near extended relations, the notion of a nuclear family comes to prominence, and life is intentionally fragmented into social, political, religious, economic, educational, public, and private spheres.

The aim of education in the town is to discover ways to make nature (and other humans) serve humans. Education serves as a means to discover laws and deduce all-encompassing theories, propositions, and principles that can be used to order and control the world. The aim of education is also to master these rules, thereby becoming a technical expert. Mastery is not limited to the natural world, though the natural sciences and mathematics are central, but includes mastery of human behavior in terms of the social sciences, such as psychology, organizational behavior, marketing, and political science.

Learning is the discovery of laws and principles from which it is possible to deduce systematic and all-encompassing theories. Fundamental axioms provide the basis for further learning. These axioms are primarily learned by rote as given constants and are not necessarily based on observation and experience as they are in the village. Knowledge is built up slowly, but with certainty through a rationalistic scientific method, so that knowledge can be passed on in systematic processes. One need not reinvent the wheel in order to gain the advantages of the learning of prior generations. Learning should continue to advance the total knowledge base. The processes and content of learning are analyzed and processes are designed to maximize the efficiency of subject mastery. Educational testing for learning is akin to quality control testing in manufacturing. Ideally, anyone should be able to master any knowledge since it is public and not subjective. Learning develops from broad subjects and principles and moves towards narrower and deeper specialization.

The ideal image of the learner is the specialist who has mastered a subject matter. Becoming adept at the mechanical learning process and learning both facts and theories at the appropriate pace achieves this. The learner acquires and builds upon the broad knowledge of prior learners; however, the learner needs to be adept when working with abstract laws and principles. In some versions of the town, not only levels of achievement differentiate learners, but also styles of learning. The learner is largely age-graded both in terms of being processed through the school system by age and also when assessed by expected age-appropriate attainment. In some forms of town education, learners are not differentiated by gender, socio-economic level, race or ethnicity, religion, or other factors other than age. An underlying view of the learner is a common, or universal, human being who is, for the purposes of education, abstracted from all contextual influences. This is an extreme form based on an extreme mechanistic view of humans and the process of learning. While this may be an extreme end of the spectrum, much town education is abased by the assumption of the efficiencies of mass produced public education where both the raw material and the processes are largely uniform.

There is an explosion of knowledge associated with towns. Laws and principles are built into coherent structures of theories, philosophies, theologies, morals, and other systems that are taught through textbooks. The foundations of these laws and principles are basic axioms that are held to be self-evident. Knowledge is unified but also based on different axioms. If we take physics as an example of the type of knowledge in which towns excel, then we note that not only does each type of physics rest on its own axioms and result in its own knowledge, but attempts are then made to unify the knowledge of the various types of physics, such as with particle physics and gravitational physics. This illustrates the twin poles of fragmentation and unification. Subjects are initially disaggregated and studied in isolation of contexts and the subjectivity of the learner. Knowledge is often split between knowledge of a subject and use of that same knowledge, between theory and practice. Highly specialized knowledge and mastery of a subject is often tied directly to greater economic productivity and reward, showing that the fragmentation of knowledge into specialized domains leads to greater power. The explosion of knowledge does, in fact, lead to greater mastery and productivity, but it also leads to increased isolation. The tendency towards unification comes at the usefulness of isolated knowledge, either as the limits of the knowledge is reached or when external challenges warrant harnessing various perspectives.

Schools are organized by age and further into subjects or disciplines. Teachers are specialists by age or by subject, and schools follow the patterns established in the views of knowledge and learning. The school day is normally divided into time periods that focus on isolated subjects. Experiments in integrated learning try to recombine the once integrated world that the process of schooling fragmented. The focus of the school is knowledge formation, or information. It is not as concerned with cultural formation. Realms such as culture and religion are subjects to be learned about, but their values are not to be promoted in the schools. That becomes the responsibility of a different fragment of society.

City

Delbert describes the city with much less confidence, though with great insight. He is undecided whether it is a collection of prior stages or a new kind of reality. What is certain is that the city represents a much greater sense of fragmentation without boundaries (villages), or centers (towns), though these prior stages find form within the larger city. There is no single common reality in the city that provides a coherent way of life. The cultural grammars of the city are simply different from one another with their own inherent rules. The political economy is marked by plurality, fragmentation, and diversity. Politics, economics, and social life move dynamically between multiple, often discontinuous, spheres simultaneously. It may seem as if there is a pick-and-choose way of living, but cities also reveal remarkably routine and durable pathways of existence in spite of the diversity of options. Energy can be released at a frenetic pace with growth and decay happening at once. Delbert is careful not to denigrate the city completely, but is wary of the personal and social effects. His analysis of the transitions from village to town to city uses language of movement from unity to fragmentation, which reveals a preference for that which was perceived as present before it became fragmented. This is the language of decay or decline from a more golden age. I share some of Delbert's experience with village culture, but I am less inclined to give it preference. I argue that the city has as much power to overcome the local idolatries and xenophobia of the village as it does to create a fragmentation. The city is a place where the power of the town is unleashed on a grand scale, but there is also potential for unmasking the hubris and self-serving nature of that power. The city, like the village and the town, is a mixture of good and bad, positive and negative qualities. New possibilities and challenges emerge that require careful reflection and devotion, not wistful thinking for the way things had been. New wineskins are needed for this new wine.

The aim of education in the city is to gain skills to be whatever is needed at any moment; flexibility and adaptability are paramount. Tried and true cultural patterns of the village are quaint in the city. The confidence of the town to control an ever-increasing amount of life is hubris. Life changes quickly in the city and the variations increase daily. The ability to be adaptable is, perhaps, evident in the form of core competencies, such as written and oral communication, quantitative reasoning, critical thinking, and information literacy. I would add to these mediated and multi-lingual communication and cultural competence. This is not content mastery, but a set of skills for use in multiple content areas and socio-political contexts. These do not replace content specialists, but they help them to adapt and interact. The village aims at living within natural and social limitations, the town aims to master the natural and social arenas, and the city might aim to manipulate those arenas for one's own purposes as it lies somewhere between an awareness of human limitation and human ability.

Many of the processes of learning in the city are derived from those of the village and the town. The diversity of the city allows for more variations, experimentations, and specialized approaches to learning. I will point out just one feature of learning that becomes heightened in the city: access is a key issue in being able to take advantage of the richness of learning. Cities value many forms of unfettered access, including transportation, communication, socialization, wealth production, education, and a host of other services. However, it also values limits in the forms of gates, passwords, memberships, and so forth. Delbert points out what he considers to be a darker side of learning in the city. He notes that in the lack of coherence in the city where many parts are viewed as interchangeable, one learns an unhealthy subjectivism. This may surface in the forms of disregard for context-appropriate behavior, lack of coherent psychological unity, narcissism, manipulation, and facile engagement and limited mastery. This may, in part, explain the value of both access and limit. The process of learning in the city includes discovering and developing skills in accessing within limits, which partially explains the emphasis on critical thinking skills (thinking within rational limits) and information literacy (access with proper acknowledgment of the work of others).

Delbert claims that the ideal learner in the city is the pop hero or virtuoso. It is not enough to have deep learning of a narrow subject, but it has to be something in demand and the learner must show rapid adaptability. The term perhaps best associated with this learner is "excellent." The term is virtually devoid of content other than to be better than most at something. It becomes a relative term of social comparison. Another term that can be associated with the ideal learner is "wonder." The city becomes so filled with variations that the learner can explore seemingly endless avenues. Wonder is also a result of being overwhelmed with unity, beauty, and inexplicability in our experiences. The plurality of the city can result in a loss of sense of integration, pursuit of trivia for the sake of stimulation, or abuse of people and the world due to the loss of a sense of connection and accountability. However, the plurality can also result in new and creative integrative designs and care for others and the world. Wonder is often associated with an idealized stage of childhood. In order for adults to renew their sense of wonder, they tend to retreat into nostalgic recovery or fantasies. In order for the adult learners to live productive, meaningful lives in the city, they need to nurture a sense of wonder, think in divergent patterns, bring creativity to new challenges, and to act responsibly in light of larger realities. They will need to learn to connect to others to form new communities and connect to the world they inhabit.

Knowledge in the city can be trivial and disconnected, or it can be meaningful, productive and connected. The challenge is discerning between activity and fruitfulness. The lack of direction towards either communal wellbeing or mastery of the world can lead to knowledge being the development of abilities to manipulate and serve only one. The question is whether knowledge itself is different in the city, or whether it is the recognition of the limited nature of any type of knowledge and the ends to which knowledge is used that is different.

Schools in the city may look like schools in towns, but with the greater possibility of being specifically focused, or special interest based. Charter schools, magnet schools, experimental schools, and special subject schools abound. Those that will take the most advantage of these opportunities are those who not only have access, but who can generate productive uses for the type of education provided. The increasing number of schools can make it difficult to distinguish which schools are providing useful experiences and which are lining their pockets at students' expense. Education in the city remains a necessity, but will be increasingly associated with cynicism and wariness. Educational institutions are constantly under pressure to demonstrate their ability to deliver on their promises. Beyond this reality is the need for people in the city to develop a sense of where education plays a meaningful role in the life of the individual and the community. As much as educational reform may be needed, a vision of life in the city, and education's role in that life, is needed.

Delbert and I have shared vigorous conversations about the pros and cons of the village, town, and city. The value of the tripartite model for my students is to give them a grammar for understanding the dynamics they face in their schools and careers as educational professionals. The grammar or map that the model provides helps them to understand the multiple expectations and often mutually exclusive demands that they face. A student-parent conference at school may include grandparents who are from a literal and figurative village, parents who bring expectations of the town, and a student who is growing up in the complexities of the city. Classrooms may have students from village-like enclaves, towns, and cities, each bearing the contributions and challenges of that stage. These teachers rarely face the subtraction of demands, only the layering on of more. They need to learn the ability to untangle the expectations and determine how they can best work with the student, the family, and the school system given their own interests and abilities. The value of "Village" is in simplifying their problems by providing a model to understand and do something with what they are given. A dangerous mind is not only one that challenges existing structures and advocates for change; a dangerous mind also enables one to see existing, all-too-familiar, realities in new light. An increase in knowledge results in the dangerous situation of having more tools and responsibility to do something to bring change.

I have attempted to share my summary of "Village" in the hope that others might gain a glimpse of the continuing usefulness of this piece. There are many places where I was tempted to fill out the model or argue against it. I would also have liked to demonstrate how Fresno Pacific University, from the days of Pacific Bible Institute to its current state, fits within this model, including the Fresno Pacific University Idea statement that guides the lives of faculty and students. I will end rather with a simple statement of gratitude for being allowed to teach a course pioneered by Delbert and to use one of his own works as a driving source. It never fails to stimulate my thinking and understanding of the values in school and society.

Section 3

Essays

10

Pagans and Galatians
Reading Galatians 5:12

W. Marshall Johnston

Do not be deceived; God is not mocked, for you reap whatever you sow.

GALATIANS 6:7[1]

A "Delbertian" Problem

PROFESSOR WIENS' (HENCEFORTH, DELBERT)[2] career has been based on asking out-of-the-box questions that help us understand our Christian walk (not to mention our human condition): in studying the ancient world, he asks how to interpret the collision of the classical and Christian mindsets, and in observing today's world he asks how to ex-

---

1. All scripture translations are from the NRSV (except as noted). I owe a deep debt of gratitude to Charlie Castanon for helping me think through some of the implications of the ideas expressed herein, as well as for major effort on his part in philological inquiry.

2. See note on the naming custom in our community in "A *Liber Amicorum*," *supra*. In other essays, I have honored the writers' particular approaches to nomenclature.

plicate the collision of the premodern and modern worldviews. Since I am a classicist, I will work on a conundrum in the former category. My solution to the meaning of Paul's shocking comment at Galatians 5:12 is submitted in his honor, though the shortcomings reflect only my inability to live up to his example. Delbert has worked for the last ten years on an attempt to consider Romans 1:16—2:11 in its proper context (especially given its importance to current Church dialogues);[3] I use that impressive work as my *exemplum* and inspiration for this consideration.

I believe that Delbert's role is significant in the history of classical scholarship (or at least in our corner of that diachronic conversation) because he was in the generation of Christian scholars who clearly realized the study of Judeo-Christian backgrounds and classical history have to be taken as two sides of the same coin, and who showed the ability and training to master the interrelation of those areas in their teaching and scholarship. I understood how creative, valuable, and signal that approach is when a student working on the some significant Near Eastern inscriptions (specifically, the Kurkh Stele) was not able to find as much scholarship on their relevance to the interpretation of the Hebrews as he and his thesis committee expected. In the last generation this shortcoming is changing quickly, and I submit my interpretation of Galatians as a small addition to that developing frisson. Delbert himself points out, with characteristic humility, that the clear connection of the disciplines in modern scholarship is to be found already in the nineteenth-century higher criticism of the Germans, but I think Delbert's work, and perhaps this volume, help to show that the Anabaptists have added a meaningful, serious, and, very importantly, pious piece to that venerable construct.

The Letter to the Galatians, like most of Paul's writings, is not easily datable to a specific year, though I am in the camp that believes it is among his first, or perhaps the very first, of the extant letters. Here he writes this *Magna Carta* for Christian freedom out of concern and even anger at how the new converts are being misled in Galatia.[4] This letter is a forceful, thorough, and compelling attempt to explain why the expectations of those becoming Christians are not necessarily tied to Jewish

---

3. I hope that this work of Delbert's will reach publication, but his key idea is that these verses juxtapose pagan worldviews with Christian ones, and are not actually responding to Christian shortcomings. I was fortunate enough to be called upon to respond to his ideas on a proper reading of Romans at the Council of Senior Professionals' meeting at Fresno Pacific University in the fall of 2013.

4. See Boice, *Galatians, inter alia.*

observance—a delinking that is the heart of Paul's identity and mission as "The Apostle to the Gentiles." When my classes work through the aspects of the appeal of early Christianity from the perspective of the classical world, the Christian connection to a venerable tradition always figures prominently. My subject for this contribution, however, focuses on how to understand the way the Galatians would have heard Paul, and so I will provide background only to the extent that it will illuminate matters that touch most closely upon their world: my view of how the "Table" debates or epistolary chronology might be parsed is best reserved for another venue.[5] The Galatians need to know what is expected of them.

There are two very significant passages in the New Testament on what is to be expected of Gentile converts to Christianity. In Acts 15:29, after the Jerusalem Council (ca. 49 CE), in which James expresses the rationale for not "troubling" the Gentiles, we see that the agreement for the converts involves abstinence "from what has been sacrificed to idols, and from blood, and from what has been strangled, and from sexual immorality." The announcement continues: "If you keep yourselves from these, you will do well."[6] In Galatians we see Paul recalling an even greater narrowing of the expectations of converts—"They asked only one thing, that we remember the poor, which was actually what I was eager to do."[7] So while we will continue to argue over the place of faith and works among Christians, how they relate to justification and sanctification, and we try to understand the book of James' admonitions in the context of our lives,[8] there were and are very few outward requirements of the faith, and that stark (by the standards of ancient religions) lack seems in the above passages to have been agreed upon by all of the major figures of the apostolic generation.

There are certainly other ways in which we might understand our requirements in accepting Christ and becoming part of the community that would come to be called Christian. The Gospel of John in chapter 21

---

5. My student Ray Sanchez did a better treatment of these questions than I will ever do in his Fresno State history MA thesis. See Sanchez, "Chronology."

6. Likely these requirements were based on what was forbidden to Noah's sons. See note on Acts 15:20 in Metzger, *NOAB*.

7. Gal 2:10. Paul Toews makes an admonitory point about how the issue of orthodoxy and orthopraxy continue to be fraught. Toews, "Singing," 89–102.

8. James is in a sense counter-sloganeering and should be seen in that context. See Metzger, introduction to "Letter of James," in *NOAB*, 331NT. It is the case that the orphans and widows were in the foreground of concern, thus making the insistence quite closely related to the summary in Galatians. Jas 1:27.

instructs, "tend my sheep . . . feed my sheep," and "follow me." Likewise it is the case that Scripture honored by the early Christians, such as Micah 6:8 (to return to the venerable tradition mentioned above), would illuminate a context for actions outside literal adherence to the law: "What does He require but to act mercifully, do justice, and walk humbly with God?" Christ gives us two great commandments, clearly derived from the Pentateuch: "Love the Lord your God and love your neighbor as yourself."[9] Paul beautifully connects these themes at Romans 13: "Love does no wrong to a neighbor, therefore love is the fulfilling of the law."[10] In Matthew's Sermon on the Mount we are admonished to understand how things have been conceived, and go beyond: to exceed the law. We should especially remember this last, because the Anabaptist tradition is often seen as a way of living out the Sermon on the Mount: what do, e.g., the Beatitudes look like in practice?

Delbert and I share a common interest in how chapter 13 of Hebrews provides valuable insight for the requirements of Christianity. We should imitate the faith of our godly leaders. We should be always hospitable. In a passage that has rung in my own ears throughout my life, not only should we confess Christ, but we should "do good and share what we have."[11] In Delbert's frequent phrase, "we must seek a city with foundations."

Paul Picking Up the Telephone

Paul's letter begins by addressing the church in and around the Roman Empire's province of Galatia, and provides the Apostle's credentials to be speaking to, and to be taken seriously by, them. Paul emphasizes the need to cleave to the real message of the gospel, and not to be misled. The promise to Abraham precedes the law. The letter supplies an allegorical understanding to illuminate how the followers of Christ can interpret their relationship to God. A warning about the compulsion to follow the

---

9. E.g., Mark 12:30–31. Gal 5:14 gives a culminating reason Paul's anger as the false teachers: the law is summed up in the phrase "love your neighbor a yourself."

10. Rom 13:10.

11. The chapter also reminds us to avoid strange teachings, suggesting a very similar theme to Galatians' admonitions against ritual, and perhaps a significant admonition to high church Christians like me! One of the FPU students who has retuned from graduate work to teach with us is Sam Musgrave. As an undergraduate he made a very compelling case that Apollos was the author of Hebrews.

law and legalism figures prominently in Paul's admonition—he is concerned that their over-reliance on it will cause them to turn back to "weak and elemental spirits."[12] In a framing device to parallel his call to the true gospel at the first,[13] the letter then excoriates teachers who are, presumably knowingly, misleading those new to Christ. In an endearing turn, Paul provides a personal insight on the letter's composition, and exhorts mutuality, before summing up that Christ-followership is not about circumcision, but about a new creation.

Paul is very angry at those who are misleading the Galatians: it is obvious that quite dramatic requirements were being made of the new Christians. Are the local demands on the Gentile converts the same as the ones we see corrected in Acts 15?[14] Who are these false teachers being addressed and admonished by Paul? Delbert has mentioned numerous times the famous one-way phone conversation aspect of Paul's letters. One of his Yale Divinity School professors, Paul Minear, encouraged him always to question who was on the other side of the call: to what comments or situations was Paul responding? In some cases, we even know there were other responses and interactions, such as another Corinthians letter, that we do not possess. Delbert has faithfully pursued Minear's advice throughout his career, in presentations, classes and writing—we must likewise begin to investigate what the situation was among the Galatians that motivated Paul's comments, and what their world might have looked like, without our modern preconceptions. Since my approach is usually inductive, we should start with a specific verse and work to the larger narrative issues.

The difference in the pagan and Christian beliefs is brought into clear relief by an allusion to the very physicality of the pagan ritual. Daniel Crosby has elsewhere in this volume shown how vulgarity of pagan mythology was used as an argument against those conceptions by early Christians.[15] It follows, then, that we should expect at least the strong possibility of a very literal reading of Paul's jarring comment, "I wish

---

12. Gal 4:9.

13. Delbert has spent a career especially alive to *chiasmoi* in ancient literature, and thus, this device was especially interesting to me. His book-length work on Stephen's sermon and its chiastic rhythms is ingenious, as are his recent insights on *chiasmoi* in Romans 1–2. Wiens, *Stephen's Sermon*.

14. It may be that Paul's comment in this letter giving an even more reduced "troubling" of the Gentiles reflects his minimalist stance in the Jerusalem Council.

15. See "Arrows Fletched from Their Own Wings," *infra*.

those who unsettle you would castrate themselves";[16] or, "Would they would cut off themselves, those who are troubling you. . . ."[17] Commentaries have frequently tried to avoid the significance of "cutting off," but really the evocation cannot be circumcision, for which there is very well established vocabulary, but castration. And this verb choice makes it clear that there is more evoked than a metaphorical "cutting off" from the community; this excision is literal.[18]

Of course, there may also be a symbolic or metaphorical level to Paul's anger. The church father Origen suggests that there are always multiple scriptural levels—he called them the body, soul, and spirit.[19] But the statement connects directly to the practices of the pagan priests nonetheless, as we shall see. If he had meant a "cutting off" of community, there are other ways he likely would have expressed it: I think of Romans 9, "for I could wish that I myself were accursed and cut off from Christ for the sake of my own people, my kindred of the flesh."[20] The notion in the case of Romans is that he would be removed from "the book," as in Exodus 32:32. This passage points out the term ἀνάθεμα that Paul would likely have used had he wanted to emphasize his desire for these teachers to be shunned.

It is never wise to ignore Augustine on such matters as this one, even if his programmatic approach to understanding the passage might seem a little forced. He is always alive to determining how a blessing is delivered by biblical injunctions, since in his view Paul must be infallible, and would not deliver a curse.[21] In this case, how would emasculation result in a blessing? If the result of the emasculation were to be a closer walk

---

16. Gal 5:12 NRSV.

17. Gal 5:12 KJV. Ὄφελον καὶ ἀποκόψονται οἱ ἀναστατοῦντες ὑμᾶς. I will provide the Greek of two of the key passages for those able to work with the language. I will limit my linguistic comment in the text to two of the most important words Paul uses. I include two translations of the passage to give a sense of the range of meaning, and thus a like range of interpretation.

18. As, e.g., "The simple meaning is, I think, that Paul wished that the authors of these errors and disturbances were excluded from the church." Barnes, *Notes*, 381.

19. Origen, *Peri Archon* 4.

20. ηὐχόμην γὰρ ἀνάθεμα εἶναι αὐτὸς ἐγὼ ἀπὸ τοῦ Χριστοῦ ὑπὲρ τῶν ἀδελφῶν μου τῶν συγγενῶν μου κατὰ σάρκα. Rom 9:3.

21. Plumer's edition is a most valuable version of Augustine's commentary on Galatians. See especially his view of Paul's inspiration. Plumer, introduction to *Augustine's Commentary*, 92.

with Christ. Thus, his connection of the deprecation to a gospel passage: they would be made eunuchs for the kingdom.²²

What Does Paul Mean?

We should assume that the punishment Paul suggests would fit the crime, and thus, Paul's anger drives him to a pronouncement that may be hyperbolic, but likely has a clear meaning in context. The significance of meaning derived from narrative in the ancient world is obvious—from the pagan cosmology of Hesiod's *Theogony* to foundational tapestry of Stephen's sermon, about which Delbert has written a book-length unpacking. Paul knows that these narratives can mislead as well as affirm. The idea that there is a story—an allegory—by which to understand the Christian gospel would be familiar to the ancient people of Galatia. The narrative making spiritual claims rather than temporal or physical ones is the new and different piece. Given that Paul quite comprehensively explains the meaning of the narrative of Abraham to Christians, what story would have been familiar to the Galatians?

Robin Lane Fox has brilliantly encapsulated how different the world of the pagans was from that of the Christians. There had to be a literal carrying out of orthopraxy, a literal visitation of the god, unlike Christianity, where the narrative did not have to be so specific, primal, and basic, "elemental." The Christians, who did not outstrip the pagans in enthusiasm, also did not encounter the pagans' "failure of nerve" in an "age of anxiety."[23] Yet they were responsible for a specific allegiance that made no sense to the pagans. The idea of devotion to an otherworldly reality and transcendent expectations seemed infantile. Nonetheless, these Christians encouraged a separation from worldly concerns and a childlike faith.

Delbert's interests have frequently touched upon how to use concrete imagery to explain abstract ideas. The practice often goes beyond metaphor to be an allegory—such as the seminary student returning to talk to the old farmer in Corn, Oklahoma. They both have some of the truth, but it is very difficult for them to learn from and understand each other. Paul helped to

---

22. Matt 9:12. Associate Editor Daniel Crosby has pointed out a kind of counter-Augustinian view based on the same assumption about the meaning. That is, by insisting that they castrate themselves, there will be no "seed" to carry on their objectionable ideas. This notion would clearly have both literal and metaphorical significance.

23. Fox, *Pagans*, 64.

work out how the Hebrews and the Gentiles could both function in the early church. Their connection to the story of the resurrection, and the "faith once delivered," presented a new way to understand the world, yet one that happened within it, and that was told in its lingua franca. The narratives that were more common among the ancients, from animist tales to those of mystery religions, were almost always derived from explanations of natural phenomena, and not oriented toward telling the tale of a community, much less a voluntary community of faith.

The story of the recurrent cycle of nature typified by the Magna Mater—Cybele—and the sacrifice of Attis has a prominent local connection. Cybele was worshipped as a meteor in Asia Minor. It was a Phrygian cult, and since the Celts invaded Asia Minor, northern Phrygia came to be called Galatia. Pessinus was the most important center of worship. The priests of Cybele were even called *Galli*. These particular Celts are called Gallic peoples because of their relation to those who settled in France. Attis was probably originally a god of vegetation, who castrated himself for Cybele, died, and was resurrected. Thus, he could represent the cycle of the seasons to priests and worshippers.

The story of Attis' sacrifice for Cybele must have been well known to the Romans, because they forbad her worship even when they imported her meteoric representation with much pomp and ceremony during the Second Punic War. Evidence from the early Christian centuries shows that the obsession with Attis' blood and testicles anticipates the medieval Christian fixation on relics.[24] A powerful poem of Catullus from the middle of the first century BCE shows its presence among the Romans—and the terror it evoked. Romans were not allowed to be Galli. My translation of the key lines:

> Goddess, Great Goddess, Cubebe, Mistress of Dindymus,
> Far from me may all your furor be, Mistress,
> Push others to enthusiasm, push others to disease.[25]

---

24. See Fox, *Pagans*, 41, 71. We believe that the actual boxes priests would use to preserve their frenzied act have been found. D. W. J. Gill, "Behind the Classical Façade," 80n25. Gill continues: "For further detailed discussion with earlier references see L. Budde and R. Nicholls, *Catalogue of the Greek and Roman Sculpture in the Fitzwilliam Museum, Cambridge* (Cambridge: CUP 1964), 77–78, pl. 41 no. 125 (where it is described as a possible altar)." This material is cited in D. W. J. Gill, *Book of Acts*, 393. The famous British archaeological find of a Cybele Priest buried with two stones almost certainly representing the testicles.

25. Dea, magna dea, Cybebe, dea, domina Dindymi,

One of the reasons that commentators may have been unwilling to deal with this rather obvious connotation of Galatians 5:12 head on is certainly discomfort with the subject matter. It was long a custom in classical translation to place passages that were deemed less proper in a different language from the one into which the passage was translated, or even to keep them in the original. Such an approach was taken, for example, in the Loeb translation of Suetonius' account the activities at Tiberius' villa on Capri. Barnes was unwilling to explain Koppe's view of Paul's meaning in English—he wrote in his commentary about this "monstrous" interpretation: "*Non modo circumcidant se, sed, si velint, etiam mutilant se - ipsa genitalia resecent.*"[26] He says that he prefers a "simple" meaning of being cut off from communion, even though the literal interpretation is supported by "Chrysostom, Theodoret, Theophylact, Jerome, Grotius, Rosenmuller," and others.

Clarke finds the clearest parallels in 1 Corinthians 5:6–7. While I concur that Paul specifically and figuratively is referring to the dangers of false teachers in these two passages, they are two very different ways of addressing the problem.[27] He is not simply suggesting that such a group be excommunicated. On the other hand, Vincent agrees with how I claim this passage has to be understood, but I think draws the wrong conclusion. It seems likely he is swayed by Augustine:

> Paul says in effect: "These people are disturbing you by insisting on circumcision. I would that they would make thorough work of it in their own case, and, instead of merely amputating the foreskin, would castrate themselves, as heathen priests do. Perhaps that would be even a more powerful help to salvation."[28]

The verb in question, ἀποκόπτειν, is used several times in the Septuagint (the Ptolemaic Greek version of the Old Testament / Hebrew Bible) and the New Testament. Thus, a philological inquiry is in order to see if

---

Procul a mea tuus sit furor, omnis, era, domo:
Alios age incitatos, alios age rabidos. Catull. 63.91–93.
Among the stunning effects Catullus uses in the poem is the gender of the pronouns. When he is castrated, Attis becomes a "she": *citata*, line 8.

26. "Not only would they circumcise themselves, but, if they should wish, they would even mutilate themselves—they would cut off (their) very genitals." Koppe *via* Barnes, *Notes*, 381, trans. my own. Barnes, like Clarke in the next note, is a classic monumental nineteenth-century exposition.

27. Clarke, *Commentary*, Gal 5:12, 231.

28. Vincent, *Word Studies*, 162.

my suggestions are corroborated. Of the seven uses of the verb in this version of the Hebrew Bible,[29] the only time it does not refer to a literal "cutting off," a severing of some kind, is in a poetic sense in Psalm 76, and in that case the cutting off occurs with the abstract idea of mercy. For humans it is exclusively associated with an involuntary amputation.[30]

Since the Old Testament and New Testament Greek forms are likely two centuries apart, we need even more carefully to observe the word's context in the latter. The verb is used five times in the New Testament.[31] It is always used of a physical severing. In the very same chapter of Galatians that the word is used, earlier Paul does suggest a cutting off from the community: "You who want to be justified by the law have cut yourselves off from Christ; you have fallen away from grace."[32] In this case, he uses the verb καταργεῖν, "to abolish, set free," suggesting a more obvious way to refer to cutting off from community.

Paul provides a counter-narrative to the "elemental" pagan one; in Paul's allegory, we can see the triumph of faith. We are minors under the law. Abraham showed that it was through his belief and faith that we are saved. The child of the slave was born according to the flesh, the child of the free woman was born through the covenant.

I began this essay with the famous quote from the letter: "you reap what your sow."[33] Paul adduces here the most challenging aspect of Christianity. Though we are no longer under the law, nonetheless we will be identified by our fruit—we must not follow false teaching, even if it comes from an angel. Paul understands how Christianity can reclaim the notion of narrative from the pagans. The story he tells is an allegory of how Christians claim God's grace, and the hearers would know the comparison is not just to the narrative of the earthly child, but is also to the narratives that pagans told of the children of the Earth Mother in Central Anatolia.

It is especially valuable to reflect here on the "phone conversation" behind the letter to the Galatians, because the Anabaptist and Mennonite

---

29. LXX Deut 23:1; Deut 25:12; Judg 1:6, 7; 2 Kgs 10:4 (marked as 2 Sam 10:4 in non-Septuagint texts); Ps 76:8 (77:8 in some Bibles); Isa 18:5.

30. De Boer, *Galatians*, 325, summarizes the modern views of why this voluntary act would be characterized in this way; that is, by asking the false teachers to "go a step further." He also includes Lucian of Samosata's description of the act.

31. Mark 9:43–45; John 18:10; John 18:26; Acts 27:32; Gal 5:12.

32. Gal 5:4.

33. Gal 6:7.

Brethren tradition puts a very high premium on a narrative understanding of our journey. We should be able to tell the story of our personal and communal redemption. The Galatians were in danger of losing that authentic narrative, and Paul intervenes. In the sixties, Delbert saw the danger for the Mennonite Brethren, and gave them the prophetic "Wineskins." The danger of trusting to narratives is that they can be opaque. Paul realized he had to be quite graphic about what was at stake.

Bibliography

Barnes, Albert. *Notes on the Old and New Testament.* Vol. 22. Grand Rapids: Baker, 1962.

Boice, James Montgomery. *Galatians/Ephesians.* Grand Rapids: Zondervan, 1995.

Clarke, Adam. *The Holy Bible: Containing the Old and New Testaments.* . . . New York: Phillips & Hunt, 1883–84.

De Boer, M. C. *Galatians.* Louisville: Presbyterian, 2011.

Fox, Robin Lane. *Pagans and Christians.* New York: Knopf, 1989.

Gill, D. W. J. "Behind the Classical Façade: Local Religions of the Roman Empire." In *One God, One Lord in a World of Religious Pluralism*, edited by A. D. Clarke and R. W. Winter, 72–87. Cambridge: Tyndale, 1991.

———. *The Book of Acts in Its Graeco-Roman Setting.* Grand Rapids: Eerdmans, 1994.

Metzger, Bruce, ed. *The New Oxford Annotated Bible: With the Apocryphal/Deuterocanonical Books.* New York: Oxford University Press, 1994.

Plumer, Eric. Introduction to *Augustine's Commentary on Galatians: Introduction, Text, Commentary, and Notes.* New York: Oxford University Press, 2003.

Sanchez, Ray. "Chronology, Conflict, and Covenant." MA thesis, California State University, Fresno, 2001.

Toews, Paul. "Singing the Christian College Song in a Mennonite Key." In *Mennonite Idealism and Higher Education: The History of the Fresno Pacific College Idea*, edited by Paul Toews, 89–102. Fresno: Center for Mennonite Brethren Studies, 1995.

Vincent, Marvin R. *Word Studies in the New Testament.* Vol. 4. New York: Scribner, 1889.

Wiens, Delbert. *Stephen's Sermon and the Structure of Luke-Acts.* North Richland Hills, TX: Scott, 1998.

11

A Dangerous Mind and Dangerous Times
The Rain Miracle of Marcus Aurelius and the Second-Century Church

Richard Rawls

As Delbert Wiens' "Wineskins" nears its fiftieth anniversary of composition, the publication that caused people to warn that he possessed "a dangerous mind" merits fresh scrutiny. Although the second half of his publication perhaps created the most consternation, it is the first half that is of interest to this chapter. In that first part, Wiens narrates the story of the Mennonite Brethren encounter with a world that was radically changing. He argued that shifting times require changes in *Weltanschauung*, in how one approaches the world. Indeed, the genius of Wiens' article is that while he specifically discussed Mennonite Brethren attitudes to culture, the dynamics he described relate not just to one ethno-religious tradition within Christianity but broadly speaking to the Christian tradition itself.

This contribution will briefly describe Wiens' ideas as set forth in "Wineskins" before subjecting them to investigation through the example of a specific incident within the second century of early church history. Because the church began to understand itself as one culture within a considerably larger and pluralistic world, the early second-century church is a good place to localize this investigation. While the church had both understood and positioned itself in a way that saw the world as hostile to its beliefs, such a view was incompatible with its own universalizing tendencies. A church that understood Jesus' encouragement to "go therefore and make disciples" could not just hide from Greco-Roman culture, which was, after all, partially its own culture.[1] Perhaps nowhere is this more evident than during the reign of the emperor, Marcus Antonius Aurelius (161–180 CE). A unique incident in the history of both Aurelius' reign and the church sheds light on the Christian reevaluation of the relationship between religion and culture early in the second century CE.

Wiens and the Question of Culture

Delbert Wiens attempted to "imagine" a stable society and world in which, as he observed, "life can be lived according to the customs handed down from parents to children."[2] The Mennonite world of his forebears reflected an early consensus on their attitude toward "outside" culture. The first generations of the Christian church also enjoyed a consensus that was enforced by forces hostile and external to the church itself. What emerges in these early communities is a folk wisdom passed down through the generations. There is a problem, however, with this folk wisdom, as Wiens rightly recognizes: namely, the world and its demands do not remain static. The folk wisdom must change to deal with a world in flux, but this produces tension in the community. One response to this tension is for the community to repeat verbally the principles of faith but quietly practice the new solutions.[3] When principle conflicts with reality, insist, in other words, that the faith community is adhering to the old forms of belief while subtly changing to acclimate to the world. The community thus adjusts while repeating the old declarations of faith. Another response is to draw a line around the faith community even if it means becoming isolated and insular.[4] If change demands adjustments to the faith that make the community uncomfortable, then perhaps the community can retreat from the "world." Becoming insular, however, requires a homogeneity that is difficult to maintain over time. This remains especially the case when the world marches headlong into ceaseless change.

---

1. Matt 28:19 NIV.
2. Wiens, "Wineskins," 8.
3. Ibid., 7.
4. Ibid., 9.

At some point, an encounter and dialogue with the world becomes necessary. That dialogue makes the old separations practically impossible. Wiens noted in this respect:

> We must develop a new definition of separation, one that permits us to distinguish within an activity what is the good and the bad of it. For the world cannot be kept safely "out there." It is also "in here," in all "here's." This will complicate what we had hoped to keep simple, and it will require ethics.[5]

The outcome, as "Wineskins" reflected, was a dialogue with the world. Dialogue implies many things, including a give and take between two different communities, but it also suggests a dialogue within those communities. "One must talk," he noted, "when one is forced to explain to outsiders what has happened."[6]

As an ancient historian (University of Chicago, PhD) as well as a theologian (Yale Divinity School), Wiens was cognizant of the early church and its patterns. It is an old story repeated over and over throughout the world: the initial retreat towards insularity is followed by a discomfort with reaching out to one's neighbors; next, followed by a turn towards treating the faith as an ethical system; finally, superseded by more meaningful dialogues with both one's neighbors and within one's faith community. Indeed, just as occurred in the early church, Wiens predicted that the failure to handle adequately these various tensions would lead to a type of shattering, an increase in scandal and fanaticism to trouble the church.[7] At some point, the failure of the old coping mechanisms compels the faithful to reach out to communicate with non-believers. For this dialogue to prove successful, the church needs to find common ground with its neighbors, to realize that "the consensus of the past will never be restored," and new levels of consensus-making will need to emerge.[8] To various degrees, this dialogue has both succeeded and failed, but the encounters with the world have also benefited the faithful. In attempting to describe their story to outsiders, the faithful are compelled to do a number of things: (1) face a level of discomfort that Wiens describes well in "Wineskins"; (2) refine their story to take into account "outsiders"; (3) engage in an intellectual defense or even "apology" in the Greek sense of

5. Ibid., 10.
6. Ibid., 4.
7. Ibid., 28.
8. Ibid., 24.

ἀπολογία, to provide an intellectual rationale for why the faithful hold the beliefs they observe; and (4) provide guidance to insiders in terms of navigating the intellectual demands of changing times. Wiens did this well in his "Wineskins," and now it remains to show how these same dynamics transpired within the early Christian church at one hundred twenty years into its existence, roughly the same amount of time as the Mennonite Brethren church had existed when Wiens composed his piece.

The second century posed a number of challenges to the early church. The church had existed now for over a century. Christians increasingly came to Roman attention, and Christians began to suffer persecutions for their faith. Though sporadic and localized at first, these persecutions caused some Christian communities to turn inward, others to run away from the "world," and still others to begin to figure out how to dialogue with their pagan neighbors. In the midst of these dynamics, the rain miracle of Marcus Aurelius occurred. In order to understand how it relates to Wiens' ideas and the early church, we need to understand it from Roman eyes.

The Rain Miracle, Various Views, and Imperial Propaganda

A detachment or vexillation of Roman soldiers fighting between 172 and 174 CE under the auspices of the emperor Marcus Aurelius found themselves surrounded by hostile members of an antagonistic tribe, the Quadi.[9] Outnumbered and enervated by hunger and thirst, the Romans vacillated behind defensive lines hastily established upon a hillside. The barbarian forces facing Rome's troops figured they had time on their side.[10] If the Romans attempted to muscle their way out of the predicament, they faced certain annihilation against overwhelming numbers. If they waited much longer, dehydration would claim their lives. At that moment, a civilian or a centurion or perhaps even the emperor himself urged the soldiers to pray to their respective gods. Although we cannot ascertain the person or people exhorting others to pray, it appears the "gods" listened. According to all accounts, both pagan and Christian, a

---

9. The precise date of the event is unknown. See Zwikker, *Studien*, 206–26, for the earlier date. Morris, "Dating the Column," 37–40, provides an argument for the later date.

10. Dio Cass. 72.8–10, trans. Cary. Note Xiphilinius' comments on Dio's narrative at 72.9.

rainstorm miraculously appeared and acted as the salvific event by which the Romans rehydrated themselves and battled their way out of peril. Some accounts claimed lightning further struck barbarian positions.[11]

While the Roman campaign against German and Sarmatian tribes ended soon after, the resulting peace witnessed an emerging public-relations contest regarding the rain miracle. The emperor controlled and employed imperial and official propaganda, including coinage, victory monuments, parades, and other resources, and it was his version of the event that first received prominent mention. Later, however, Christians and pagans composed their own interpretations. None disputed the historicity of the event. Instead, each asseverated his or her god was the deity responsible for the deluge and deliverance.

Proclaiming the superiority of one's deity was nearly a pedestrian enterprise in the ancient world. At least four interpretations of the event emerged over time. Two will be of concern here: (1) the official, imperial portrayal of the event and (2) the Christian version. A third and fourth account circulated. The third credited an Egyptian priest named Arnuphis and the god(s) Mercury-Hermes-Thoth, and like the first two, it was nearly contemporaneous with the event.[12] The fourth tradition connected Julian the Theurgist with Marcus Aurelius during the rain miracle. The Julian Theurgist tradition first received mention, however, in the eleventh century. It is so spurious that the historian Garth Fowden observed that all other accounts were obvious explanations advanced soon after the event, but the "Julian version is neither obvious nor, it seems, historical."[13] These third and fourth versions will not receive additional mention because they do not necessarily contribute significantly to our understanding of culture and religion in the second-century imperial period.[14] The emperor's propaganda will instead be the focus here. Understanding it

11. E.g., SHA *Marc.* 24.4. The only other ancient source to link the two events was Dio Cass. 72.8, whose work might have informed the *Scriptores Historiae Augustae*.

12. Ibid., 72.8.

13. Fowden, "Pagan Versions," 93. Sozomen, a fifth-century ecclesiastical historian, also mentioned Julian in the content of another miracle, which a local bishop refuted by an even larger miracle. Even then, Sozomen said nothing about Julian's role in the Marcus Aurelius rain miracle. Sozom. *Hist. eccl.* 1.18.7.

14. The third version cannot be addressed here, but that is not to say it is insignificant. Some scholars have thought it represented a different version of events than the "official line." For a recent harmonization of the official line with the Arnuphis, Mercury-Hermes-Thoth version, see Israelowich, "Rain Miracle," 96–102.

will help us articulate both the worldview that the Christians were arguing against and their critics.

Roman imperial propaganda attributed the rain miracle and the wider victory over Rome's enemies to Marcus Aurelius and to Jupiter. One may observe in the literary, numismatic, and archaeological evidence what scholars have described as the "official line" of imperial propaganda.[15] Since both the relationship between the emperor and Jupiter and the associations of victory with Roman religion were extremely complex, the official line gave several possible interpretations, all of which remained mutually inclusive. First, Jupiter functioned as the traditional God of Rome and lord of the elements. Rome's victory, with Jupiter's help, informed Rome's conception of itself as imposing order over the forces of chaos, especially weather. Jupiter had long been depicted as *fulgor*, the source from which lightning was sent, and in imagery evoking control of the sky: *Pluvialis, Imbricitor, Serenator, Serenus*.[16] Jupiter's spiked thunderbolt reminded the Romans of both his powers of destruction and his capacity to bless his devotees. As father of the gods, Jupiter scatters red lightning, hurtles thick fires, and strikes terror into the hearts of humans.[17]

A scene on the Marcus Aurelius victory column portrays lightning destroying an enemy siege tower. The scene thereby depicted Jupiter as both pulverizing the enemy and blessing Rome's soldiers. Although the victory column pictured the lightning event as separate from the rain miracle, not all sources considered them separately.[18] The *Scriptores Historiae Augustae* (not always reliable, but especially helpful on Marcus Aurelius) linked the two events: "By his [Marcus Aurelius'] prayers he summoned a thunderbolt from heaven against a war-engine of the enemy, and successfully besought rain for his men when they were suffering from thirst."[19] These depictions and portrayals accorded well with imperial ideology. From the inception of the principate, Jupiter was described along with the emperor as partners in the struggle against chaos and evil.

Second, Jupiter's association with the emperor imparted legitimacy to the emperor and his office. Marcus Aurelius faced no danger to his

---

15. Fowden, "Pagan Versions," 87.

16. Fears, "Cult of Jupiter," 19. See, e.g., Ov. *Fast.* 3.285–392 and Plin. *HN* 2.52–55 (138–42).

17. Ov. *Fast.* 3.285–290.

18. Becatti, *Colonna*, scene 9.

19. SHA *Marc.* 24. 4; cf. Dio Cass. 72.8.

rule, but since Octavian (63 BCE–14 CE) emperors validated their position as commander-in-chief through victory. Military success confirmed the emperor's right to rule.[20] Emperors now succeeded in battle not by means of "luck" or "chance" or even military prowess, but through the merit of their *virtus*.[21] The qualities inherent in this *virtus* involved goodness, prayers, divinity, as well as masculinity at war. Battlefield victories, therefore, established the emperor's spiritual authority to rule and testified to the fact that the gods favored a particular ruler.

Next and closely related, the rain miracle confirmed the emperor's status as Jupiter's vicegerent. By associating himself with Jupiter's rain miracle, Marcus Aurelius aligned himself precisely as participating in the tradition of the emperor as Jupiter's vicegerent. This tradition enjoyed nearly two hundred years of association by the time of Marcus Aurelius' reign. Ovid (43 BCE–17/18 CE), for example, praised Augustus as Jupiter on earth, as one whose presence preserved the protection of the gods.[22] Horace (65–68 BCE) suggested that Augustus, and by implication his successors, was designated to expiate crimes against Rome and appease the wrath of the gods.[23] Later, Nero (37–68 CE) issued a coin late in his reign commemorating his liberation of Greece. The *aureus* depicted *Jupiter Liberator* as seated and holding a thunderbolt and scepter, thereby emphasizing the emperor's role as the one who satisfies Jupiter's functions on earth.[24] This simultaneous emphasis on Jupiter as the protector of Rome through his vicegerent undergirded the entire Jovian theology of imperial power at Rome. It only accumulated authority through time. For example, Pliny the Younger (61–112 CE) emphasized Trajan (r. 98–117 CE) as the elect of Jupiter in his *Panegyricus*:

> With the same reverence for the gods, Caesar, you will not allow public thanks for your benevolence to be addressed to your genius, but direct them to the godhead of Jupiter Best and Highest; to him, you say, we own whatever we owe you, and your benefactions are the gift of him who gave you to us.[25]

---

20. McCormick, *Eternal Victory*, 4.

21. Storch, "Absolutist Theology," 198.

22. Ov. *Tr.* 5.2.47–48. See also 5.2.50–55, where lightning is associated with Augustus and his judgment.

23. Hor. *Carm.* 1.2.

24. Mattingly, *Coins*, 1:214, no. 110, pl. 40, no. 15.

25. Plin. *Pan.* 52.6, trans. Radice.

Finally, Trajan recorded his investiture of power by Jupiter on his arch at Beneventum. The crown and sides of the arch portray Jupiter bestowing the thunderbolt upon Trajan, establishing the link between heavenly and earthly rulers.[26]

Fourth, the ideological proclamations following the victory sought to support a beleaguered army. The war had progressed unfavorably at times. Barbarians threatened as far south as northern Italy. At approximately the same time as war was being prosecuted elsewhere, the Costoboci burst into the Balkans and overwhelmed Thrace and Macedonia, and Moorish rebels crossed the Strait of Gibraltar to attack the Iberian Peninsula. The situation remained desperate enough for some provincials to swear vows to Jupiter if he would deliver them. Even when the Romans counterattacked, they suffered grievous defeats. The Quadi have been judged as "man for man, the most formidable," of all the enemies Rome fought in the early 170s.[27] Although they emerged victorious, the Romans grievously "felt" the horrors of the fighting. Anyone who has viewed the Marcus Aurelius victory column cannot help but feel admiration mixed with horror: admiration for an emperor who would so honestly portray the terrifying nature of war without necessarily sanitizing it or glorifying it. As one scholar has observed, Marcus Aurelius' victory column captures the terrors of the conflict in agonizing detail:

> There is a note of pathos that is only too clear, when the burning and destruction of enemy villages, and the execution of rebels and the remorseless onset of battle are displayed. . . . The war was a grim and sordid necessity. Marcus knew it, and the artists on the column clearly felt it.[28]

Victory proved both long and difficult, with an opening phase of barbarian aggression (perhaps 166–171 CE), followed by the Roman counterattack (172–175 CE), and then limited skirmishes until a final peace reached conclusion in 180.[29] The account of the Roman historian Cassius Dio further supports this impression of a protracted war involving horrific scenes of battle.[30]

---

26. Torilli, *L'arco di Traiano*, Plates CXXIX, CXXXV, CXL.
27. McLynn, *Marcus Aurelius*, 363.
28. Birley, *Marcus Aurelius*, 178.
29. Oliva, "Zur Bedeutung der Markomannenkriege," 120.
30. Dio Cass. 72.8, 10.

Support for a beleaguered army might have proven a moot point, but the revolt of Avidius Cassius (175 CE) made it clear that soldiers maintained the capacity to rebel at any time. There is some indication that Avidius Cassius had not intended to rebel but that he thought Marcus Aurelius had already passed away due to illness. Once his troops declared him emperor, he could not back down. The *Scriptores Historiae Augustae* recorded that even before Cassius' revolt Marcus Aurelius felt pressured by both military and nobility: "But because Marcus, as a result of his system of philosophy, seemed harsh in his military discipline and indeed in his life in general, he was bitterly assailed."[31] A few lines later, the author revealed the source of such pressure: "And because in this war . . . many nobles perished . . . his friends often urged him to abandon the war and return to Rome."[32] Religion worked in the emperor's favor. For instance, the overwhelming majority of dedications to Jupiter Optimus Maximus in the military frontiers of the Danube and Rhine regions were issued by military and imperial officials.[33] The rain miracle provided Marcus Aurelius the opportunity to restore morale and the confidence of his army and nobility while propitiating their anger. An appeal to traditional Roman religion and its confirmation on the battlefield could be portrayed in coins, columns, and other forms of communication. These enabled him, in the words of Ido Israelowich, "to convey a public image that suited Roman ideals."[34]

Finally, one cannot rule out the possibility of what Marcus Aurelius may have considered to be a "legitimate religious experience." The central role of Jupiter in imperial ideology was not entirely a calculated political fabrication of skeptical emperors. It was customary to associate Jupiter as the savior of the current emperor.[35] People at all social levels throughout the Latin-speaking portions of the empire believed in Jupiter as a personal deity who intervened in both personal and state affairs. Because it is frequently difficult—if not impossible—to distinguish religious theology from political ideology, it is more than plausible that Marcus Aurelius personally believed in the beneficence of the gods and of Jupiter in particular. "There are gods," he insisted in his *Meditations*, "and they

---

31. SHA *Marc.* 22.5–6.
32. Ibid., 22.7–9.
33. Fears, "Cult of Jupiter," 501.
34. Israelowich, "Rain Miracle," 94.
35. Birley, "Religion," 1511.

do concern themselves with human things."[36] It was this same devotion to both the gods and his own "state" that later led Marcus Aurelius to permit sporadic and localized persecutions of Christians in Lyons and elsewhere. We cave into Hollywood versions of events if we consider Roman persecution of Christians as engaging in bloodlust and not motivated by piety. Strange as it seems to us, the Romans thought they were being pious in persecuting those whose beliefs clashed with that of their ancestors.[37]

Christian Use of the Rain Miracle

Christians generally endeavored to assuage the fears of imperial authorities that they were a seditious group failing to contribute to or for the commonweal. They were not popular, and indeed the second century generally witnessed an increase in the persecution of Christians. The rain miracle provided them with the perfect opportunity to elucidate the intellectual defenses of the faith that they were already formulating. By asserting that their god delivered the Romans from the barbarians on account of Christian soldiers praying for deliverance, they sought to reinforce several political and religious points at once. We shall focus on the six most prominent positions and how the Christians inserted them into their justifications of their beliefs. We shall further examine the claims of the apologists for signs that they were struggling with the same issues to which Wiens alluded in *New Wineskins*. Perhaps as important as the content of their messages, the apologists' efforts suggested a type of "New Wineskins for Old Wine." Far from rejecting Greco-Roman culture, the Christian message suggested a type of acceptance of certain aspects of the culture in which they lived. This acceptance will enable us to scrutinize what it meant for someone like Tertullian (160–225 CE) and others to claim that Christian soldiers served in the military.[38]

The first Christian use of the rain miracle was to insist that Christians supported the empire in general. They had no choice but to insist upon this message. As events leading up to the rain miracle make clear,

---

36. M. Aur. *Med.* 2.11, trans. Haines.

37. Wilken, *Christians*, 48–67.

38. The leading proponents of the idea of early Christian pacifism are: Bainton, *Christian Attitudes*; Cadoux, *Early Christian Attitude*; and Harnack, *Militia Christi*. Helgeland, "Christians," 735–71, provides a delightful summary of various positions on Christian pacifism and convincingly proves that the early church held no coherent, consistent position regarding military service.

Rome's populace remained in an angry mood and harbored grievances against those suspected of disloyalty. When times become tough, a populace will look to insure that all of its members support the body politic. Society may look for a scapegoat or sacrificial victim.[39] The empire had already been enfeebled by an earlier war with Rome's eastern neighbors during the Parthian War, 161–166 CE. Marcus Aurelius' own adopted brother and co-emperor, Lucius Verus, fell victim in 169 CE to one of several plagues circulating throughout Eurasia. Rome's population was so decimated by fighting and plague that it could not muster enough manpower to relieve northern Italy in the late 160s. Since Roman people had grown unaccustomed to wars on Italian soil, they desperately appealed for assistance. The army eventually accepted slaves as volunteers, formed gladiators into special units, turned bandits of Dalmatia and Dardania into soldiers, and hired mercenaries of Germanic origins.[40] The author of the *Scriptores Historiae Augustae* emphasized the gravity of the situation when he related that Marcus Aurelius sold imperial palace furnishings in order to secure the fiscal resources required for his impending counteroffensive.[41] Since some Christian communities remained pacifist and others refused to make the required oaths and sacrifices to and for the emperor, pagans interpreted Christian behavior as a shirking of their duties as citizens.

Even Marcus Aurelius voiced a grievance in apparent reference to Christians and their failure to support their country: "Yet to have the intelligence a guide to what they deem their duty is an attribute of those who do not believe in Gods and those who fail their country in its need and those who do their deeds behind closed doors."[42] The emperor's charge of atheism, unpatriotic feelings, and forming a secret society echoed the three typical pagan criticisms of Christians.[43] It was not just the emperor making such observations. The pagan philosopher Celsus composed his piece, ἀληθής λόγος or "True Doctrine," at approximately the same time. Although Celsus' text is no longer extant, the specifics of his argument found preservation in the writings of Origen of Alexandria: "Then Celsus next exhorts us [Christians] to help the emperor

---

39. Girard, *Violence*, 2–4, 12, 39–67.
40. SHA *Marc.* 21.5–8.
41. Ibid., 21. 9–10.
42. M. Aur. *Med.* 3.16. See 63n7 in Haines' trans.
43. Green, *Christianity*, 120–32.

with all our power, and cooperate with him in what is right, and fight for him and be fellow-soldiers if he presses for this, and fellow-generals with him."[44] Celsus' point, within the overall framework of Origen's work and especially the eighth book, related not to early Christians as pacifists but rather that they refused to assist the society from which they benefited.[45]

Demonstrating physical support for the empire was the first and foremost function of Christian apologetics. When the rain miracle provided them with an opportunity to work on their image, they incorporated it into their apologetics. Four apologies were addressed to Marcus Aurelius between 166 and 177 CE by Athenagoras of Athens, Melito of Sardis, Apollinarius of Hierapolis, and Miltiades. All emphasized the loyalty of Christians to the emperor, and Melito and Apollinarius specifically broached the subject of Christians in the *Legio XII Fulimanata*. These appeals to the rain miracle followed shortly after the event itself! Apollinarius lived close to the camps, and he was the first Christian, about whom we know, to assert Christian participation in the miraculous rainfall. Apollinarius may have misunderstood the facts about the name *Fulminata*, but his proximity to the camp of the twelfth legion and his being the first Christian to produce a Christian version has provoked considerable contemporary discussion among scholars.

The church historian, Eusebius of Caesarea (ca. 260–340 CE), later circulated Apollinarius' assertion that the twelfth legion, the *Legio XII Fulminata*, "Thundering," was so named because of its presence at the event.[46] This claim about the name *Fulminata* is widely discredited today, and for two reasons: (1) *Fulminata* is a perfect passive participle, meaning "thunderstruck or having been struck by thunder," not a present active participle, which would mean "thundering"; (2) the title *Fulminata* in reference to the twelfth legion can be traced back to the reign of Octavian Augustus.[47] Despite the error in the origins of nomenclature, most scholars consider it entirely plausible that the emperor might have pulled vexillations or detachments from eastern legions, including the *Legio XII*. It is important to remember that Eusebius composed his history in the fourth century, long after the event transpired. Moreover, it was apparent that Eusebius had read not only prior Christian accounts of the event

---

44. Origen, *C. Cels.* 8.73, trans. Chadwick.
45. Wilken, *Christians*, 118.
46. Euseb. *Hist. eccl.* 5.5.
47. Ritterling, "Legio," 1186–1829.

but also pagan ones such as the one by the Roman historian Cassius Dio. Nobody doubted the historicity of the event. What was at issue was the religious origin of the event and, therefore, its cultural and political ramifications. It was precisely the cultural and political support of the empire that Apollinarius and Melito wanted emperors to notice, and the rain miracle provided them with that opportunity.

Christians utilized the rain miracle as a means of elucidating a second fact: they brought both spiritual and material benefits to the empire as a consequence of their religion. Tertullian informed Scapula that Christians were responsible not only for the battlefield rainstorm but also for ending droughts by their prayers: "When, indeed, have not droughts been put away by our kneelings and our fastings."[48] Tertullian declared that in addition to their cosmological benefits, Christians prayed and sacrificed for the emperor's safety in a manner commensurate with their religion:

> We are ever making intercessions for all the emperors. We pray for them a long life, a secure rule, a safe home, brave armies, a faithful senate, an honest people, a quiet world, and everything for which a man and a Caesar can pray.[49]

Like Tertullian, Athenagoras of Athens assured Marcus Aurelius of Christian prayers in both the beginning and the end of his pleas for the Christians. This was a constant refrain of Christian apologists.

A third assertion of the apologists closest in date to the rain miracle was that Christians had participated as soldiers at the event itself. Although the Carthaginian theologian Tertullian was not the first to circulate the story with a Christian interpretation, he seized upon it some twenty years after the event itself. Tertullian, in fact, testified about it in more than one place, writing in both an *Apology* to a Roman emperor and an epistle to Scapula, a Roman proconsul in North Africa. He insisted not only that the God of the Christians had performed the miracle but also that Christian soldiers were present:

> Also, during the German campaign, Marcus Aurelius was successful in obtaining rain during the well-known drought when Christian soldiers prayed to God. And, when in fact have even droughts failed to be avoided by the prayers and fasts of our people? On that occasion the people, acclaiming "the god of

---

48. Tert. *Ad Scap.* 5.4, trans. Thelwall.
49. Tert. *Apol.* 30.4, trans. Glover; cf. Tert. *Ad Scap.* 2.

gods, who alone is mighty," gave tribute to our God under the name of Jupiter.⁵⁰

The claim of Tertullian in 192 CE that Christians were responsible for the rain miracle was, therefore, directly meant to counter pagan charges that Christians failed to share their responsibility for supporting the emperor and army.

Tertullian seldom refrained from entering the verbal fray, and the rain miracle gave him additional material for discourse. He boldly declared Christians were present during the battle and secured divine assistance. He insisted that in addition to sailing and fighting with and for Romans, the ubiquitous Christians participated in nearly all facets of Roman life:

> We have filled all your things [places]: cities, islands, forts, towns, market-places, the [military] camp itself, tribes, town councils, palace, senate, forum; we have left nothing to you except your [religious] temples.⁵¹

Although Tertullian's attitude towards the Roman Empire later shifted along with his gradual "conversion" to Montanism, his works exhibited an intentional effort to portray Christians as satisfying the physical and military requirements requisite to imperial citizenship. Furthermore, Tertullian continued to appeal to the Christian presence during the rain miracle even after he assumed the intransigent position of a rigid Montanist.⁵²

Tertullian further articulated a fourth theme closely related to the rain miracle. Mainly, he averred that not only had Christians served with imperial forces during the rain miracle but that they had also helped to suppress the revolt of Avidius Cassius in 175 CE. Indeed, the emperor had taken ill in the early 170s, and at one point he may have lingered in that liminal space between life and death. The evidence hints that Marcus Aurelius' wife became so concerned that, anticipating her husband's death, she encouraged Avidius Cassius to become emperor because her son, Commodus (161–192 CE), was not quite ready as a juvenile to

---

50. Tert. *Ad Scap.* 4, trans. Thelwall.

51. Tert. *Apol.* 37.4, trans. Glover.

52. Even though Tertullian wrote *Ad Scapulam* late in his life, he demonstrated no remorse for Christian military service. His "hostile" stance with Christians serving in the military concerned the religious oaths soldiers were compelled to swear and not the service per se. See, Helgeland, *Christians*," 738–44.

assume responsibility.[53] By the time Cassius realized the emperor had lived, it was too late. He was technically already in open revolt notwithstanding Marcus Aurelius' notorious clemency. This revolt provided Tertullian with an opportunity to contrast the behavior of Christian Romans with non-Christian Romans. Non-Christian Romans supported Cassius' revolt, they later attempted to seize the palace after Commodus died, and they murdered Commodus' successor, Pertinax (126–193 CE), who had been a leading general under both Marcus Aurelius and Commodus. Meanwhile, Christians had not only solicited the rain miracle, but they had remained faithful to Marcus Aurelius during Cassius' revolt.[54] Ever the master of verbal pugilism, or in the words of Frank McLynn, a "pathological controversialist,"[55] Tertullian further compared Christian fidelity to the emperor with that of others:

> Every one of them [plotting against the emperor], right up to the moment of the outburst of impiety, was offering sacrifice for the health of the emperor, was swearing by his genius, some outdoors and some indoors, and you may be sure they were giving Christians the name of public enemies.[56]

Tertullian was not the only one to make this comparison. Apollinarius also alluded to this fact as well as to the fact that the *Legio XII* was involved in suppressing the revolt of Cassius. This was the same legion he credited for the rain miracle.[57]

To move from Christian presence as providing spiritual and material benefit to advocating their God as "The God" was a logical fifth position. Since the Christians considered their presence and prayers for the emperor as efficacious, the battlefield intervention of their God implied not only their God's benevolence but also their own presence as blessing Roman society and not as hostile to it. Indeed, what better way for Melito, Apollinarius, Tertuallian, Origen, and later, Eusebius, to legitimize this proposition except through the battlefield intervention of their God? Melito's writings demonstrate this fact. Although his *Apology* to Marcus Aurelius is no longer extant, Eusebius conveyed a portion of it in his *Ecclesiastical History*. Melito insisted that the mere presence of

---

53. Dio Cass. 72.22.2–28.2. See also, SHA *Avid. Cass.* 7.
54. Tert. *Apol.* 35.9–10.
55. McLynn, *Marcus Aurelius*, 283.
56. Tert. *Apol.* 35.10, trans. Glover.
57. Grant, "Five Apologists," 4.

Christians and their "philosophy" (to be understood as their *way* of life) conveyed blessings upon Rome:

> Our philosophy first grew up among the barbarians, but its full flower came among your nation in the great reign of your ancestor, Augustus, and became an omen of good to your empire, for from that time the power of the Romans became great and splendid. You are now his happy successor, and shall be so along with your son, if you protect the philosophy which grew up with the empire and began with Augustus.[58]

Eusebius' inclusion of Melito indicated one of the points of Eusebius' own work: namely, the advent of both Christ and the Roman Empire demarcated the boundaries of a new age that would witness the continued revelation of the "true God."[59]

A sixth and final point of the apologists related to acceptance of the Roman Empire and acceptance of Roman culture if even not all of it. It ought to be acknowledged before turning there, however, that not all Christians wanted to embrace the empire. Some saw it as so infused with Greco-Roman paganism, and by implication as so hostile to God, that it ought to be avoided at all costs. Therefore, some Christian communities became insular, isolated, and deliberately as separate as possible. Other communities sought to live by other rules. The Christian community in the first three centuries was, in fact, a patchwork of *praxis* as well as theologies.

In the midst of divergences of practice and belief, Tertullian became increasingly hostile to the Roman Empire and all for which it stood. In his later years—well after the rain miracle—he wrote his famous words, "What indeed has Athens to do with Jerusalem? What concord is there between the Academy and the Church? What between heretics and Christians?"[60] Such hostility is, on one hand, understandable because North Africa witnessed more martyrdoms from persecution of the church than did any other region of the empire. On the other hand, Tertullian represented the attitudes of some who had not experienced persecution but who envisaged a bifurcated world in which a holy remnant needed to remain pure from the polluting influences outside of the church.

---

58. Euseb. *Hist. eccl.* 4.26, trans. Lake.
59. Chesnut, *First Christian Histories*, 98–102.
60. Tert. *De praescr. haeret.* 7.

Tertullian was not the only one whose hostility to Roman culture has survived. Tatian (ca. 120–180 CE) emerged as another figure in the early church who delighted in attacking Greco-Roman culture and religion. He labeled the Greeks as arrogant for claiming to invent many things that had actually originated in other cultures.[61] Moreover, even in areas where the Greeks excelled, such as philosophy, they still committed serious errors calling into question the coherence of their ideas. He further asserted in contrast to the pagan philosophies, that the Christian philosophy or *way* of life remained far superior. Pagan philosophers concerned themselves with the way people looked, judged people by their external appearance, and made decisions based on other ephemera.[62] Christians, in contrast, judge others by personal character, strength of mind, and in compliance with their beliefs. Although he insisted he paid his taxes, he also maintained that while he once excelled at Greek philosophy, he now rejected it and all for which it stood.[63]

The cases of Tertullian and Tatian point to an irony captured well in the words of R. M. Grant: "Tatian says he is turning his back on Graeco-Roman culture, though he uses rhetoric to say goodbye."[64] In other words, he who was claiming to renounce Greco-Roman culture was utilizing a very typical and culturally mediated, rhetorical form in which to accomplish it! As Grant further observes, "Such ambivalence was to be shared by Tertullian, but not by all Christians either then or later."[65] No matter how hard the likes of Tertullian and Tatian tried to isolate themselves and draw a line between culture and religion, they found it was impossible in the words of Wiens to keep the "out there" away from the "in here."

A contemporary of Tertullian, Origen of Alexandria, characterized the evolving attitude of pragmatism maintained by other Christians. Though the early church fathers and mothers might not have concurred with Origen, a pacifist, about the role of Christians in the military, they all would have affirmed what he stipulated about their God and the Roman Empire:

---

61. Tatianus, *Ad Gr.* 1.
62. Ibid., 32. E.g., Thersites was judged as much for his appearance as his behavior in the *Iliad*.
63. Ibid., 1, 4.
64. Grant, "Five Apologists," 13.
65. Ibid.

> God was preparing the nations for the teaching, that they might be under one Roman emperor, so that the unfriendly attitude of the nations to one another, caused by the existence of a large number of kingdoms, might not make it more difficult for Jesus' apostles to do what he commanded them when he said, "Go and teach all nations."[66]

It was this conviction that undergirded the logic of those willing to deal with Roman culture, their interpretation of contemporary vicissitudes, and subsequently, their ideology: God worked through the history of other nations and cultures to carry out the divine plan. As the Christians like Eusebius would later stipulate, this included divine intervention on the battlefield in instances like the rain miracle and at the Milvian Bridge.

It would be convenient to say that with the conversion of the emperor Constantine (272–337 CE) the church wrapped up a neat and tidy consensus about its ways of life and forms of belief, but that would be disingenuous to declare. Dialogue requires time, and the early church could not openly have a dialogue until it was safe to do so. Moreover, the first ecumenical council of the church only met in Nicaea in 325 CE. Such dialogues required centuries because the church faced the demand of agreeing upon a definition of such complex theologies as Christology (involving the nature and person of Jesus), soteriology (theory of salvation through Jesus Christ), and ecclesiology (theological nature, role, and purpose of the church), to name just a few. The early church and Late Antique Christian discussion remained heated, passionate, and contentious. Such conversations transpired before but especially after the fourth century. The theologian Gregory of Nyssa (334–395 CE) marveled how the penchant for theological discussion remained so great that one could scarcely talk with shopkeepers or even public bath attendants without becoming engaged or even embroiled in theological conversation.[67]

By the fifth century, a rough consensus about culture had emerged within the church. As was so often the case in the church's first six centuries, it is best represented by a bishop from North Africa. The Bishop of Hippo, St. Augustine (354–430 CE), frequently faced the same questions as intimated in Wiens' "Wineskins." St. Augustine wrestled more with culture than most of us can imagine. His priestly duties and earlier life as an imperial official helped him to feel the tension quite acutely. Should

---

66. Origen, *C Cels.* 2.30, trans. Chadwick.
67. Gregory of Nyssa, *Diet fil.* column 557.

he, for example, use his old pagan-derived skills of oratory in a court of law to rescue a parishioner who had run into trouble? Ought he to use the works of Cicero in preparing ministers for the responsibility of preaching? Cicero was, after all, one of the best speakers in the history of the Roman world, if not in history itself. What about the use of medicine and its Greco-Roman origins in the cult of Asclepius? What about the use of education theory as developed by philosophers as diverse as Plato, Isocrates, and Quintilian? How about understanding tricky passages in the Bible? Was not Greek, after all, originally a pagan language? Yet, it was the language of New Testament composition. Authentic study of the Bible might require all kinds of skills originating with the pagans. Augustine possessed an intellectual conviction not unlike that of Wiens when he declared in his *De Doctrina Christiana* (*On Christian Doctrine*) that new forms of understanding would have to emerge. The church would not have to accept pagan superstition, but it would need some of the skills of its culture in order to serve Christian faith:

> If those who are called philosophers, especially the Platonists, have said things which are indeed true and are well accommodated to our faith, they should not be feared; rather what they have said should be taken from them . . . and converted to our use.[68]

Given the circulation of Augustine's writings, his opinion helped further solidify the emerging consensus about religion and culture within the sixth-century church and beyond.

Conclusion: The Second Century and the Twentieth Century

Delbert Wiens envisioned a dialectical process in which the church could not simply withdraw from the world. The church had to remain engaged with the world over changing times because the consensus of the past not only will never be restored, but it also cannot be restored. Would we really want such a restoration in light of the changes that our technology, instant communications, and shifts in production have produced in the world? Would a return to older pieties cause us to make idols out of our own consensus instead of leaving us open to the ongoing revelation of

---

68. August. *De doctr. Chr.* 2.60, trans. Robertson.

God's spirit? Revelation, as Wiens observed, further necessitates dialogue because humans find it difficult to stay quiet about it! Equally important, this dialogue serves to keep the church honest. As Wiens noted, Mennonite Brethren piety, like all pieties, are just another form of human belief and ethics. Important things happen in this dialogue over consensus, however:

> Ultimately, *all* our culture forms are of this world. Only after we have been saved from our pious forms will we be able to receive these forms again. We will not see them anymore as absolutes for all mankind, but as God's gracious gift and live command to us. Then this way will be our free calling, not our childish slavery to a law."[69]

Consensus about culture might, moreover, be difficult to find. The church is complex, and the world is complex. Recognizing this fact, Wiens maintained, "We will have to develop several levels of consensus, matching to some extent, our stages of maturity and differences in our economic and cultural settings."[70] Indeed, as the church in the second century reconciled itself to a long-delayed *parousia*, it too had to come to grips with its pious forms, its social and cultural context, and its realities. The rain miracle of Marcus Aurelius helps us to see that the dynamics Delbert Wiens described in the Mennonite Brethren Church are part of the wider church's story throughout the centuries.

---

69. Wiens, "New Wineskins," 23.

70. Ibid., 24.

Bibliography

Bainton, Roland. *Christian Attitudes towards War and Peace.* New York: Abingdon, 1960.
Becatti, Giovanni. *La Colonna di Marco Aurelio.* Milan: Editoriale Domus, 1957.
Birley, Anthony. *Marcus Aurelius.* Rev. ed. London: Batsford, 1987.
Birley, Eric. "The Religion of the Roman Army: 1895-1977." In *Aufstieg und Niedergang der Römischen Welt,* 2. 16. 2, edited by Wolfgang Haase, 1506-1541. Berlin: de Gruyter, 1978.
Cadoux, John. *The Early Christian Attitude towards War.* London: Headley, 1919.
Chesnut, Glen F. *The First Christian Histories.* Vol. 46 of *Theologie Historique.* Paris: Beachesne, 1977.
Fears, J. Rufus. "The Cult of Jupiter and Roman Imperial Ideology." In *Aufstieg und Niedergang der Römischen Welt,* edited by Wolfgang Haase, 3-141. Berlin: de Gruyter, 1981.
Fowden, Garth. "Pagan Versions of the Rain Miracle." *Historia* 36 (1987) 83-95.
Girard, Rene. *Violence and the Sacred.* Translated by Patrick Gregory. Baltimore: Johns Hopkins University Press, 1972.
Grant, Robert M. "Five Apologists and Marcus Aurelius." *Vigiliae Christianae* 42, no. 1 (1988) 1-17.
Green, Bernard. *Christianity in Ancient Rome.* London: T. & T. Clark, 2010.
Harnack, Adolf. *Militia Christi: Die christliche Religion und der Soldatenstand in den ersten drei Jahrhunderten.* 1905. Reprint, Darmstadt: Wissenschafliche Buchgesellschaft, 1963.
Helgeland, John. "Christians in the Roman Army from Marcus Aurelius to Constantine." In *Aufstieg und Niedergang der Römischen Welt.* II. 23. 1, edited by Wolfgang Haase, 735-71. Berlin: de Gruyter, 1979.
Israelowich, Ido. "The Rain Miracle of Marcus Aurelius: (Re-) Construction of Consensus." *Greece & Rome* 55, no. 1 (April 2008) 83-102.
Mattingly, Harold. *Coins of the Roman Empire in the British Museum.* Rev. ed. Vol. 1. London: Trustees of the British Museum, 1976.
McCormick, Michael. *Eternal Victory: Triumphal Rulership in Late Antiquity, Byzantium, and the Early Medieval West.* Cambridge: Cambridge University Press, 1986.
McLynn, Frank. *Marcus Aurelius: A Life.* Cambridge, MA: Da Capo, 2009.
Morris, John. "The Dating of the Column of Marcus Aurelius." *Journal of the Warburg and Courtauld Institutes* 15 (1952) 33-47.
Oliva, Pavel. "Zur Bedeutung der Markomannenkriege." In *Marc Aurel,* edited by Richard Klein, 53-61. Darmstadt: Wissenschaftliche Buchgesellschaft, 1979.
Storch, Rudolph H. "The 'Absolutist' Theology of Victory." *Classica et Medieaevalia* 29 (1972) 179-206.
Torilli, Mario. *L'arco di Traiano a Benevento.* Rome: Instituto Poligrafico dello stato, 1972.
Wiens, Delbert. "New Wineskins for Old Wine: A Study of the Mennonite Brethren Church." *Christian Leader,* October 1965.
Wilken, Robert. *The Christians as the Romans Saw Them.* New Haven: Yale University Press, 1984.
Zwikker, Wilhelm. *Studien zur Marcussäule.* Amsterdam: N.V. Noord-Hollandische Uitgevers MIJ, 1941.

12

"Arrows Fletched from Our Own Wings"
The Early Church Fathers and the "Delphi of the Mind"

Daniel J. Crosby

As a student at Fresno Pacific University, I was in some ways the intellectual grandchild of Dr. Delbert Wiens, for he and his colleagues had designed the first versions, and thus the interdisciplinary character, of the undergraduate classes that directed me towards the study of the classical world. I had never met the man, though, until after I was offered the opportunity to contribute and assist in the process of editing this volume. Through my conversations with him and through reading many of his publications, I came to discover a few elements of what a few of my fellow contributors have called "Delbertian thought" that seem to be ever present in my own mind: a fascination with the connection between the classical tradition and Christianity, a desire to bring abstract thought to life with what has been called "sticky" ideas, and a refusal to shy away from treating tough issues regardless of the potential backlash from the "orthodox." (Whether this commonality came through my training in the programs that he helped to build or another fortunate circumstance, I will never know.) In this way, I have endeavored to do honor to my grandfather by writing a contribution in the same vein as these three ideas, which I have come to identify with Dr. Wiens.

Introduction

In the span of less than one hundred years, the status of the Christian faith had gone from persecuted, to tolerated (Edict of Toleration, 311) to legalized (Edict of Milan, 313) to sanctioned (Edict of Thessalonica, 380).[1] During this same time, the Greco-Roman religion and its sanctuaries and practices, some of which had been around for more than a millennium, seem to have fallen progressively out of favor. In 341, Constantius II issued an edict to stop pagan sacrifices; in 382, Gratian confiscated the incomes of the pagan temples and shrines; and by 392, the Theodosian Decrees had effectively issued a ban on paganism. Although one can debate the effectiveness of these edicts, it is difficult to avoid the conclusion that the rise of Christianity was responsible for the decline of the Greco-Roman religion based on the events of the fourth century.

Naturally, the early church fathers were a large part of the advancement of Christianity; however, their apologetics argued not only in favor of Christianity but also against paganism. With regard to their indictments against paganism, there was one institution of particular importance and interest, the Delphic Oracle. The evidence suggests that many of the arguments against the legitimacy of the oracle that the early church fathers raised had either been made previously by pagan skeptics or were merely different perspectives on those arguments. This contribution has two purposes. First, it will be necessary to elucidate and comment on the assault made by the early church fathers against the Oracle of Delphi. In the process, it will become apparent that the early church fathers felt compelled to change the perception of the most honored institution of the Greco-Roman religion despite the fact that it had long been in decline, and that they borrowed extensively from the pagan tradition of philosophical skepticism to effect that result. The second purpose is to indicate the greater implications that these evidences hold for Delphic scholarship as a whole.

The Oracle of Delphi

The Oracle of Delphi was the most venerated institution in the Greek world. Located in the region of Phocis in a natural depression beside the southwest slope of Mt. Parnassus, Delphi held a more central geographical

---

1. Dates are given in years CE unless it is stated otherwise.

position in Greece than the oracular shrines like Didyma, Dodona, and Zeus Ammon, which, no doubt, contributed to its popularity. In fact, the Greeks recognized Delphi not only as the geographic center of the earth, but also as a cultural and spiritual center.[2] Here, mankind was afforded a kind of direct communication with the divine, more specifically with Apollo through the agency of his priestess, the Pythia. Both Greeks and barbarians brought their inquiries concerning issues of state and of personal importance, and the Pythia, believed to have been inspired in some manner by Apollo, would make a prophetic response while seated upon the holy tripod.[3] The institution that was the arbiter of orthopraxy in Greek religion seems to have come into prominence in the Archaic Period.

The Debts of Our Fathers

Emperor Julian is once credited to have complained, "We are shot by arrows fletched from our own wings."[4] The statement indicates that some pagans from the time period believed that the Christian apologists implemented the arguments of certain earlier philosophers, who were skeptical of the traditional Greco-Roman religion, as weapons against paganism. The sentiment rings true even if Julian never spoke the words. In the mid-fourth century, paganism was in serious decline, and the early church fathers were leading the assault.

The authority of the oracle was one particular issue, and there were a few different approaches to criticize the institution that had developed a reputation as the most truthful oracle in the world. First, the apologists attacked the perceived ambiguity of the oracles. Eusebius (mid-third to mid-fourth century) believed that the oracles of the Greeks were "well-furnished for deception" and consciously "composed in an equivocal

---

2. The mythology surrounding the *omphalos*, the dome-shaped stone lying in the temple of Apollo, indicates that some Greeks believed this stone to be the "navel of the earth" (ὀμφαλὸς τῆς γῆς). According to the myth, Zeus sent two birds in flight, one east and one west. He marked the place where the two met with the *omphalos*, e.g., Pi. frg. 54 (260) *via* Paus. 10.16.3 and Eust. *Comm. Hom. Il.* 1057.57. Pindar calls the *omphalos* "the navel of the well-treed mother." Pi. *P.* 4.74, trans. Race; cf. Hsch. T.1134.

3. Perhaps the most famous examples of state and private consultations are the oracle received by the Athenians concerning their defense against the Persians by means of "wooden walls" (Hdt. 7.141) and the consultation of Chaerephon concerning the wisdom of Socrates (Pl. *Ap.* 20E–21A), respectively.

4. Theodoret, *HE* 3.4.

and ambiguous sense."[5] To demonstrate his argument, Eusebius claims that the Delphic Oracle was responsible for the destruction of its own faithful patrons, offering a quotation from Oenomaus the Cynic (second century), a pagan who believed that Apollo betrayed Croesus. In this instance, Croesus, who had lavished Pythian Apollo with his most exquisite dedications, was only told that if he should cross the Halys River, a great empire would fall, and believing the great empire to be that of the Persians and not his own, he attacked.[6] Clement of Alexandria (mid-second to early third century) was also aware of this ironic and unfortunate episode, saying, "He [Apollo] betrayed his friend Croesus, and, forgetful of the reward he had received . . . , led the king across the river Halys."[7] To the early church fathers, Pythian Apollo was a traitor to his faithful patrons.

The argument that both Clement and Eusebius made was a legitimate one, but it was definitely not original. Oracular institutions, and the Delphic Oracle in particular, had a reputation for ambiguity going back at least as far as the philosopher Heraclitus (late seventh to early sixth century BCE), who famously said, "The lord whose oracle is in Delphi neither tells nor conceals, but gives a sign."[8] Cicero (first century BCE) cites the example of Croesus, too, and adds about the oracles in general, "Some were so intricate and obscure that their interpreter needs an interpreter and the oracles themselves must be referred back to the oracle; and some so equivocal that they require a dialectician to construe them."[9] According to Dio Chrysostom (first century), Diogenes the Cynic warned

---

5. Eus. *PE* 4.1, trans. Gifford.

6. Eus. *PE* 5.20–21. Oenomaus wrote a work called *On the Detection of Impostors*, in which he ridicules credulousness, particularly the belief in prophetic oracles. The book became a gold mine for Christian polemicists eager to tear down the foundations of pagan beliefs and institutions. For the incident on Croesus, see Hdt. 1.53.

7. Clem. Al. *Ex. Gr.* 38P, trans. Butterworth. Lipsey cleverly quips, "Herodotus would have been floored to learn that his tale could be interpreted as an indictment of the greed and pitilessness of Apollo." Lipsey, *Have You Been to Delphi*, 211.

8. Frag. 93 DK. Fontenrose, a notable scholar of Delphi in the last century, argues against the understanding that the Delphic Oracle had a reputation for ambiguity. Fontenrose, *Delphic Oracle*, 236–38. His argument is essentially a systematic dismissal of the evidence for oracular ambiguity outside of the oracles themselves. About the fragment of Heraclitus, he says that scholars who use the fragment in support of equivocalness ignore the context of the passage within Plutarch's work. The context, however, cannot tell us anything about the meaning that Heraclitus intended; it only tells us how Plutarch and his interlocutors understood his meaning. Plut. *Mor.* 404D.

9. Cic. *Div.* 2.115, trans. Falconer.

a man traveling to Delphi to be cautious of the response that the Pythia would give to him, lest he unwittingly cross his own Halys.[10] Delphic ambiguity was such a well known topic in the Greek world that Lucian (second century) could mock Apollo, whom he portrays as hedging his bets in his prophecies, for the amusement of his audience.[11]

The early church fathers also attacked the foundations of the Delphic Oracle by challenging the source of its oracular inspiration. In other words, the apologists were able to cast a measure of suspicion on the oracle by redefining the nature of and relationship between Apollo and the daemons. The Greek understanding of the cosmological order of δαίμονες evolved much over time. The essential element of daemonology from the Classical Period is Plato's supposition that daemons were intermediaries through which the gods and men interacted, bridging the gap between the opposing realms of mortal and immortal that could not intermingle.[12] Therefore, daemons were responsible for relaying prophecy from Apollo, the prophetic god, to the Pythia, his oracular priestess. To Porphyry (mid-third to early fourth century), and Theophrastus (early fourth to early third century BCE), upon whom Porphyry seems to have relied, all sacrifice was a defilement, an unholy and shameful act, in the sight of the gods and worthy only of the daemons. "He who cares for religion knows that nothing which has life is offered to the gods, but to the daemons either good or bad."[13] Some Greek philosophers, then, not only recognized that there was a distinction between good and evil daemons, but also that all sacrifice was an element of daemonic worship.

The early church fathers pursued the argument of the Hellenistic philosophers to its ultimate conclusion. Eusebius says, "He [Porphyry], appealing to Theophrastus as witness, says that the sacrifice of animals is not fit for gods, but for daemons only: so that, according to the argument of himself and Theophrastus, Apollo is a daemon and not a god."[14]

10. D. Chr. 10.23–26.

11. Lucian, *DDeor.* 18(16).1; *JTr.* 28.

12. Pl. *Sym.* 202E. Daemons are semi-divine spirits that were known in Greek popular religion since at least the time of Homer, e.g., *Il.* 1.222. Daemons were not immortal; otherwise there would be no distinction between them and gods. Being subject to corruption, these souls could be workers of good or evil. This theory allowed Plutarch to believe that the decline in the importance of the Delphic Oracle that he perceived in his own time and had read about in the past was due to the defection of the daemons that were responsible for relaying Apollo's prophecy. Plut. *Mor.* 418C–E.

13. Eus. *PE* 4.10, 15, trans. Gifford; cf. Plut. *Mor.* 417C–D.

14. Eus. *PE* 4.10, trans. Gifford. Eusebius indicts Apollo especially, whose oracular

If sacrifice is only fit for the worship of daemons, and the gods demand sacrifice, then the gods must, in fact, be daemons. However, Clement of Alexandria and Eusebius were not merely content to prove that the Greco-Roman gods were daemons; they desired to prove that the gods, and Apollo in particular, were deceitful, man-hating daemons in order to discredit the Delphic Oracle. They accomplished this task through various means, but the most powerful argument used was an appeal to natural law.[15] "If the offering of irrational animals was called by the philosophers execrable and . . . unworthy of the gods, what are we to think of the offering made by human sacrifice?"[16] Both Clement and Eusebius go through a litany of historical examples of this practice, and thus, the Greco-Roman gods are consigned to the ranks of the evil daemons by the common perception that human sacrifice is immoral.[17] Apollo's Oracle at Delphi could not have been truthful because its source was evil. In this instance again, we see that the early church fathers employed a pagan tradition, specifically the theology that developed out of the pagan, philosophical schools of the Classical and Hellenistic periods, to assault the basis for the oracle's authority.

Another method for discrediting the Delphic Oracle was through an appeal to sexism. The common thread of Greek, male chauvinism is clearly seen in Plato and in the works of other philosophers: women are, by their very nature, inferior to men.[18] The argument appears most clear-

---

pronouncements endorsed sacrifice to the gods, but the argument extends to the whole pantheon. Eus. *PE* 4.9. Origen appears to be alluding to a similar line of reasoning, citing an uncertain Pythagorean commentary on the *Iliad*. Origen, *C. Cels.* 3.28; 7.6, 35; 8.62.

15. Clement of Alexandria relies mostly upon mythology, stories of the gods being on earth, living human-like lives, and dying, as a means to discredit the "deathless" ones. Clem. Al. *Ex. Gr.* 2.24P–31P; cf. Origen, *C. Cels.* 6.2. Eusebius points out the disparity between mythology and the opinions of the philosophers, both of which were supported by oracular pronouncements at different times. Eus. *PE* 3.14–15. Additionally, Apollo, who was supposed to be the sun, could not descend in order to bring inspiration. Eus. *PE* 3.16. Finally, Apollo recommended an inquirer to sacrifice to an evil daemon in an oracle. Eus. *PE* 4.20.

16. Eus. *PE* 4.10, trans. Gifford.

17. "Should any one say that the custom of human sacrifice is not wicked, but was most rightly practiced by the men of old, he must at once condemn all of the present day, because none worship after the manner of their fathers." Eus. *PE* 4.20, trans. Gifford.

18. When, and only when, his partners in dialogue are willing to suspend their objections based upon societal preconceptions, Plato's Socrates lays something of a

ly in Origen (late second to mid-third century). "If the Delphic Apollo were a god . . . ought he not rather to have chosen as his prophet some wise man or, if such a man could not be found, at least one who had made progress in that direction?"[19] Origen plays to the sexist mindset that was prevalent in Greek society by questioning the tradition of Apollo's priestess. If we can agree that even a wisdom-inclined man is superior to a wise woman, then why is the Pythia a she and not a he?

The answer that was adduced by the church fathers would have appeared, at first glance, to be a shock to the reverent Greek. They unabashedly attributed to the mantic session the sensational and the burlesque. "While the prophetess of Apollo is sitting at the mouth of the Castalian cave she receives a spirit through her womb; after being filled with this she utters oracular sayings. . . . The oracular spirit, Apollo, free from any earthly body, passes into the so-called prophetess seated at the Pythian cave through her genitals."[20] In one sense, his description conjures up images of the treatment of certain gynecological diseases, vaginal fumigation (θυμίασις/ὑποθυμίασις); in another sense, Origen is clearly representing the inspiration of the Pythia as the result of sexual interaction between the god and his priestess.[21] The inspiration of the Pythia by this spirit produced an odd symptom. In addition to the ability to pronounce oracles, the spirit "fills the woman with madness, and she with disheveled hair begins to play the bacchanal and to foam at the mouth, and thus

---

foundation for a more positive view of the female sex in Greek society, granting that they are at least capable of preforming the same functions as males, although to an inferior level of ability. This train of thought is an appreciable departure from the Greek societal views concerning the accepted role of women and their abilities. Pl. *Rep.* 455B–C; cf. Arist. *Pol.* 1.1254B10–14 and *NE* 8.1158B11–14.

19. Origen, *C. Cels.* 7.5–6, trans. Roberts and Donaldson.

20. Origen, *C. Cels.* 7.3, 3.25, trans. Roberts and Donaldson; cf. "This same Pythoness then is said, being a female, to sit at times upon the tripod of Apollo astride, and thus the evil spirit ascending from beneath and entering the lower parts of her body." John Chys. *Ep. Cor. Homil.* 29.2, trans. Chambers. Clement of Alexandria may be indicating this same perception of oracular consultation when he says, "Others were excited by demons, or were disturbed by waters, and fumigations (θυμιαμάτων), and air of a peculiar kind," but he does not specifically cite Delphi. Clem. Al. *Strom.* 1.135.2–3, trans. Roberts and Donaldson.

21. The process of vaginal fumigation calls for a woman to be seated over a cauldron of smoldering spices in order to adjust the position of uterus within the body, which was thought to inform the overall health of a woman, e.g., Littré, *Oeuvres complètes d'Hippocrate*, 444. See discussion in Sissa, *Greek Virginity*, 44–49.

being in a frenzy to utter the words of her madness."[22] Thus, the church fathers could draw an interesting dichotomy: the Hebrew prophets were superior not just because they were men but also because they prophesied in a sober state of mind.[23]

There was nothing new here. Strabo (mid-first century BCE to early first century CE), Plutarch (mid-first to early second century), and Pausanias (second century), just to name few, were aware of the tradition of a prophetic πνεῦμα ("breath" or "spirit") at Delphi.[24] There is even some indication that the obscene images of the Pythia that were conjured up by the Christian apologists were not entirely without precedent. Certainly, the position of tripod over the supposed source of the πνεῦμα is suggestive of vaginal fumigation, in and of itself, not to mention the fact that the symptoms of certain conditions in women, for which the prescribed treatment might be fumigation, included bacchant-like behavior popular in later characterization of the Pythia.[25] Additionally, Longinus says, "The Pythian priestess, when she takes her seat on the tripod, where there is said to be a rent in the ground breathing upwards a heavenly emanation, straightway conceives (*gravidam*) from that source the godlike gift of prophecy, and utters her inspired oracles."[26] The Pythia is literally impregnated by the prophetic *halitus* ("breath" or "spirit"), and their

---

22. John Chys. *Ep. Cor. Homil.* 29.2, trans Chambers.

23. Origen, *C. Cels.* 7.3-4; John Chys. *Ep. Cor. Homil.* 29.2. If we are to imagine the inspiration of the Pythia as a sexual act between god and priestess, might we also see the result of the inspiration, the uncontrollable madness, to be her sexual ecstasy?

24. Str. *Geo.* 9.3.5; Paus. 10.5.7. "Certainly it is foolish and childish in the extreme to imagine that the god himself . . . enters into the bodies of his prophets and prompts their utterances, employing their mouths and voices as instruments." Plut. *Mor.* 414E, trans. Babbitt. Ammonius' objection is that it is beneath the dignity of Apollo to enter the Pythia for himself, not that this was not their conception of the means of inspiration. The agent responsible was a daemon. Plut. *Mor.* 417A. Πνεῦμα has a broad range of meanings in Greek literature. *LSJ*, s.v., "πνεῦμα."

25. One gynecological treatise describes such symptoms as rolling back of the eyes, grinding of the teeth, and flowing of saliva. Littré, *Oeuvres complètes d'Hippocrate*, 32. Sissa remarks that in the case of the Pythia "it is as if a well-known image of a traditional therapy had been distorted for the purpose of representing the disease that it was intended to cure." Sissa, *Greek Virginity*, 48.

26. [Longinus], *Subl.* 13.2; cf. "The spirit endeavored to show him the light of the Tripod, which, as he said, shooting through the womb (κόλπος) of Themis, fell upon Parnassus." Plut. *Mor.* 566D, trans. Babbitt. Themis, in certain versions of Delphic Succession Myth, was said to have held authority at Delphi. e.g. E. *IT* 1259-70.

offspring is the oracular pronouncement.²⁷ Giulia Sissa concludes that the obscene nature of the process of oracular consultation at Delphi is the reason for much of the silence that we encounter in the primary sources of the Classical Period on mantic session at Delphi. "It evokes what ought not to be seen: an inspired pregnant woman in a temple—a woman who simultaneously opens her mouth and her vagina."²⁸ The Christian fathers could hardly have kept themselves from pointing out such a salacious fact.

The Christian apologists were also able to demonstrate the superiority of Christianity to paganism by calling upon the Delphic Oracle as a witness. We are told by Eusebius that when the Nicaeans went to inquire at the oracle about a certain sacrifice to Apollo, the Pythia said, "Nought can restore the Pythian voice divine enfeebled by long ages, it hath laid the keys of silence on the oracle. Yet still to Phoebus bring your offerings due."²⁹ A similar declaration is made in an oracle given by Philostorgius (late fourth to early fifth century), a heretical church historian. The emperor Julian's emissary to the Oracle was told, "Tell the emperor that my hall has fallen to the ground. Phoibos no longer has his house nor his mantic bay nor his prophetic spring; the water has dried up."³⁰ It is clear by the admission of the Pythia herself that there is no oracular power left at Delphi! The decline of the oracle, however, had come much earlier, and the Pythia had foreseen that the end would come. According to Eusebius, Augustus asked the Oracle of Delphi who would rule after him. The response he received was, "A Hebrew boy, a god who rules among the blessed, bids me leave his house and go back to Hades."³¹ In

---

27. *OLD*, s.v., "halitus."

28. Sissa, *Greek Virginity*, 52. The word στόμα in Greek is used for both the mouth and the mouth of the womb. *LSJ*, s.v., "στόμα."

29. PW 475; Fontenrose Didyma 41. Parke and Wormell note that sixteen of the twenty-four significant works are *hapax legomena* in the corpus of Delphic oracles. Parke and Wormell, *Delphic Oracle*, 2:194. Fontenrose' case that this is a pronouncement of the Oracle at Didyma is based on the observation both that the Pythia's silence would not be claimed by a speaking Pythia if it were genuine and that the oracle immediately preceding this in Eusebius' work is attributed to Didyma. Fontenrose, *Delphic Oracle*, 427.

30. PW 476; Fontenrose Q263.

31. PW 518; Fontenrose Q250. This was not the only oracle to speak of Christ. John of Euboea (eighth century) provides an interesting example. "After a time one will come to this earth and will become flesh without sin. By his divine decree he will banish destruction caused by incurable passions, and he will incur the ill will of an unbelieving people and be hanged on high, condemned to death, which he will willingly

the same words, the Pythia proclaims the eventual victory of Christianity and consigns herself to damnation! That these oracles are very likely to be forgeries should at least be suspected considering the fact that our witnesses for these oracles are the Christian apologists themselves, but they demonstrate that some of the early church fathers were perfectly willing to rely upon the authority of the oracle to further the Christian cause.[32] Perhaps the reason was that the Hebrew prophecies of Christ would have persuaded the Greek little, but Greek oracles about the coming of the Messiah would have held a much more persuasive power.

Julian's lament that early Christian apologists constructed "arrows fletched from our own wings" was, indeed, an accurate metaphor. We can clearly observe how significant those borrowings were in this case study on the Delphic Oracle, and we ought not to be surprised. Although the use of Delphic literature in order to discredit Delphic literature has an inherent irony, it was through this literature that the argument could be made most convincingly. It is as Faustus the Manichean (late fourth century) suggested: a pagan was more inclined to be persuaded by arguments that were working within a tradition with which he was familiar (i.e., oracular institutions) than one with which he was not (i.e., Hebrew prophets).[33]

The "Delphi of the Mind"

The course of Delphic scholarship has swung rather pendulum-like over the last century. During the excavations begun by the French Archaeological School in 1893, it was revealed that no chasm existed beneath the temple of Apollo, contrary to what some of our ancient literary sources

---

endure; and he will rise from death to eternal life." Fontenrose Q268.

32. Eusebius certainly consulted Pophyry's *On the Philosophy to Be Derived from Oracles*, but how scientifically Porphyry went about gathering his sources and authenticating them is the issue here.

33. "The Christian Church, which consists more of Gentiles than of Jews, can owe nothing to Hebrew witnesses. If, as is said, any prophecies of Christ are to be found in the Sibyl, or in Hermes, called Trismegistus, or Orpheus, or any heathen poet, they might aid the faith of those who, like us, are converts from heathenism to Christianity. But the testimony of the Hebrews is useless to us before conversion, for then we cannot believe them; and superfluous after, for we believe without them." August. *Contra Faust.* 13.1. Hardly any of the early church fathers would have agreed with Faustus that the Hebrew prophets were of no value to the Christian converted from paganism. Augustine himself spends the next several sections arguing against Faustus' claim.

say and more modern research suggests.[34] This dramatic refutation began the swing of the Delphic pendulum between trends of syncretism, which endeavored to harmonize the ever-growing wealth of archaeological evidence with the literary sources, and skepticism, which sought to disregard any witness that did not agree with the archaeological evidence.[35] Recently however, one scholar has attempted to view the issue from a different angle. Rather than attempting to reconcile the literary evidence with the archaeological evidence, Roger Lipsey proposed the existence of two Oracles of Delphi.

> From the beginning there were two Delphis [sic]: the Delphi of fact and the Delphi of the mind. Throughout ancient times, the two followed generally parallel courses, linked to one another by pathways however slim, yet likely to diverge because Delphi lived richly in the minds of men and women, most of whom would never visit the holy city or enjoy the privilege of inquiring there. Delphi drew to itself, as if magnetically, both the refined inventions of poets, orators, and playwrights and the rough storytelling of the common people. Even when historical figures about whom we know a great deal visited Delphi—for example, the model of Roman virtue, Cicero—the recorded results seem to swerve gaily from the verifiable realm of history to the imaginative realm of story, which may or may not be wholly "true."[36]

Lipsey uses a story about the cynic philosopher Diogenes of Sinope, recorded by Dio Chrysostom, to introduce the "Delphi of the mind." Diogenes meets a man who is on his way to Delphi, and the two strike up a conversation about the famous inscription, "know thyself." Lipsey's point is that, although Dio Chrysostom may have invented this story,

---

34. Str. 9.3.5; D.S. 16.26; Oppé, "Chasm at Delphi," 232. For a more recent reanalysis of the geomorphology of Delphi, see de Boer et al., "New Evidence," 707–11.

35. The pendulum of opinion can be observed in scholarship with regard to several Delphic issues, but one example will have to suffice for the purposes of this contribution. The ancient chasm that was said to be located below the temple of Apollo at Delphi was not found in the excavations. This fact prompted a pair of responses. Some scholars, like Flacelière and Dempsey, suggest that the frequent earthquakes, to which Delphi is prone, were responsible for erasing all trace of this chasm or fissure. Flacelière, *Greek Oracles*, 48; Dempsey, *Delphic Oracle*, 59. On the other hand, Oppe and Fontenrose prefer to scrutinize the literary sources than the expertise of the French geologists and archaeologists. Oppé, "*Chasm at Delphi*," 214–31; Fontenrose, *Delphic Oracle*, 197–203. More recently the evidence of a chasm at Delphi was reexamined and demonstrated as a real probability by de Boer et al., "New Evidence," 707–11.

36. Lipsey, *Have You Been to Delphi*, 2.

it nonetheless may contain a kernel of truth—in this case, the Delphic injunction above was considered one of the most thought-provoking phrases in Ancient Greece and was, therefore, part of the "Delphi of the mind" that affected the ancients. The point of the author's book is to revive the philosophical "Delphi of the mind," and to that effect, he provides commentary on a number of popular Delphic tales like the one above.[37] The stories and commentary he presents, however, do not as adequately show that the "Delphi of the mind" existed in the minds of the ancients as might have been hoped, only that its elements may, at times, be observed by the modern mind in these stories. It seems a far more interesting argument to Delphic scholarship to demonstrate that the "Delphi of the mind," as an intellectual entity, was just as real as the "Delphi of fact" in ancient times.

A systemic refutation or confirmation of various aspects of Delphic tradition, creating a divide between the elements belonging only to the "Delphi of the mind" and those belonging to the "Delphi of fact," is both impractical and unoriginal; such a work would occupy numerous volumes, and much of the scholarship of the last century on Delphi has been done in this way. Additionally, it is apparent that there may always exist controversy over which elements belong to which Delphi. Thus, the easiest and quickest approach is to look for the effects of the "Delphi of the mind" rather than its constituent elements, and the best place to look for those effects is where the two diverge most significantly.

It should be evident from the vast amount of literature, from Herodotus to Plutarch, that the Delphic Oracle and Pythian Apollo occupied a special place of honor in the heart of the reverent Greek. However, Plutarch, one of the priests of Apollo at Delphi, could discuss a decline in the importance of the Delphic Oracle in a treatise that came to be called *On the Obsolescence of Oracles*. This decline was evident to Cicero even earlier. He said, "Now, therefore, its glory is lesser . . . the oracles of Delphi are no longer issued in our own time."[38] In fact, the cause of this decline seems to have been as popular a topic in the ancient world as it is to modern scholars of the oracle.[39] In any event, it is clear that

---

37. Lipsey, stating the purpose of his book, says, "The project of this book is to stake a claim in rocky Pytho on behalf of modern minds for which *some* Delphic material—not all, by any means—can be uplifting and provocative, as it was for many ancient listeners and readers." Lipsey, *Have You Been to Delphi*, 7.

38. Cic. *Div.* 1.37-38, 2.117, trans. Falconer.

39. For a few possible reasons for the decline of the Oracle, see Dempsey, *Delphic*

by the first century BCE the effects of numerous destructions by earthquakes and enemies, the depopulation of Greece and decentralization of Delphi in the Hellenistic period, and the developing trend of skepticism in philosophy, to name but a few reasons, left behind a skeleton of the "Delphi of fact" that had once been, despite several attempts to revitalize the institution, most notably under the emperors Trajan and Hadrian.

The early church fathers were very aware of the decline of the Oracle at Delphi. Clement of Alexandria, Eusebius, and Gregory of Nazianzus (fourth century) all declared that the prophetic spring was dried up.[40] This fact, however, did not stop them from casting a dark shadow on the legacy of the oracle or stripping the Pythia naked.

Why would the early church fathers spare a full quiver of shafts for the Delphic Oracle when, by their own admission, the institution was only of negligible importance to paganism during the empire? The answer must be that the early church fathers felt compelled to respond in their apologetics not to the declining institution at Delphi, the "Delphi of fact," but to the collective, literary tradition of Delphi that had left a deep impression on the Greco-Roman mind, the "Delphi of the mind." This reality demonstrates that the "Delphi of the mind" was every bit as real as the "Delphi of fact" in ancient times, and by the time of the early church fathers, it was far more real.

As the romance of the oracle captured the hearts and minds of the ancients, material accreted to its tradition. Sometimes the material was true, sometimes false, but it is the full scope of that tradition that encompassed the Greco-Roman perception of the oracle, not just the "Delphi of fact." Many Greeks and Romans in late antiquity would not have had the opportunity or even the inclination to visit the Delphi, and thus, the most common way to access the oracle was through the more readily available and portable Delphic literature. It is through the study of the full tradition that historians can discover what Delphi truly was and meant to the ancients.

ΤΔΘΧΤΔΗΤΝΔΤΚΗΙΧ

Oracle, 167–81; Flacelière, *Greek Oracles*, 72; Parke and Wormell, *Delphic Oracle*, 1:277–81; Heineman, "Decline of Delphi."

40. Clem. Alex. *Protr.* 2.1; Eus. *PE* 5.16; Greg. Naz. *Or.* 5.32. Eusebius draws extensively from Plutarch as evidence for the decline of the oracle.

Bibliography

De Boer, J. Z., J. R. Hale, and J. Chanton. "New Evidence for the Geological Origins of the Ancient Delphic Oracle (Greece)." *Geology* 29, no. 8 (August 2001) 707–11.

Dempsey, T. *The Delphic Oracle: Its Early History, Influence, and Fall.* Oxford: Blackwell, 1918.

Flacelière, Robert. *Greek Oracles.* Translated by Douglas Garman. New York: Norton, 1965.

Fontenrose, Joseph. *The Delphic Oracle: Its Responses and Operations with a Catalogue of Responses.* Berkeley: University of California Press, 1978.

Heineman, Kristin M. "The Decline of Delphi." PhD diss., University of Newcastle, 2012.

Lipsey, Roger. *Have You Been to Delphi: Tales of the Ancient Oracle for Modern Minds.* Albany: State University of New York Press, 2001.

Littré, Émile, ed. *Oeuvres complètes d'Hippocrate.* Vol. 8. Paris: Bailliere, 1853.

Oppé, A. P. "The Chasm at Delphi." *Journal of Hellenic Studies* 24 (1904) 214–40.

Parke, H. W., and D. E. W. Wormell. *The Delphic Oracle.* 2 vols. Oxford: Blackwell, 1956.

Sissa, Giulia. *Greek Virginity.* Translated by Arthur Goldhammer. Cambridge: Harvard University Press, 1990.

13

From the Pueblo to the City

Salvador Diaz

MIGRANTS DO NOT LEAVE their home, their family, and their culture behind on impulse, they do so out of necessity. Just as the Mennonite Brethren left behind their ancestral homes in Europe, so too have many immigrants from Latin America come to the United States looking for the often-elusive "better life." The journey is often harrowing, and the promise of work, once they arrive, is uncertain. There is a cultural shock for these strangers in a strange land, and among the many things that they find alien and discomforting is the plurality of religious expressions that coexist here in the United States. Back home in the small *pueblos* (villages) of Mexico, or Central America, there was only the dominating monolith of the Catholic Church, which offered guidance, moral structure, and salvation to the people. In those farming communities, where *masa* (corn dough) for tortillas is made with the sweat of one's brow, most of the hardworking and pious *campesinos* (farmers) never met a person of any other piety, be it a different Christian denomination, Jewish, or Muslim. The lack of exposure to other traditions has created an incapacity to understand and relate that has traveled north, across cultural and national borders, as if bundled with the language, values, and customs of the immigrant.

Roman Catholic apathy is not the only problem; there is a stringent resistance on the part of many Protestants to view the Catholicism of the immigrants as a valid Christian faith. Perhaps what is lacking is context. In a region as culturally diverse as California's Central Valley, a little bit of empathy can go a long way. The story of Latin American Catholic immigrants should resonate with the Mennonite community; there are similar trials and tribulations and the same growing pains as the immigrant community seeks acceptance and attempts to make the transition from the small and familiar "pueblo" of their culture to the larger and more complex American "city."

In the pueblo where I spent my early formative years, the *cura* (priest) is more respected than any secular government official, whom most people cynically assume to be corrupt and almost useless and appointed through nepotism. In those little pueblos, where local elections are fraught with problems and indifference, the *presidente* (the mayor) is the person with the most clout/land/money. Once he is in office, he appoints his staff and the chief of police; usually a cousin, brother, neighbor, or friend without any real training. The chief of police then selects his own men based on favors or bribes. Regardless of this obvious deficiency of lawful structure, growing up in those little pueblos of a few hundred inhabitants was peaceful and safe—I do not remember my parents ever having to lock our front door. Neighbors knew each other well and would help each other in any way possible.

The few international tourists that came to our town were usually on their way from Guadalajara to another major city. They would stop in our town out of curiosity or need of rest after descending through the narrow and winding roads of *la barranca* (the mountainside). They never talked of religion; they would sometimes go to our church—small but built of heavy cut stones—to take pictures and often commented, with their limited Spanish, on the fragrance of flowers and incense that surrounded the altar. Some would respectfully "cross themselves" as they approached the altar to take pictures of the grisly statue of the crucified Jesus. Others would not and this perceived disrespect would often incite negative comments among the local adults.

As is common in most small communities in Latin America, the church was within the plaza, the central courtyard of the pueblo. Arranged around the plaza were the schools, the *presidencia* (government offices), houses, shops, and small stores. Ambulatory merchants would set up around the plaza and sell all kinds of goods, mostly food, which ranged from roasted peanuts to full meals consisting of rice, vegetables, beans, and a variety of meats. Transcending its central location, the church was also the fulcrum of our cultural expression and our collective identity; the major festivals of Mexican history, the holy days of the patron saints and Virgin Mary, Easter, and Christmas were all celebrated within the church and in the open court that surrounded the church. In these festivals and celebrations one can still recognize the blending of Catholicism and native religious ideas.

In the pueblo there is no such thing as a secular education. Our teachers would just as easily tell us the history of Mexican independence from Spain as they would tell us of the miraculous appearance of the Virgin Mary on Tepeyac Hill—where, according to legend, she asked for a church to be built in her honor. Priests figure prominently in Latin American history; Mexico's first attempt at independence from Spain in 1810 was led by Father Miguel Hidalgo. Just as the United States has within its origins the stories of Puritan Pilgrims participating in the first Thanksgiving and sharing the gospel with Native Americans, so too Latin American history has priests and missionaries cast in the most benevolent of lights: educating, protecting, and inspiring the downtrodden Amerindians.

In the last generation the United States has seen a great influx of peasants coming from southern Mexico and Central America. They leave their pueblos and *ranchos* (small settlements) due to hardships created by inflation, monetary devaluation, and the crippling market competition arising from the North American Free Trade Agreement (NAFTA). Once they arrive, they find that it is nearly impossible to make a smooth transition to a radically different culture. Everything is unfamiliar: the food, the language, manners, and the expressions of faith. They feel unwelcome; they are afraid, anxious, and suspicious of everything and everyone. Some may have family connections to provide assistance and guidance, but many others do not. Due to their limited skills, when they finally find employment, it is doing difficult menial work that no one else wants.

One of the cultural structures that could help to soothe their anxiety, the Catholic Church, is present, but they find that it is not the familiar church of their pueblo. In the village, religion was communal and an integral part of their identity; here it is personal and separated from the daily routines of society. They are not versed in the type of Catholicism that inhabits American churches, with rituals that are aimed for a flock of European descent. Irish, French, Portuguese, and Italian Catholics practice a brand of the faith that is somewhat foreign to them. Latin American

Catholics find these churches plain and lacking the warm spirit that exists in their churches back home. They do not find the niches along the walls covered in the overflowing wax from candles that can be lit to pray for a dearly departed one, or to ask for a blessing/favor from God. There are no large icons of the apostles, the saints, or the Virgin Mary that were often elegantly dressed and carried on the shoulders of believers during a holiday procession. Access to the priest is made through parish secretaries and limited by appointments and schedules. The churches are open only at certain times of the day and they are far from the center of town, often surrounded by a crowded parking lot, not the airy open spaces where they celebrated their festivities. Catholic churches here are inconspicuous places of contemplation and prayer; in their pueblos, they are the beating heart of the community.

To understand the central position of the church, perhaps it is worthwhile to understand the nature and uniqueness of the religion of the pueblo. Latin American Catholicism is not an exact copy of the European Catholicism with which most Protestants are familiar. While their faith derives from European traditions, native religious ideas have heavily influenced its present state. This syncretism was actually facilitated by the Catholic priests and friars that followed in the footsteps of the Spanish conquistadors. The early attempts at conversion were based on principles of replacing the native beliefs and ceremonies with Catholic ideology. The Roman Catholic Church can often prove to be an undeserving mother as it savages its own children rather than accept the merit of their beliefs. To signal the absolute victory of Catholicism and the utter defeat of paganism, the friars induced the native peasants to build churches on top of the shattered temples of the old gods. The missionaries also buried or destroyed the natives' idols and codices, and demanded that natives subject themselves to the sacraments and services of the Church—from baptism to the last rite.

To their dismay, the missionaries realized that their coercive approach was not working. The converts, especially adults, were ambivalent about their conversion and could not easily internalize Christianity at the expense of their own identity. In order to ease the transition from paganism to Catholicism, the missionaries allowed some rituals and ideas from the pre-Christian past to filter into the doctrine. An amalgam was created as they cast the new content from old molds. The saints and Mary replaced the pantheon of spirits and gods that inhabited the pre-Columbian cosmos. The foods and oblations that were made for the old gods were now offered to saints, the Apostles, Mary, and Jesus. And the shaman and practitioners of the old medicine continued healing and cleansing people of evil spirits, but these rituals were now performed in the name of Christ, and the demons that they were casting out were allies of Satan.

Through this accommodation the native beliefs in maleficence and superstition, and their reliance on *curanderas* and *sobadoras* (healers) for medical help rather than modern medicine, remained—as did many of the colorful traditions that adorn Latin American social mores. These are the beliefs that spring from the soil of the pueblo and the campesinos could not easily divest themselves from them, for it would be like shedding their own identity. Instead, the foreign religion of the missionaries was forged into a more familiar faith that could be nurtured in the pueblos. These pueblos still exist in rural Mexico and Central America, and these villages are ones who feed many of their sons and daughters to a United States that is hungry for cheap labor.

Perhaps more disconcerting than the different atmosphere and expression of the Catholic churches in the United States, is the immigrant's encounter with diverse Christian beliefs. I vividly remember my first experience with this realization. Soon after we moved to California, a polite and well-dressed couple knocked on our door, my mother answered and talked to them for a couple of minutes. My siblings and I gave in to our curiosity and approached the door to hear their conversation. They spoke fluent Spanish and wanted to give my mother a thin magazine and an invitation to their church. My mother had never experienced this but apparently she had been warned about it by my aunt who had lived here for many years. She respectfully refused their offer and told them that we were faithful Catholics and were not interested. When they left, I asked my mother about her interaction with the strangers. She seemed anxious and told us they were *Aleluyas* (derisive term for "Protestants"), and we were to never open our door to them again if we saw them. I did not know what "*Aleluyas*" meant and they seemed perfectly courteous and harmless but my mother was not in the mood to explain.

It was not until my father came home from work and my mother told him about the visit that I understood: they were from "*otra religion*" (a different religion), Jehovah's Witnesses, and they were not welcomed. My parents were not hostile to them, but they did seem bothered by their visit, almost as if it had been a personal slight. When we went to mass on Sunday, my mother approached the priest and told him of the incident, he told her that what she had done was right, the best thing to do is to just say no and not open the door to them again—as if they were intruding salesmen. And if she did not want to be bothered again she could put a small postcard sized sign that read "*Este Hogar es Catolico*" ("This is a Catholic Home") on our door.

That was our first experience with a Christianity that was different from ours. In fact, in the opinion of the priest and my parents, they were not even really Christian. I was further educated over the coming years about Protestantism, almost always in a negative light. One Sunday we stopped over my aunt's house to go to church together and one of my uncles that had come over for a visit was in the living room watching Jimmy Swaggart. This was the fiery, pre-"I have sinned" Jimmy Swaggart. He was moving from one side of the stage to the next, extolling the audience to repent and to "Praise the Lord" with a phone number scrolling at the bottom of the screen. "Call and ask for blessings and prayers and give donations to ensure that God hears you." Nothing helps God listen like money does. I asked my uncle who the man on the television was, and he, noting that I had never seen such a spectacle, tried to explain it using Catholic imagery so that I could understand—or, more likely, so I would stop bothering him. He told me that Swaggart was a priest. "But he's wearing a suit and tie, and he's yelling, and weeping," I replied. "The *cura* back in Mexico did no such thing, and neither did the priests at the Catholic churches here in the US." My uncle just shrugged, as if to say *este si* ("this one does").

My mother walked into the room and told me to hurry to the car or we would be late for mass. She told my uncle that he should go, too, he jokingly replied, "I just did. I've been watching for an hour." That is when my mother paid attention to the screen and her face turned from inquiry to horror as she realized that he was watching a televangelist. My mother hurried to the kitchen and related this unacceptable situation to my aunt. They both marched in and asked me to leave. I grudgingly obeyed. On my way out my mother leaned towards me and told me to never watch this type of liars again on television, that it was a sin. They then began berating my uncle under basically the same premise, that he was committing a sin and was insulting God and pretty much everything holy by watching Jimmy Swaggart. Soon everyone in the living room was yelling, and my father, other uncles, and my older cousins also got caught up in the argument. It quickly spiraled into a major religious controversy that only served to harden the hearts of my Catholic relatives in regard to Protestantism.

The core of the argument was my family's unwillingness to accept the religious views of Protestants as genuinely Christian. They share this reluctance with many immigrants who have come to the United States over the past fifty years and who do not see the intense veneration of *los Santos* (the saints) and the Virgin Mary among the Protestant denominations. They find this odd and discomforting, almost as if the Protestants were deliberately and nefariously diminishing the sanctity of the Catholic objects of worship. Where does this view come from? Although the Catholic Church here in the United States is not the same as the Latin American version, it is still Roman Catholic and parish priests often exacerbate the division by constantly repeating to their flock that Protestants are not true followers of Jesus, that only those who recognize the authority of the pope in Rome (because of the Petrine Doctrine) are legitimate Christians. Protestant denominations are lumped as a whole and labeled as liars and deniers of the truth. Through this misinformation, the Catholic immigrant develops a distrust in Protestants that is not easy to overcome. This is not to say that outside of religious confines this unease continues; social interaction is friendly and normal, but when it comes to religion, the tension can be palpable.

I cannot speak for the Protestant reluctance to accept Catholics as true Christians, but it may be rooted in the same ideas expounded by dissenters during the Reformation. These include: defiance of the centralized system of control that emanates from Rome, a preference for communal integration and participation in religious rituals, and basic disagreements over the meaning of sacraments. Most important were the ability to translate (and read) the Bible into the vernacular and the principle of practicing a purer Christianity found in the Scriptures, not in the dogma of the Catholic Church. While different denominations may have other concerns with the Catholic Church, it should not prevent us from recognizing each other's Christianity. Regardless of the acrimony that has set our journeys on different paths, it is time to perceive that although we inhabit different branches, we are all part of the same tree; ours should be an organic relationship based on respect and acceptance.

Mennonite Brethren and the campesinos from the pueblos have had very similar experiences: a culture rooted in the soil and the language; a story of defiance, accommodation, and migration; and the values of the village that were passed from generation to generation. The two also share in the reluctance of subsequent generations to continue with past mores and values as their worldview is shaped into new forms by the global culture of the United States. Catholic immigrants from Latin America often despair when they notice that their children do not have the same respect for the church and that their life is not centered on religious activities. Fewer and fewer of the youth attend church regularly or learn the prayers and rituals of their ancestors. The elders have to grudgingly accept that there is a different modus vivendi here in the United States. Change may not come easy and may not originates from those in leadership positions, but it is we at the local level who can begin to foster relationships and understanding, after all, it is in the community, whether a village, a pueblo, or our California towns, that our values survive. The things we have in common are greater than those than set us apart.

14

On Building the Kingdom
A Heresy in the Fresno Pacific Idea

Peter Smith

THIS ESSAY BEGINS AS a testimony, since my own journey as a scholar and an instructor in higher education owes much to my experience with Delbert Wiens. After providing a few snapshots of my personal experiences with Delbert, I move the essay in the direction of critically exploring a theme—the reign of God in the Fresno Pacific Idea—with which I believe Delbert would resonate. Specifically, I argue that our institutional understanding of God's reign (or kingdom) has drifted from its biblical roots and has come to resemble imperial pretensions that we would do well to query in our quest for faithfulness. But let me begin with a bit of personal story.

Going off to college was a pivotal time for me, a kind of rite of passage filled with potential and opportunity. While I did not make quite the same journey from the village to the city in my move from Spokane to Fresno that Delbert did in his own move from Corn, Oklahoma, to Yale University, as an undergraduate I resonated with his depiction of the dissonance and wonder opened up by the world of higher education. One of the first courses I took at Fresno Pacific College was Literature of the Ancient World taught by Professor Delbert Wiens. In this course, I was challenged to read Genesis (in particular) with fresh eyes, to hear

Scripture as a literary voice seeking to have its say in the narrative contest of ideas that shapes the social landscape. By method of compare and contrast, Delbert guided us through the dissonance of experimenting with new readings and new information and provided us with frameworks that made the insights of those long dead important for young college students. The texts of ancient civilizations came alive as they were put into conversation with the biblical texts and set in the wider cultural milieu of the ancient world.

So it was that in this first course of my college experience, the intrigue of higher learning was inculcated. History—with its formative ideas and worldviews—became alive and compelling, though I do not know that I was able to name it as such quite yet. It was not until my second year, when one must declare a major, that I took stock of my experience. The second semester of my sophomore year did not glow for me in the same way as previous semesters. I wondered why. It occurred to me that a key difference between that semester and all the others was that I was not taking a course that really got me thinking about the big ideas of human civilizations. From this insight, I deduced that I was missing historical studies in that semester and decided to pursue a major in history. While I moved into theological directions for study after college, my sensibilities for thinking about trends, engaging complexity in diverse perspectives, and critiquing assumptions were shaped by that first course, and then subsequent courses, with Delbert Wiens.

In my senior year in college, Delbert invited me to work with him as a teaching assistant for the freshman course that had first captured my attention: Literature of the Ancient World. I jumped at the opportunity. Mainly, I assisted with grading quizzes and exams and functioning as a tutor for those freshmen feeling lost in the course. However, some weeks into the semester, Delbert indicated that he would need to be out of town for part of a week and asked that I fill in for him during the class lecture time. I was not quite sure how I was going to be able to carry this out, but Delbert freely shared his class notes with me in the weeks prior to my time at the lectern so that I would be prepared for the instruction students needed during those two class periods. Leading the class in discussing and understanding concepts of the ancient world was a profound experience for me. I enjoyed it immensely and having a few students affirm my ability to communicate what these ancient texts were saying birthed in me a sense of calling to become involved in teaching. I trace my vocational path—circuitous though it has been—to this formative teaching experience under Delbert's tutelage.

As noted above, Delbert often expounded upon the movement from what he called "the village to the city."[1] These ciphers pointed toward the shift from concrete, localized communities toward abstracted, heterogeneous contexts that were increasingly characterizing modernity and the experiences of the Mennonite Brethren of his generation. While my growing up experience was not on a farm in a rural, Mennonite Brethren community, the tensions that Delbert was naming and with which he wrestled resonated with me, in my limited experience. Mainly, this had to do with my move from home to a college campus in Fresno, which initiated a series of profound intellectual encounters. At the risk of overstating, they were earth-shaking to me because of the sense of finding that my prior categories or language for reality were shown to be provincial and rather ill-equipped for the college-level learning on offer. I know that this experience is not unique to me. It is repeated quite often in many college-age young people. Indeed, this tension of breaking open of the old and constructing of something new, even when simply talking of intellectual frameworks, is part and parcel of what higher education purports to impart. Yoder suggests that this process of personal development is like leaving one's monolingual village for the poly-lingual diversity of the city and then seeking "to interpret the embarrassment of [one's] particularity, which drives people to seek validation beyond themselves."[2]

The Fresno Pacific Idea and the Kingdom of God

This drive for validation in the context of embarrassment or uncertainty is a point that I want to dwell upon below. At this juncture, I move to attempt to follow in the steps of Delbert in an analysis of the use of the phrase "building and extending the kingdom of God" in the Fresno Pacific Idea. What I mean by following in Delbert's footsteps—which I hope is honoring to him, at least in its attempt—has to do with his propensity to take seemingly innocuous notions and subject them to provocative scrutiny. For an example of this, one need look no further than the title for his essay: "The 'Christian College' as Heresy," which appears in Paul

---

1. Wiens, "Village."
2. Yoder, *Pacifist Way*, 41.

Toews' volume exploring the history of the Fresno Pacific Idea.³ In that essay, Delbert suggests that heresy expresses a partial truth and that what the Christian college seeks to do is fundamentally founded upon heretical assumptions about community—the abstracted, heterogeneous kind—that we would do well to acknowledge and scrutinize in our quest for what faithful Christian living looks like in our contemporary world.

So, allow me to engage in scrutiny in that same spirit. In the current version of the Fresno Pacific Idea, adopted in 1995, we find this sentence: "On this foundation, the university seeks *to build and to extend the kingdom of God* by enabling persons to serve church and society" (emphasis mine). On its surface, this sentence seems unremarkable, perhaps even inspiring, as it casts its vision of a worthy project to which the university community is called to rally. But, I suggest that this sentence is problematic theologically and that it issues in a distortion of discipleship for the community. The particular phrase which I wish to scrutinize is "to build and to extend the kingdom of God" because this terminology contributes to a distorted discipleship by mis-telling the gospel narrative that situates Christian living. To show how this is so, I will sketch a brief account of how this language came to be a part of the Fresno Pacific Idea, then show how this terminology serves to distort discipleship and, finally, suggest a faithful expression of this theological conviction more consistent with the Jesus story.

History of the Idea

The Fresno Pacific Idea was first formulated in 1966, then revised in 1982, and again revised in 1995. In reviewing the language of the various versions with an eye on the "kingdom language" usage, the appearance of (what I suggest as) the troublesome language does not appear until the 1995 revision. Indeed, the explicit use of the term "kingdom of God" does not even appear in the original Idea of 1966, though there are several implicit references. In the 1982 revision, the Idea speaks of seeking to be consistent with the "Believers' Church tradition . . .[by encouraging] voluntary acknowledgement of the sovereignty of God and the triumph of his kingdom. . . ."⁴ By the 1995 revision, the kingdom-of-God language had grown into a commitment "to the ideals of God's kingdom" and

3. Toews, *Mennonite Idealism*, 43–65.
4. Ibid., 159.

retention of the language from 1982: "the triumph of God's kingdom" in addition to the quote noted above.[5]

Let me be clear: I am not trying to make an argument regarding a slippery slope that shows how kingdom-of-God language comes to "pollute" the Pacific Idea and then leads to mishandling. To be sure, I affirm the presence of kingdom language in the Idea and I contend that the language that is used in the 1982 revision is solid theologically and can serve to guide the corrective that I suggest. But, at this point, the question remains, how did the Pacific Idea evolve from containing no explicit kingdom-of-God language, to the community acknowledging the triumph of the kingdom, to the community building the kingdom? What accounts for this movement and the assumptions that undergird it?

An important piece to this puzzle can be found in the historical development of Fresno Pacific, a story that cannot be completely retold here. However, in briefly tracing certain outlines of the story, we can decipher some of the crucial forces at play that illumine the movement in theology that takes place. In a masterful chronicling of the dynamics at work in Fresno Pacific history, Robert Enns identifies the ideological ambiguities and dilemmas inherent in the growth of the small, denominational, Pacific Bible Institute into the more complex and diversified Fresno Pacific College.[6] From the outset, argues Enns, the institution embodied its dual heritage in both Mennonite Brethren-Anabaptism and evangelical-fundamentalism. Indeed, the diversity and complexity lies not only at the theological orientation level but also is inherent in the numerical growth of the student and faculty populations, portending changes in the demographic temperament of the Fresno Pacific community and calling upon the institution to make programmatic changes to keep pace.

In the context of this discussion of historical development, the tumultuous 1970s stimulated the need for the college community to revisit the Pacific Idea in the early 1980s. The institutional guide for the first decade and a half needed to be reconsidered, a normal occurrence in organizational life. As noted above, the 1982 version of the Pacific Idea is the first to explicitly utilize kingdom-of-God language. This appearance is not surprising given some of the currents in biblical scholarship of the time, to which many professors at Mennonite Brethren-owned Fresno Pacific College were attuned. One thinks of important books by the likes

---

5. Ibid., 151.
6. Ibid., 66–88.

of Ladd, Schweitzer, Chilton, Braaten, and Perrin that were published from 1964 to 1975 with "kingdom" in the title.[7] Indeed, it would be remiss in this context to overlook John Howard Yoder's generative text, *The Politics of Jesus*. For though Yoder's book does not include "kingdom" in the title, that topic is certainly thematic in Yoder's Anabaptist-Mennonite discussion of how Jesus' orientation and ministry provide a normative ethic for Christian living.[8] Thus, it makes sense that the Pacific Idea would incorporate the renewed emphasis upon the kingdom of God that was shaping the way that Christian theology was conceived, inviting the Fresno Pacific community to "voluntary acknowledgement of the sovereignty of God and the triumph of his kingdom."[9] This constitutes a recovery of kingdom-of-God language in the life of the institution as portrayed in the Pacific Idea, drawing on biblical sources to affirm doxologically that "[God's] kingdom is an everlasting kingdom, and your dominion endures throughout all generations."[10]

Another aspect of the story that informs the evolution of the Pacific Idea in terms of kingdom-of-God language has to do with the growth and development of professional programs at Fresno Pacific. With a long history of respect for the value of education, the Mennonite Brethren who formed Pacific College moved in the first years of the 1970s to establish a teacher credential program. As the decade progressed, professional development courses and a graduate program in the field of education were introduced. Indeed, these became some of the flagship drivers of Fresno Pacific's public identity, facilitating a wider reputation and one with more links to professional ranks in society. But, it should be noted, the teacher credentialing, professional development, and graduate education programs were geared to a different audience from the undergraduate learning community that was primary in the vision of the Pacific Idea. Thus, there was an underlying tension in the coexistence of these thrusts at Fresno Pacific College, which is not necessarily negative, but this is a tension worth reflecting upon. Tensions can issue in creativity. Tensions can also issue in a search for validation, often as a way to ease them.

John Henry Yoder, former Dean of Graduate Studies at Fresno Pacific, suggests that the 1985 Graduate Program Mission Statement is a

7. Braaten, *Eschatology and Ethics*; Chilton, ed., *Kingdom of God*; Ladd, *Jesus and Kingdom*; Perrin, *Kingdom of God*; Schweitzer, *Kingdom of God*.

8. Yoder, *Politics of Jesus*, 2nd ed., 21–59.

9. Toews, *Mennonite Idealism*, 159.

10. Ps 145:13. All biblical quotations from NRSV.

document that sought to bring purpose and legitimacy to these professional education programs.[11] It worked at articulating the basis for doing professional education at the graduate level, employing both creativity and validation. Notable in Yoder's description of this mission statement is the claim that "the statement was built upon the implicit proposition that the Kingdom of God can be carried forward by a program that moves persons or institutions in some way closer to the realities of the 'Kingdom ethics' of love and concern for individuals, that such programs are, in their own right, legitimate expressions of the college's broader ministry."[12] Here, then, is a trail that can be followed in regard to this limited quest to see how and in what ways kingdom-of-God language came to be used in the Pacific Idea. Having noted that the 1982 Pacific Idea speaks of the triumph of God's kingdom, the graduate programs sought to articulate a sense of their mission in this light. But it would appear, at least in the telling of John Henry Yoder, that the understanding of the kingdom that informed the graduate programs was one of kingdom-of-God as progress, a notion more rooted in liberal theology and the social gospel movement of the early twentieth century rather than the biblical scholarship that animated the kingdom-of-God recovery in 1964 through 1975.[13] Some in Christian history have sought to lessen the tension of God's kingdom as being both "now and not yet" by positing that Christians are to be making society into the kingdom of God through reforming efforts.[14] The kingdom of God, then, would be less of a rupture in the fabric of existing kingdoms and less of an expectation for consummation and more of a progressive shaping and molding of society such that the kingdom of God is realized by human effort deftly employed.

My reading of this flow of thought in the institutional life of Fresno Pacific would seem to be substantiated by Yoder's description of the 1992 version of the The Graduate Program's Mission Statement which "begins with the assertion that the central purpose of all divisional activity is to

---

11. Ibid., 133–51.

12. Ibid., 141.

13. For an extensive study to understand currents in liberal theology, particularly its reformist character and its commitment to make Christianity credible and socially relevant, see Dorrien, *Making*, vol. 1, *Imagining*; vol. 2, *Idealism*; vol. 3, *Crisis*. The social gospel movement is largely associated with the work of Rauschenbusch. See *Righteousness* and *Christianizing*.

14. Ladd, *Presence of Future*, 218–42.

'build and to extend the Kingdom of God.'"[15] In this sense, it would appear that simply "acknowledging the triumph of God's kingdom" was no longer a sufficient validation for professional/graduate studies. Thus, it is not surprising to see this phrase—"to build and to extend the kingdom of God"—adopted into the 1995 version of the Pacific Idea, particularly when one considers the ongoing tensions alluded to earlier, which even visiting accreditors were able to observe. The ambiguities of institutional identity were noted in the 1993 WASC review such that pressing problems of the institution were related to "the need to articulate a mission for the College which can unify its presently disparate components."[16]

In the 1995 version of the Pacific Idea, we see the broadest usage of kingdom-of-God language in comparison with previous versions, an effort at least partially informed by the need to secure institutional identity via validation for the various initiatives that made up Fresno Pacific College at that time. Again, I suggest that the use of this language is not inherently evil, nor fraught with ill will. But it invites examination, particularly when we begin to account for the implied assumptions: that the kingdom of God is ours to build or can and should be built by human effort. While this notion of God's kingdom can provide identity and validation for institutional efforts, it also can introduce discipleship distortions, to which I will now turn.

Distortions in Discipleship

"Building and extending the kingdom of God," though misguided—I contend—needs to be heard sympathetically as well since it seeks to express a desire to contribute to something meaningful, to put one's shoulder into an effort that is worthwhile, to be part of a project larger than oneself. What is needed is not only to critique our often well-intended penchant to build kingdoms, but to offer an alternative story.

In many ways, "building and extending the kingdom" expresses the activist impulse of the social gospel and the Anabaptist emphasis on embodied discipleship. It seems quite sensible to conceive of the mission of a Christian institution as contributing to a kingdom greater than itself, a missional vision worthy of the faculty and staff of the institution as well. Nonetheless, while the desire to contribute and build has laudability,

15. Toews, *Mennonite Idealism*, 144.
16. Ibid., 84.

Christian discipleship demands that we discipline our desires in accordance with the story of Jesus. How can we take our desire to contribute toward and build better communities and put that desire in relation to the life and death of Christ?

We will need to face some things about ourselves and the world in which we live. Thus, consider two observations and the shadow side of those observations. First, the drive to contribute and build is a normal, human impulse that accounts for much that is good in the lives that we lead. This drive ought not to be denigrated. It is not uncommon to hear people talk about a turning point in their lives in which they assessed the path they were on and realized that they were not really making a significant contribution to those around them and were too caught up in self-interest or other distracting goals. They then gave themselves to more voluntary service and being in relationship with those in need, finding much greater satisfaction in what they were doing. There is much to affirm in this push to contribute authentically to human flourishing.

At the same time, we do well to acknowledge the shadow side of our drive to build and construct. An aspect of this shadow side has to do with the continuing legacy of the Enlightenment, which so often shapes current thinking. Part of the Enlightenment impetus was the quest for certainty: how can we be sure of what we know and of reality itself? In this light, the quest to "build and extend the kingdom of God" seems to share in the need to secure that which is otherwise uncertain. If we can build the kingdom, then we will know where it is, what it is, and we can be sure to defend it from attack. But it is a distortion in our discipleship to think and live in this way, confusing the gift of the kingdom for a possession or accomplishment.

The shadow side of our drive to build can be an expression of our need to justify ourselves or to seek validation as those who are good and who prove themselves to be good by the contributions that we make. A commitment to "building the kingdom of God" may, in fact, put us in a position similar to those that Jesus spoke of:

> Not everyone who says to me, "Lord, Lord," will enter the kingdom of heaven, but only the one who does the will of my Father in heaven. On that day many will say to me, "Lord, Lord, did we not prophesy in your name, and cast out demons in your name, and do many deeds of power in your name?" Then I will declare to them, "I never knew you; go away from me, you evildoers."[17]

---

17. Matt 7:21–23.

In this passage, we learn that it is rather common (signaled by Jesus' use of "many will say") to do good things (e.g., did we not build the kingdom in your name?) and find that we have missed out on the kingdom of God. The caution here is that in adopting the language of "building the kingdom," the validation of professional efforts may boost our identity and secure some sense of prestige and purpose while at the same time putting us out of sync with the in-breaking of God's kingdom.

In a second distortion to consider, the language of "building and extending the kingdom" positions us as central actors in a drama that is not ours to control/direct. The observation, here, is that we *are* indeed called to participate in what God is doing to change and redeem this world. This observation stems from the Genesis narrative in which God calls forth humankind to a kind of partnering stewardship in God's bountiful creation.[18] Clearly, humankind is an actor in the unfolding drama that God sets in motion wherein people will learn to live in the reign of God. Human actions do matter, for Jesus remarked that it is those who do "the will of my Father in heaven" who will enter the kingdom.[19] So, we must consider, is it the will of God for God's people to build God's kingdom? It would seem that the obvious answer is affirmative. However, here, we can take our cue from Jesus and note the ways that he was remembered to talk about the kingdom of God, as captured in the gospels: "the kingdom has come near";[20] "the kingdom is among/within you";[21] "my kingdom is not from this world";[22] and, most often, "the kingdom is like . . ."[23] One does not get the sense that Jesus had a program for constructing the kingdom of God. Indeed, George Eldon Ladd, in his landmark study *The Presence of the Future*, expressly concludes that Jesus does not ever speak of building or bringing in the kingdom as what he was doing or what he expected of his disciples.[24] In the gospel accounts, Jesus announced and welcomed the arrival of God's kingdom, but he did not speak of his work as "building the kingdom."

---

18. Gen 1:26–31; 2:15–17.
19. Matt 7:21.
20. Matt 3:2; Mark 1:15.
21. Luke 17:21.
22. John 18:36.
23. Matt 13.
24. Ladd, *Presence of Future*, 333.

To return to the metaphor of the drama used above, Jesus appears to have seen himself as following the lead of God as the chief thespian who directs and acts in the drama of salvation.[25] It is an orientation that emphasizes God as central actor, God as savior, God as builder. Again, Ladd contends, the realization of the kingdom comes through the intervention of God, not via the gradual efforts of disciples to overcome evil within history.[26] Or, put another way, without a sense of eschatological urgency—that the kingdom is both now and not fully yet—the people of God lose orientation, become absorbed in a foreign script, and set out to do the best that we can in our confusion: we seek to build the kingdom. In this frame of reference, we become the chief actors, the directors, the ones who must "make history come out right" so as to justify our efforts in the world.[27] Readers of John Howard Yoder will recognize in this phrase a recurring theme in his work, which often sought to highlight the church's problematic absorption into the world via the "Constantinian compromise."[28] Yet, as Yoder would remind us, it is not up to the people of God to make history come out right. Put differently, it is not up to us to ensure that the drama has a happy ending, one in which the heroes (whom we assume are us) save the day and build a better world. Thus, the well-intended language of "building and extending the kingdom of God" adds to our disorientation by casting us as heroes and controllers of a script that is not ours to write or direct. Indeed, the more biblical language of building that we would do well to recover is in a passage like the one which invites us to imitate Jesus, the original "living stone," and take our places on stage as living building materials rather than the builders.[29] The passage goes on to admonish disciples that, in seeing ourselves as living stones in the hands of a master craftsman God who is building a spiritual house, we find our true calling as dramatic actors: "in order that you may proclaim the mighty acts of him who called you out of darkness into his marvelous light."[30] Rather than builders, we are building materials. Rather than leading actors, we are part of the supporting chorus pointing to what God is doing.

---

25. John 8:28–29; 17:6–8.
26. Ibid., 335.
27. Yoder, *Christian Attitudes*, 71; Yoder, *Politics of Jesus*, 228.
28. Yoder, *Nations*, 103–24; Yoder, *Original Revolution*, 52–84, 107–24, 140–76.
29. 1 Pet 2:1–10.
30. 1 Pet 2:9.

Therefore, we as disciples are invited to resituate ourselves by regaining a proper understanding of the business of building in God's economy. God's kingdom does not come by human effort; it is a gift of grace to which we give witness as it is seen and received. Our Christian role is one of "faithful presence" in the world, as helpfully outlined by James Davidson Hunter.[31] As has been noted, while we seem to have a strong desire to build something with our efforts, this desire can lead us into a disorientation that places too much emphasis upon what we are doing and how it will serve to make for a satisfying narrative outcome. But we need to be disciplined by the narrative of Scripture, paying attention to how the story is told so that we can rightly participate in it. That story always begins in grace, with the saving action of God to call out mercifully a people who will give witness to God's gracious light. We see it in the calling of Abraham, to leave the heart of civilization (where grandiose building is always taking place) and to move into a liminal space of vulnerable sojourning where God will provide and God will "build" Abraham into a great nation.[32] Abraham is called to follow, but it is God's initiative to call him and God's work to make him into a "great nation." When Jesus appears on the scene, it is not as part of Herod's royal dynasty, which would enable the building of great structures or empires, though certainly there was a craving in Israel for a messianic leader who would build a great state once again. Yoder reminds us that when the writer declares, "And the Word became flesh and lived among us,"[33] the sense of the Greek is that "the Logos camped among us/set up a tent" which speaks to a gift of grace and a stance of vulnerability as part and parcel of how God is incarnated.[34] To seek to "build and extend the kingdom" then comes to be seen as a misunderstanding of how God moves and what kind of response is befitting the good news of grace that the kingdom is near. "We do not go out to find or to build the kingdom but only to meet it."[35]

The language of "building and extending the kingdom" has more in common with the story of that hubristic construction project in Genesis known as Babel than it does with the calling of Abraham and the

---

31. Hunter, *Change the World*.
32. Gen 12.
33. John 1:14.
34. Yoder, *Pacifist Way*, 58.
35. Ibid.

Incarnation of God among us. For it is in that story that we find humans saying to one another, "Come, let us build ourselves a city, and a tower with its top in the heavens, and let us make a name for ourselves; otherwise we shall be scattered abroad upon the face of the whole earth."[36] The impulse on display in this account is one of seeking security and certainty, of building a reputation and providing self-validation for one's efforts. Thus, I contend, the language of "building the kingdom of God" introduces distortions in Christian discipleship that need to be addressed.

Seeking Kingdom Faithfulness

Let me attempt now to weave together the historical and the theological strands that I have traced in this essay so as to move toward a more faithful explication of Christian conviction related to the kingdom of God. Historically, Fresno Pacific, as a Christian institution for higher education, has sought to be responsive to its immediate context as well as to biblical narrative. The articulation of the Fresno Pacific Idea over the decades has provided a sense of missional identity, tying together the various initiatives and impulses of a dynamic and tension-filled community. The movement that we see in the various versions of the Pacific Idea from implicit kingdom-of-God language to more explicit is welcome, yet has also fostered unhealthy perspectives for Christian discipleship that skew the sense of mission.

The motivation to "build and extend the kingdom of God" sets disciples on a path of proving our relevance and capacities in the terms of the society around us. That is, what this language of "building the kingdom of God" implies is that we have grown uncomfortable with postures of vulnerability that are coherent with discipleship in the way of Jesus. Our thinking seems to be the following: higher education and professional studies ought to lead to professionalism, and professionals are those who shape, mold, and create—these are the great ones of society, the "movers and shakers," the ones who can really build the kingdom in significant ways. The implicit hope in this kind of thinking seems to be that insofar as we are legitimized by the wider society as being useful and nonthreatening, then we will be able to realize progress toward the kingdom of God.

---

36. Gen 11:4.

But Jesus did not call his followers to "build and extend the kingdom of God." An instructive passage in this regard is the one in which Jesus commissions seventy followers to replicate his ministry and proclaim the kingdom of God.

> After this the Lord appointed seventy others and sent them on ahead of him in pairs to every town and place where he himself intended to go. He said to them, "The harvest is plentiful, but the laborers are few; therefore ask the Lord of the harvest to send out laborers into his harvest. Go on your way. See, I am sending you out like lambs into the midst of wolves. Carry no purse, no bag, no sandals; and greet no one on the road. Whatever house you enter, first say, 'Peace to this house!' And if anyone is there who shares in peace, your peace will rest on that person; but if not, it will return to you. Remain in the same house, eating and drinking whatever they provide, for the laborer deserves to be paid. Do not move about from house to house. Whenever you enter a town and its people welcome you, eat what is set before you; cure the sick who are there, and say to them, 'The kingdom of God has come near to you.' But whenever you enter a town and they do not welcome you, go out into its streets and say, 'Even the dust of your town that clings to our feet, we wipe off in protest against you. Yet know this: the kingdom of God has come near.' I tell you, on that day it will be more tolerable for Sodom than for that town.[37]

We can note several themes that inform a Christian understanding of our role in the story. The first is the image of the harvest that is already bountiful. Even though Jesus has seemingly not yet been to the villages to which the seventy are sent, their instructions are not to till the ground, to sow the seed, or to water the tender stalks. Instead, the kingdom of God appears as a gift of God's action, as a field already bursting with produce that merely requires those willing to collect the bounty. This situates followers of Jesus as co-laborers, yes, but not as central actors in the story, not as "movers and shakers" who cause great things to appear by their heroic efforts to shape history.

A second, notable theme from this passage in Luke is the vulnerability of those giving witness to the kingdom of God. They are sent "like lambs into the midst of wolves" with very little in the way of outfitting.[38] Their equipment is minimal and their mode is Abrahamically itinerant.

37. Luke 10:1–12.
38. Luke 10:3.

The message of the kingdom of God is one that offers peace, the shalom of God that entails wholeness, such that the speaking of peace is matched with healing works for those who show receptivity and hospitality to the message-bearers. But the message of peace, though vulnerable, is not always welcome.

A final, third theme to note from this passage is that the message of the kingdom of God appears to threaten some who encounter it, so resistance and dissonance are not unexpected. The announcement of the in-breaking kingdom of God carries with it the implied judgment that all existing kingdoms are under threat, news that may not sound like good news, depending on one's commitments. The Jesus story is one of seeking to gather in the lost sheep of God's people (not unlike Luke's harvest metaphor), a mission that is undertaken in vulnerability and without a grand scheme to build something. And the story of disciples is one that follows in this same pathway, responding to the gracious salvation that God is performing, living by the lights of the in-breaking kingdom. Thus, vulnerability and gift remain as hallmarks of the advent of the kingdom of God, for it comes near to many but can always suffer rejection.

Of course, the conundrum for an institution like Fresno Pacific University is that it is not solely concerned with following in the way of Jesus. It is an institution for higher education and carries institutional assumptions. Institutions, by nature, are not interested in vulnerability and unpredictability, in the sojourn of tents. Indeed, institutions are formed to combat these very things so as to secure the future by means of planning and organization. Thus, we are confronted with a fundamental tension in how institutions can play a role in giving witness to the kingdom of God, a way of life that is rather foreign to the logic of institutions. To move toward an adequate engagement with this tension, I suggest we need to revise our posture, vision, and language.

Posture

While the language of "building and extending the kingdom of God" means well in its call to contribute to a project larger than ourselves, it also sets us on a grandiose path of accomplishment and self-righteousness. But postures of accomplishment and self-righteousness are not consistent with discipleship in the way of Jesus. One thinks of a rich man who kneeled before Jesus—which seems an appropriate posture—and asked what he could do to inherit eternal life.[39] When Jesus tells him that he ought to practice the commandments, his reply—"I have kept all of these from my youth"—displays his true posture, one of Babelian self-righteousness and accomplishment. However, as Jesus points out to the man, a more faithful posture is needed for discipleship, one that flows from humility and vulnerability: a posture of repentance. Christian community and service ought to be characterized by a repentant posture, in large part because the unfolding of our salvation is one of increasing recognition of our previous blindness, malice, and deception. The good gift of the kingdom that God is making available to humanity is often mishandled. As Jesus noted, "From the days of John the Baptist until now the kingdom of heaven has suffered violence, and the violent take it by force."[40] For this reason, even as those who seek to be in alignment with the kingdom of God, we would do well to inhabit postures of repentance so as to receive the gift of the kingdom. Hand in hand with such a posture we can find resources for renewed vision of our role as disciples.

Vision

We must ask ourselves, to what role are we called in this world as disciples of Jesus? This question is important because it goes to how we see: our vision. Too often, we as Christians have been tempted to see ourselves as chaplains to the social order around us. In such a vision, we are tasked with blessing and making a little more bearable the death and destruction that is wrought around us. Such a vision orients us toward lending a helping hand and being a kinder, gentler presence in the world, which sounds like a good thing, and is, to a certain extent. But this vision does not seem worthy of Jesus and the path he walked in announcing the arrival of God's kingdom, a message that was heard by the powers that be as a threat to their social order. Thus, our sense of our role as disciples is one integrally related to vision, because the people of God are called to live by the lights of the in-breaking kingdom. This requires eschatological vision: eyes that can see the dawning reality in Christ that is being made available as a gift, as new life, in the midst of the decaying structures of the present age. As such, eschatological vision sees beyond the immediate horizon and trains disciples in offering prophetic voice in the wider

---

39. Mark 10:17–22.
40. Matt 11:12.

world rather than functioning as assuring chaplains. This prophetic witness is the alternative community made possible in Christ. So, while the witness is lived out in history, it would be misleading to say that it is built by Christians. Indeed, "building the kingdom" speaks of a vision devoid of eschatology and lacking a sense of expectation of the intervention of God in history. Instead, it assumes that we have the capacity to construct God's kingdom for (or with) God in the here and now, rather than to receive it and give witness to it, vulnerably, in the dynamic tension of the now and not yet. Thus, our vision needs to be trained on the horizon of God's in-breaking kingdom that serves notice on this present age that is passing away.

Language

If I have sufficiently problematized the terminology of "building and extending the kingdom of God," then one might ask what alternative language is recommended for use in the Christian community. Indeed, one might first ask if we ought to simply adopt a passive role, sitting around with folded hands while God is at work. Tyler Wigg-Stevenson addresses a similar charge by noting the following:

> There is no contradiction in laboring as Christians to serve the kingdom that is "at hand" and "near to us" while believing that such efforts are distinct from its final consummation. In fact . . . because we know that the work is God's to bring about, we can labor without the anxiety of imagining that the welfare of history rises or ebbs on the tide of our own blood, sweat and tears. And we can rejoice at those foretastes of the kingdom that we are privileged to behold in our own time.[41]

Of course, there are many alternatives for language use, and I will only suggest a few, with the caveat that many of these may need further critical consideration. But this acknowledgement of the place of critical revision serves to remind us that theology is not a fixed science but an interpretive dialogue over time and space, so the language that is adopted will necessarily change and require some flexibility in search of understanding.

Working from the revisions in posture and vision suggested above, it follows that the language that we use to describe our relationship to the

---

41. Wigg-Stevenson, *World*, 22.

kingdom of God ought to be both humble and eschatological. In terms of the repentant, humble posture, we may do well to anchor our speech in the gracious gift of the kingdom and to speak of receiving the kingdom in the various ways that it appears in the world around us. For God does not withhold the kingdom from anyone or any place, but as the Scripture says, "he makes his sun rise on the evil and on the good, and sends rain on the righteous and on the unrighteous."[42] This gracious giving by God puts us into the role of receivers and as those who might assist others in recognizing the good work of God among us.

Another way of speaking that would also seek to emphasize that Christian actions are in the best sense always a response to God's gracious initiatives—saving action that always precedes us—would be to speak of cooperating with the kingdom of God. Such cooperation will typically be of the ad hoc variety, as Christians discern where and how the Spirit is moving at a particular time to liberate creation into the freedom of the children of God.[43] Indeed, such cooperation may well look like a celebration of what God has done, not unlike the many characters in the gospels who were healed and could not help but talk about how the kingdom had come near to them as a gracious gift in the person of Jesus. Thus, the phrase "cooperating with the kingdom" provides a promising corrective to "building the kingdom" and, as I have traced it, leads us in the direction of classic biblical language: witness.

The people of God are called, first and foremost, to witness to the reality of the gracious reign of God that is being made available to inhabit in time, though not fully realized yet. As such, witness provides not only a humble language (for a witness does not control or construct) but also an eschatological language. Witnesses are not responsible for fabricating the substance of that to which they point, so the temptation to (arrogantly?) deliver on the kingdom come can be avoided. Witnesses speak the truth of the coming age, even when that truth may not be particularly welcome. Witnessing to the kingdom of God reminds us that the advent of that reign—though vulnerable—is subversive and disturbs the status quo of the human kingdoms that are passing away. Instructively, the longest segment of the Beatitudes in Matthew is given to affirming the blessedness of those who are persecuted for witnessing to the kingdom of

---

42. Matt 5:45.
43. Rom 8:21.

God. Rather than creating certainty and validation, witnessing to God's kingdom seems to be rather precarious.

All in all, we can affirm the sensibility of seeking to situate Christian living in the context of God's kingdom that we see manifested in the historical development of the Pacific Idea. After all, this is the message that Jesus proclaimed and that his disciples should naturally take up as well to guide and inform our way of life. I have tried to show how such noble sensibilities can drift and distort our discipleship when we adopt heretical language like "building and extending the kingdom of God." But the point is not to demonize a particular phrase, for that simply issues in a form of self-righteousness for those who can manage to regularly monitor their tongue. Rather, the hope here has been to call for greater mindfulness, to examine our orienting convictions and to consider how we live so that we might be more faithful witnesses to the One whose is "the kingdom, the power and the glory, forever. Amen."[44]

---

44. Matt 6:13.

Bibliography

Braaten, Carl E. *Eschatology and Ethics: Essays on the Theology and Ethics of the Kingdom of God*. Minneapolis: Augsburg, 1974.

Chilton, Bruce, ed. *Kingdom of God in the Teaching of Jesus*. Issues in Religion and Theology 5. Philadelphia: Fortress, 1971.

Dorrien, Gary J. *The Making of American Liberal Theology*. 1st ed. 3 vols. Louisville: Westminster John Knox, 2001–2006.

Hunter, James Davison. *To Change the World: The Irony, Tragedy, and Possibility of Christianity in the Late Modern World*. New York: Oxford University Press, 2010.

Ladd, George Eldon. *Jesus and the Kingdom: The Eschatology of Biblical Realism*. New York: Harper & Row, 1964.

———. *The Presence of the Future: The Eschatology of Biblical Realism*. Grand Rapids: Eerdmans, 1974.

Perrin, Norman. *The Kingdom of God in the Teaching of Jesus*. London: SCM, 1975.

Rauschenbusch, Walter. *Christianizing the Social Order*. New York: Macmillan, 1912.

———. *The Righteousness of the Kingdom*. Edited by Max L. Stackhouse. New York: Mellon, 1968.

Schweitzer, Albert. *The Kingdom of God and Primitive Christianity*. London: Black, 1968.

Toews, Paul. *Mennonite Idealism and Higher Education: The Story of the Fresno Pacific College Idea*. Fresno: Center for Mennonite Brethren Studies, 1995.

Wiens, Delbert L. "From the Village to the City: A Grammar for the Languages We Are." Direction 2, no. 4 (October 1973–January 1974) 98–149.

Wigg-Stevenson, Tyler. *The World Is Not Ours to Save: Finding the Freedom to Do Good*. Downers Grove: InterVarsity, 2013.

Yoder, John Howard. *Christian Attitudes to War, Peace, and Revolution*. Grand Rapids: Brazos, 2009.

———. *For the Nations: Essays Public and Evangelical*. Grand Rapids: Eerdmans, 1997.

———. *The Original Revolution: Essays on Christian Pacifism*. Eugene, OR: Wipf & Stock, 1998.

———. *A Pacifist Way of Knowing: John Howard Yoder's Nonviolent Epistemology*. Edited by Christian E. Early and Ted Grimsrud. Eugene, OR: Wipf & Stock, 2010.

———. *The Politics of Jesus: Vicit Agnus Noster*. 2nd ed. Grand Rapids: Eerdmans, 1994.

Section 4

Delbert's Work

15

The Mennonite Syndrome

December 1965

DELBERT PREACHED "IMITATE THEIR Faith" at the Tabor College Spring Baccalaureate Service in 1965. Having heard it, Marjorie Gerbrandt, now his wife, asked him to be a speaker for adults at the Mennonite Brethren (MB) retreat held that summer at the Rocky Mountain National Park. He agreed to do that if he could preview the long essay on our churches that he intended to write that summer. She agreed and that retreat began their courtship. That fall he began PhD studies at the University of Chicago. After the October appearance of "New Wineskins for Old Wine" in the MB publication *Christian Leader*, the loosely organized Mennonite graduate students who regularly gathered over the 1966 New Year's break to agonize over their love/hate relationship to their heritage, invited him to speak on that year's topic. During Christmas break, he wrote this piece, proposed to Marj, celebrated with their families in Oklahoma and Kansas, and the two of them went to Minneapolis. By way of explanation, Delbert says: "I was full of *eros*."

Introduction

I understand a syndrome to be the set of symptoms that is characteristic of a particular disease. Although some have thought that the disease we are discussing is hereditary, it has been satisfactorily established that it is contracted from sustained contact with confirmed carriers. Given favorable conditions, some are driven to morbid concern over the disease. The hypochondriacs who take enough time to organize yearly sessions for comparing their stages of infection are entirely capable of proposing topics like, "The Mennonite Syndrome." Philologists will notice that *syndrome* combines two Greek roots that mean *to run* and *with*.

Because we are exceptionally self-aware, it will not be necessary to catalog our symptoms, but it may be interesting to speculate on the cause and cure of the disease. Since the attempt to do this may be seen as one of its symptoms, this attempt must be tentative. It is even true that it may be dangerous. "Cures" have often been worse than the disease. Moreover, we must not be deceived that a reversal of symptoms constitutes a cure. The anti-Mennonite syndrome may be its most virulent stage.

Though it smacks of homeopathism, many diagnosticians assume that its chronic stage is not detrimental and advise that an acute phase be allowed to run its course. There are many who believe that a moderate dose, like a vitamin-enriched vaccine, both inoculates patients against worse ills and contributes to well-being.

They prescribe patience and tender loving care for the fevered. If tender loving care is the most effective treatment, we may have a clue to the cause of the condition. On the old Greek principle that "like knows like," we can posit that the root problem is the love life of the young Mennonite. Accepting the philological hint mentioned above and begging apology for perhaps unwarranted departures from the serious scientific tone that this gathering deserves, we may rephrase our question as "What Makes Young Menno Run."

The Beautiful and the Good

It is desire for the beautiful and the good, said Socrates in Plato's *Symposium*, that draws those who seek. *All* searching, *all* inquiry, *all* creating is motivated by *eros*. But one does not desire what one already possesses. Nor, as the wise prophetess Diotima taught when he asked her the meaning of love, could he have desired that of which he had not heard. Therefore love was born of the mating of Need with Resource and always partakes of the natures of both. Love both knows and knows not, has and has not, has once possessed and therefore pursues. Love is desire for the everlasting possession of the good and the beautiful. But what is it that we have and do not have? What loss causing what desire brings us to cold Minneapolis when we should be watching football games, reassuring our parents, cramming for exams, and romancing girlfriends?

In his encomium to the god of love in Plato's wonderful dialogue, the comic poet Aristophanes had told a delightful myth on the creation of desire. Once upon a time, rounded human creatures had four arms and four legs and a face on each side of their head. Their tremendous strength and speed (they stuck out their eight limbs and rolled) had led them to dare to storm heaven. Zeus angrily cut them in half, swiveled their heads to the cut away sections, and tied up their skins at the navel. Since then, half-humans have run about seeking to find their "better halves." Aristophanes was a conservative traditionalist. Sophistication is degeneration. To be complicated is to be diseased. Let us return to a simpler past when craving was swallowed up in satiety.

At points in our young lives, our Mennonite communities seemed to fit this demand. A consensus built upon common work, customs, education, and beliefs shaped an essentially homogenous culture. One set of answers was supposed to be adequate for the questions one could legitimately ask. Originally formed by those similar enough to respond to a radical "calling out" during the Reformation and fixed by retreat to *Stillen im Lande* enclaves by persecution made intense relationships possible. Mennonites often had a strong sense of identity. We knew who we were and what we had to do.

The strength of such a group gives rise to its greatest weakness. Growing individuals could develop close relationships with a variety of *Onkels* and *Tantes*. Most children adopted one or another familiar role and sustained the culture. But this also made possible the development of strong personalities who become aware of their potential and found consensus to be constricting. Inner tensions could be intense.

When "greener pastures" lured or lack of land forced them out, a limited number of options were possible. Those who had adjusted well carried their culture with them, calculating precisely the amount of compromise with outsiders that allowed them to imagine that they had reestablished the best of Hillsboro, or Berne, or Goshen. Others learned not a final adjustment to *Mennonitentum*, but the trick of being adjustable. We were proud that these contributed admirable traits and gifts to other sorts of communities; we also sadly consigned them to the *Englisha*, our word for Gentiles.

Those who identify deeply do not have an easy time of it. The more aware of themselves they have become, the more of a problem their selfhood becomes. Their discipline and virtue brings a sophistication that sharpens their sense of the limitations of their past and that can lead them to revulsion against what had once seemed desirable.

Even this is too simple for those who are also thoughtful (namely, us). We realize that the strength of our anger depends upon the great importance the old forms had for us. They did once fit us. They do still fit many of those we love. To turn our backs upon the old forms is to sacrifice part of our own identity. To reject *Mennonitentum* is to reject relationships stronger than have shaped the lives of many who grow up in the anomie of a mass culture.

But Socrates was sure that Aristophanes was wrong about one thing. Strong as is the pull on us of a simpler wholeness, it becomes impossible to deny truth, beauty, and goodness. And so, though driven by the beauty we have known, we wish to share it with those we continue to love.

Of course, the beauty we have known now suffers in comparison with more engaging maidens. To speak in metaphor, the girl back home has become too plain, too limited, too domestic; but we are not ready for exotic damsels. Even when their virtue equals their charms we are often held back from wooing them.

Our desire has become grotesque. We desire to possess the beautiful and the good. Thanks to our past, we have known what that can mean. Thanks to the strength that past has given us, we have become alien to it. Thanks to our sophistication, we know how problematic their possession is. Are not we those with that "most subtle thirst" of which Friedrich Nietzsche spoke? Is it not a community we wish again to deserve and to possess? What wholeness we have known had been found there. It was there that the beauty of an entire belonging was glimpsed. And there we seek it again. And so, a quotation:

> The difference among men does not manifest itself only in the difference of their lists of desirable things—in their regarding different good things as worth striving for, and being disagreed as to the greater or less value, the order of rank, of the commonly recognised desireable things:—it manifests itself much more in what they regard as actually *having* and *possessing* a desireable thing. As regards a woman, for instance, the control over her body and her sexual gratification serves as an amply sufficient sign of ownership and possession to the more modest man;

another with a more suspicious and ambitious thirst for possession, sees the "questionableness," the apparentness of such ownership, and wishes to have finer tests in order to know especially whether the woman not only gives herself to him, but also gives up for his sake what she has or would like to have—only *then* does he look upon her as "possessed." A third, however, has not even here got the limit of his distrust and his desire for possession: he asks himself whether the woman, when she gives up everything for him, does not perhaps do so for a phantom of him; he wishes just to be thoroughly, indeed, profoundly well known, in order to be loved at all he ventures to let himself be found out. Only then does he feel the beloved one fully in his possession, when she no longer deceives herself about him, when she loves him just as much for the sake of his delivery and concealed insatiability, as for his goodness, patience, and spirituality. One man would like to possess a nation, and he finds all the higher arts of Cagliostro and Catalina suitable for his purpose. Another, with a more refined thirst for possession, says to himself: "One may not deceive where one desires to possess"—he is irritated and impatient at the idea that a mask of him should rule in the hearts of the people: "I must, therefore, *make* myself known, and first of all learn to know myself!"[1]

Does this not explain many of our symptoms, our inability to let go, our penchant for exhibiting ourselves, our desire to shock? We wish to make ourselves known, to be rightly loved; and we wish for our own people to be worthy of our passion.

Immortality and Procreation

But Nietzsche and Plato knew that so far the answer is incomplete. It is too simple to say that we desire the everlasting possession of the beautiful, the eternal return to a once-glimpsed wholeness. If that were the entire goal of our craving, we would not progress beyond the primitive. And so a quotation from *The Symposium*:

---

1. Nietzsche, *Beyond Good*, 115–16. Due to the fact that this paper was a presentation, some bibliographic information, like the exact edition and translation, was not included from the document. We, therefore, have chosen to select fresh editions and translations of the same paragraphs that Delbert cited in his original presentation to insert in the appropriate places. –DJC.

> Very well, then. And that being so, what course will Love's followers pursue, and in what particular field will eagerness and exertion be known as Love? In fact what *is* this activity? Can you tell me that, Socrates?
>
> If I could, my dear Diotima, I retorted, I shouldn't be so much amazed at *your* grasp of the subject, and I shouldn't be coming to you to learn the answer to that very question.
>
> Well, I'll tell you, then, she said. To love is to bring forth upon the beautiful, both in body and in soul.
>
> I'm afraid that's too deep, I said, for my poor wits to fathom.
>
> I'll try to speak more plainly, then. We are all of us prolific, Socrates, in body and in soul, and when we reach a certain age our nature urges us to procreation. Nor can we be quickened by ugliness, but only by the beautiful. Conception, we know, takes place when man and woman come together, but there's a divinity in human propagation, an immortal something in the midst of man's mortality which is incompatible with any kind of discord. And ugliness is at odds with the divine, while beauty is in perfect harmony. In propagation, then, Beauty is the goddess of both fate and travail, and so when procreancy draws near the beautiful it grows genial and blithe, and birth follows swiftly on conception. But when it meets with ugliness it is overcome with heaviness and gloom, and turning away it shrinks into itself and is not brought to bed, but still labors under its painful burden. And so, when the procreant is big with child, he is strangely stirred by the beautiful, because he knows that beauty's tenant will bring his travail to an end. So you see, Socrates, that Love is not exactly a longing for the beautiful, as you suggested.
>
> Well, what is it, then?
>
> A longing not for the beautiful itself, but for the conception and generation that the beautiful effects.
>
> Yes. No doubt you're right.
>
> Of course I'm right, she said. And why all this longing for propagation? Because this is the one deathless and eternal element in our mortality. And since we have agreed that the lover longs for the good to be his own forever, it follows that we are bound to long for immortality as well as for the good—which is to say that Love is a longing for immortality.[2]

We are full of children, children of the body and of the soul, and we desire to give them birth. In the birth of children, of ideas, of poems, of all the things that endure after us, we achieve an extension of the self, a

---

2. Pl. *Sym.* 206B–207A, trans. Joyce.

relationship to the future, a kind of immortality. We seek beauty, not for beauty's sake, but because the presence of beauty opens up the creative springs by which we give meaning to our lives that endures beyond our death. We must create, and the more advanced we become, the more "spiritual" are the children that we bear. The greatest creator, the most elevated of artists, said Plato, is one who creates a community—the statesman who gives wise laws to a well-ordered state.

Perhaps this is too far-fetched; and yet it may help to explain the love/hate we bear to *Mennonitentum*. Is it not equally absurd that we young rebels continue to be obsessed with Berne and Lancaster and Newton? Is it not strange that so many of us take up history as vocation or avocation?

The gifts we received and the harmony we absorbed came to us at home. But we have gone away; we have grown; we are full of ideas. We wish to give birth—and cannot. For the lady who bore us, whose beauty we remembered, now appears to be quite plain. And so we aim to restore her charm so that she can again be the beauty upon whom we bear our children and who will build with us a larger and a finer home.

One solution is to construct a community around the old ideals that makes room for our sophistication. The girl back home has sadly "let herself go." And so we would-be artists create an idealized mistress to whom we return. We fantasize a shimmering image of our mother church, one unsoiled by hundreds of years of seduction by necessity. Rewriting history, we create an *urzeit* when the maiden was both pure and wise—and so far in advance of her time that the world has not yet had the wit to understand her charms.

Mirable dictu, having discovered the Anabaptist Vision, we are no longer rebels. We are now the maiden's only true lovers. Even more wonderful, we are not odd and irrelevant people from narrow communities. We are suddenly ahead of all those benighted folk who wonder why we do not have beards. Now we are not really "out of it." We are so truly "in" that the rest of the witless world must see us as "out." Never mind, we are the elite who dream of explaining to our elders what they had confusedly and incompletely practiced.

Back at the farm, that idealized virgin looks suspiciously like yet another foreign temptress, and even those in our Winklers and Ephratas and Hillsboros that struggle with the possibility that something like what H. S. Bender described was somehow their virgin mother and who respect a "Reba Place Fellowship" that attempts to incarnate a radically

Anabaptist Vision cannot be expected to imitate what feels suspiciously utopian. After all, a *volkskirche* is a *volkskirche*, even when claiming an Anabaptist theology and history.

And it is the theology that threatens to undo us. We were the radical left wing of the Reformation recovering first-century, non-ritualized Christian faithfulness. Surely we can now have our cake and eat it too. We can revolutionize our actual communities while claiming to be their true heirs. Hallelujah!

I am not much of a historian, but I am suspicious of attempts to rewrite our history in the light of our up-to-date ideals. I am proud of our past and believe that God was at work in it. But I doubt that there ever was a Golden Age. We are also right to react against too-rigid molds. The cocoons that once protected us threaten to become constricting tombs. Nonetheless we rebels too easily allow our shame of narrowness to tempt us to scorn those who helped us to become what we are and who remind us of what we were, and still partly are, by continuing to live there.

But we are wrong to think that our capacity to idealize our virgin lady makes us the only experts on her care and feeding—or that we immediately deserve to be honored and heard. We are even more wrong if we think that we can create a formless Christian fellowship characterized by instant love and non-resistance. There is no such thing as a continuing fellowship that does not take forms and develop molds and power structures. Even the universities that now offer freedom and unlimited opportunities can become confining tombs. Perhaps every beauty sometimes requires the comfort of a corset.

Yet it is true that new wineskins must be created so that growing persons can develop from level to level, finding models for each stage of their growth. Then our own children may have less need to react against the whole before questioning the parts.

I do not know how it will be possible for communities to contain levels of sophistication while maintaining intense loyalties. In any case, our consensus is breaking down. A church characterized by close fellowship and a rich variety of lifestyles could be the greatest challenge to which desire has led us.

Meanwhile I plead that we appreciate what we have been. We can neither despise what has made us nor mindlessly return to the past. Nor should we try too eagerly to be "at home" in the homes of others. Caught as we are by rival lifestyles, we are in an admirable position to love and transcend what surrounds us. The astonishing thing is the mediocre use we make of our fortunate chance to achieve mature sanctity. (Very well, we are still quite young.)

Perhaps the criticism of more hide-bound brothers will prove to be right. Will we be wise with the serpents and harmless with the doves and yet be integrated? Will we be able to give to our children the desire and quest for wholeness that our elders have given to us? Will it be the Rechabites—and Amish—that will endure?

But all this desire for the good and the beautiful and the true, all this idealism, all these attempts to create communities that match our theology may be nothing more than the fruit of desire—and of our quest for meaning and immortality. However exalted the sublimation, I have so far been dealing with the works of *eros*. I have not yet spoken a single sentence that is fully and distinctively Christian. Though I have alluded to a past that was much more, it has been the fear of losing a possession that has explicitly occupied my attention.

Possession and Creation

We are less likely to attain possession than was indicated in the quotation from Nietzsche, who insisted upon deserving the ownership of that which we desire to possess. What if the woman does not fully understand me or if the community is not omniscient? I cannot fully see myself as a whole when I am by myself. If I am to see more than a merely objectified self, others must reflect myself back to me. What if the mirror is dull or distorted? Then I shall never find the wholeness I seek. So far, we face only worsening desire—and despairing resignation.

Socrates was an expert on desire, but even he deferred to the wise Diotima, the one whose name spoke of honoring, and being honored by, the god. But St. Bernard of Clairvaux, Dante's guide to the highest reaches of paradise, knew of a love that goes beyond desiring. St. Bernard was sure that he was entirely understood, and loved, by God. "Readily do they love more, who understand themselves more loved." And in this knowledge he receives himself as one remade.

> For it is written of man and of all things that were made, "He spake the word, and they were made" (Ps. 148.5). But to redeem that creation which sprang into being at His word, how much He spake, what wonders He wrought, what hardships He endured, what shames He suffered! Therefore what reward shall I give unto the Lord for all the benefits which He hath done unto

> me? In the first creation He gave me myself; but in His new creation He gave me Himself, and by that gift restored to me the self that I had lost. Created first and then restored, I owe Him myself twice over in return for myself. But what have I to offer Him for the gift of Himself? Could I multiply myself a thousand-fold and then give Him all, what would that be in comparison with God?[3]

And so the stages of love were different from what they were for Plato. There is not simply the growth of desire for more and more refined and abstract objects. There is instead a return to the perfect love of self—a love that may or may not be fully experienced on earth—but one that is experienced by grace.

> Nevertheless, since we are carnal and are born of the lust of the flesh, it must be that our desire and our love shall have its beginning in the flesh. But rightly guided by the grace of God through these degrees, it will have its consummation in the spirit: for that was not first which is spiritual but that which is natural; and afterward that which is spiritual (I Cor. 15.46). And we must bear the image of the earthy first, before we can bear the image of the heavenly. At first, man loves himself for his own sake. That is the flesh, which can appreciate nothing beyond itself. Next, he perceives that he cannot exist by himself, and so begins by faith to seek after God, and to love Him as something necessary to his own welfare. That is the second degree, to love God, not for God's sake, but selfishly. But when he has learned to worship God and to seek Him aright, meditating on God, reading God's Word, praying and obeying His commandments, he comes gradually to know what God is, and finds Him altogether lovely. So, having tasted and seen how gracious the Lord is (Ps. 34.8), he advances to the third degree, when he loves God, not merely as his benefactor but as God. Surely he must remain long in this state; and I know not whether it would be possible to make further progress in this life to that fourth degree and perfect condition wherein man loves himself solely for God's sake.[4]

Where can we find the wholeness and the beauty that we seek? But where did we learn of it so that we again seek it? It is no doubt true that all communities must pay careful attention to the lower levels of *eros*. It may even be the case that our Corns and Winklers and Ephratas and Newtons

---

3. St. Bernard, *Loving God*, ch. 5.
4. St. Bernard, *Loving God*, ch. 15.

revolve substantially around the naïve extension of their tangible works and the prospect of immortality through their children.

But have we not also met those who had gone beyond *eros* to the tranquility of those possessed by God and of themselves as those who had become the beloved children of God? The wholeness I have glimpsed and continue to seek has been their gift to me. Or, I should say, it is God's gift that they have mediated to me.

Mennonites have intended to be the body of Christ Jesus. Of course they, and we, often adjusted to a *status quo*, and there are those who accept the form but experience little of the spirit. But let us not, for the sake of our ideals, our theology, our own lofty *eros*, despise those whose *eros* is less refined. For among them are those who have truly loved, and we will yet need them to help us to become whole beyond unending erotic cravings. And so, another quotation:

> "The Lord is good unto them that wait for Him" (Lam. 3.25). What will He be then to those who gain His presence? But here is a paradox, that no one can seek the Lord who has not already found Him. It is Thy will, O God, to be found that Thou mayest be sought, to be sought that Thou mayest the more truly be found. But though Thou canst be sought and found, Thou canst not be forestalled. For if we say, "Early shall my prayer come before Thee" (Ps. 88.13), yet doubtless all prayer would be lukewarm unless it was animated by Thine inspiration.[5]

Was it not back home that God *prevented* us? St. Bernard's word was *praevenire*, to go before, to precede. To understand this is to forgive and to love again our not-so-virgin mother church that is, in God's sight, the radiant bride of Christ.

Having experienced the love that goes beyond mere craving, our syndrome and its symptoms will have passed away; and it will be a question of our several callings whether we return to our communities or whether we "naturally" become those who seek to recreate the circles of discipline and beauty and wholeness that are the fruit of the Holy Spirit. Even Nietzsche laid his scorn aside to celebrate this possibility in *Beyond Good and Evil*.

> To love mankind *for God's sake*—this has so far been the noblest and remotest sentiment to which mankind has attained. That love to mankind, without any redeeming intention in the

---

5. St. Bernard, *Loving God*, ch. 7.

> background, is only an *additional* folly and brutishness, that the inclination to this love has first to get its proportion, its delicacy, its grain of salt and sprinkling of ambergris from a higher inclination:—whoever first perceived and "experienced" this, however his tongue may have stammered as it attempted to express such a delicate matter, let him for all time be holy and respected, as the man who has so far flown highest and gone astray in the finest fashion![6]

With St. Bernard, I also doubt that this comes fully to any of us. And yet it can be known in part. Having seen love that transcends *eros* in our communities, how can I scorn them for failing to measure up to my exalted desires? And immortality? I will take my chances with T. S. Eliot's mud-dwelling hippopotamus.

The Hippopotamus

"And when this epistle is read among you, cause that it be read also in the church of the Laodiceans."[7] For six stanzas T. S. Eliot compares the feeble, mud-dwelling hippopotamus whose voice "betrays inflexions hoarse and odd" to the "True Church" that never fails because "it is based upon a rock" while rejoicing "at being one with God." Then, in two stanzas, the poet hears angels singing around the hippo while he "takes wing from the damp savannas" and hears him singing in heaven while "performing on a harp of gold." Then comes the final stanza:

> He shall be washed as white as snow,
> By all the martyr'd virgins kist,
> While the True Church remains below
> Wrapt in the old miasmal mist.[8]

---

6. Nietzsche, *Beyond Good*, 79.
7. Col 4:16 KJV.
8. Eliot, *Poems*, 27–28.

Bibliography

Bernard of Clairvaux. *On Loving God.* Christian Classics Ethereal Library Edition. http://www.ccel.org/ccel/bernard/loving_god.html.

Eliot, T. S. *Poems.* New York: Knopf, 1920.

Nietzsche, Friedrich. *Beyond Good and Evil: Prelude to a Philosophy of the Future.* Translated by Helen Zimmern. New York: MacMillan, 1907.

16

Bowel Rumblings or Bone Roaring or Something[1]

Spring 1973

Introduction

This discussion is a mixture of analysis and prophecy. All prophecy must be preceded by some sort of analysis of the present. My aim in analysis is to give us all a common starting point, a point of view that usefully, I hope, organizes data and judgments on those data so that we can then get on to the more important job of prophecy. The point of view I select need not be the best one that is possible. Of course, it must not be wholly false or even hopelessly inadequate. If it is either of these, let us bury it without wasting any time. Even so, your reading it would not be a waste of time. As the history of theology amply illustrates, truth is often error's gift. Once badly stated, error calls attention to its falsity and thus points to where the fuller truth doth lie. The prophecy, then, is the thing. Alas, I am neither a prophet nor the son of a prophet. But I will

---

1. "Bowel rumblings" is a biblical allusion: "Look down from heaven, and behold from the habitation of thy holiness and of thy glory: where *is* thy zeal and thy strength, the sounding of thy bowels and of thy mercies toward me? are [sic] they restrained?" Isa 63:15. –DJC.

preach boldly, hoping by this to provoke you all to that roaring in your bones which leads to your own prophesying.

Analysis: A Point of View

Every culture, at least during its creative stages, possesses a worldview and an image of what man ought to be. And every culture works out processes and institutions which tend to bring about this ideal. These are my beginning assumptions. Of course, it is not necessary that anyone in that culture know clearly how to describe that ideal. It may, in fact, be subconscious. But it is nonetheless true that members of that culture can recognize those who more nearly approach it. And some within any culture do come closer to embodying it than do others. These are the true educators.

There are also those who come to be better than others at talking about the ideal. These become the actual educators. In the course of time, the actual educators are not the same people as the true educators. And, finally, the scribes (actual educators) foist their scribal ideals onto society as the true ideal. Then dies the culture, either stagnating or giving birth to another ideal.

The triumph of the scribes may be as much of a symptom as it is a cause of this decline. In any case, I believe there is a direct link. A viable culture must have an ideal that beckons, one that challenges individuals to mature toward it. As individuals do so, they progressively embody it. The embodiment then functions as a magnet for those farther back. These are the "heroes." But these models also make possible a more accurate description of the ideal. The hero's progress suggests the series of stages through which initiates must pass. Expertise on these various stages develops and is systematized in an educational system that is organized to "produce" its "products."

If the ideal is simple, then a large number do attain it. But at this point the ideal ceases to be a challenge. Such a culture dies of boredom. If the ideal is a rich and complex one, then the attainment is rare. But its profundity makes possible a large number of stages in the process of becoming. And its subtlety calls forth great masses of knowledge appropriate to each stage. It time, specialists become so engrossed in their area that they lose sight of the ideal and deny that there is a single process. The "worldview" which gave rise to the complexity is destroyed by what it has spawned. It may even be that the "truths" of the parts reveal the so-far-hidden contradictions within the original vision. Indeed, it is virtually necessary that this must happen for all but a finally true vision. In either case, the coherence of the culture is broken at the same time that it achieves its greatest richness.

Each area then spawns its own more-attainable ideal, and a whole series of "pop" heroes emerge. Perhaps one may illustrate this from our history. From George Washington, an aristo("best")crat who was the best general, most cultured, and richest man in the colonies, we move to business tycoons and inventors and politicians. For the young, there are Daniel Boones and Babe Ruths. Finally, when the disintegration becomes too apparent, those with eyes to see ("Look, ma, the emperor has no clothes!")[2] embody their mockery in the creation of antiheroes (Alfred E. Newman, Dustin Hoffman, Joe Namath). If some overarching religious and social sanctions remain, such a dead culture sometimes is able to maintain itself for a very long time. Where these are broken, the end is swift. The dilemma is this: a truly advanced culture must have an ideal that is real, that is progressively realized, that is true, but that is unattainable.

So much for the point of view. I would defend the first paragraph. Those that follow are more questionable. That we may "feel" their truth, if we do, may be more obvious than constructive ones. We "see" the forest burning but have harder time visualizing the forest growing. Even so, there remains the problem of visualizing the shape of the forest while in it.

Application to Colleges in General and, Now and Then, to Pacific

Using the terminology of the Danforth study that Hans Kasdorf brought to our attention, let us define the first colleges in the U.S. as faith-affirming. I would, then, broaden the definition of this term. These early colleges did not, it seems to me, define for themselves the creed they affirmed. Nor were creedal-type statements the content of the basic affirmation. The communities that created them already possessed an ideal

---

2. Delbert uses the now proverbial tale of "The Emperor's New Clothes" as a metaphor for the true nature of those antiheroes; "i.e., the mockery of heroism by those who would earlier have been nonentities, the 'famous for being famous,' and even sensationally dubious." Wiens, email to W. Marshall Johnston, January 9, 2015. –DJC.

of what it meant to be a Christian and to think Christianly. The colleges they created were the modern monasteries. They provided a place where those who could best define the common vision would have the necessary leisure and stimulation to do so. Here the common faith found intellectual self-expression. But these masters were themselves nurtured in the community. They were not the only embodiments, but they were the best of those who could also think about what they represented. They were a sort of "hero," heroes of the faith who could also think and speak. And all in those communities recognized them as legitimate heroes of the group's ideals.

At the same time these teachers were to educate future church and community leaders. Thus, they were a combination of the master (read "guru") and teacher (read "scribe" or "professor"). As teachers they taught necessary intellectual skills to students. As masters they provided a model of Christian maturity and guided the life of the disciples through one phase of what was understood, at least tacitly, to be a lifelong maturational process. (Saints are not made in a day, nor are they "made" at all.)

The entire community shared the ideal and nurtured it. The college was one aspect of that community. The graduate was not a "product" who had "arrived." It was to be expected that he went back into the community for his "graduate studies." In time, he too could become a master and be asked to rejoin his school as a teacher and master. The validity of what happened at school depended both upon what had happened to the youth before he came and what happened to him after he left. There were stages, and the student stage made sense only as it fitted the learner-disciple for higher ones to come. The community was the true locus of becoming. The college was a subsidiary of the community.

Those schools did very well. The definitions grew. And so did all the subspecialties. Gradually, the school itself became its own community. It became the place for "graduate studies." Those who learned the best might go from student to teacher without ever leaving its halls. Meanwhile the communities also changed. Industrialization brought mobility and a wide choice of occupations requiring special expertise. The schools agreed to teach that expertise. Or did it first develop there, thus making possible the occupations?

Never mind. The scribes were winning. Presidents now turn to Harvard professors instead of to old-line politicians of Bernard Baruchs. The primary communities are disappearing. But we have multiversities and little colleges cast in their image.

With the loss of the central vision of what it means to keep on becoming human, we are left with a whole series of "lifestyles" that can be put on or taken off at will. It is all a matter of putting oneself through the given process that "produces" it. One can go through a "trajectory" of lifestyles, as in Alvin Toffler's *Future Shock*, but there is no sense of organic development in this. They are, however, very "attainable." One may, in time, become so adept at changing style that one can do it with ease. Thus, the multiversity produces multiphrenia.[3] Unless it was that the multiphrenia produced the multiversity.

In any case, the condition tends to become visible wherever it is that the young gather. And the people back in the primary communities that were left, as well as the even more conservative people who left those communities without outgrowing them, reacted with alarm to what they truly saw had become a non-faith-affirming college with neither a sense of wholeness not commitment.

And so, in their alarm, they created the faith-defending college. This school teaches, for even the fearful must learn the techniques of the specialists to survive. It is anti-intellectual and anti-cultural because it rightly senses the nihilism of the university and the larger culture. But it has not understood and transcended the problem. Instead of a higher vision, it regresses to an out-of-date formulation of the old ideal as if the ritual intonation of old creeds can contain the creative Spirit. Therefore, it is defensive and lacks freedom. And it ends by producing its own "pop" heroes who embody "pop" visions. This solution works only so long as one can separate what one does from what one says one believes. The word for it is "compartmentalization," which is another word for multiphrenia, which is precisely the disease the defended hoped to escape.

And then there are those colleges ("Lord, we, only we are the left")[4] who seek to be faith-affirming. But there is a growing sense of frustration in us. For we do not anymore affirm and seek to express an ideal and a worldview that is given us by our communities. There too the integrating

---

3. I apologize for combining Latin and Greek roots into the same word. In this instance, I feel that it was necessary for the wordplay with "multiversity."

4. This is another biblical allusion. "And he said, I have been very jealous for the Lord God of hosts: for the children of Israel have forsaken thy covenant, thrown down thine altars, and slain thy prophets with the sword; and I, even I only, am left; and they seek my life, to take it away." 1 Kgs 19:10 KJV. Delbert adds: "Unlike Elijah fleeing to the desert mountain after his slaughter of the Baal prophets sure that 'only I am left,' we can cite a few colleges among the 'We, only we, are left.'" Wiens, e-mail message to W. Marshall Johnston, January 9, 2015. –DJC.

vision is disappearing. Once we could all point to certain men and know that, somehow, they embodied the kind of saintliness we too sought. Men like A. H. Unruh and H. H. Flaming come to mind. Moreover, these men emerged out of the community that was still the locus for higher becoming. Whether or not they went on to teach, they were masters who helped the young (as H. H. Flaming did for my father) both by being who they were (heroes) and through personal guidance.

But this older vision and wisdom could not maintain itself. The leaders came to be those who had gone off to school for their higher training. These schools were largely the faith-defending type. And our communities, in their progressive disintegration, also became faith-defending. They also could not maintain themselves.

It can be put this way. Once there was an ideal, a vision of the truly human, and our world was organized to make its realization possible. For us Mennonite Brethren and for Christians generally, the realization of that image had been revealed finally in Jesus Christ. But that vision cannot exist in splendid isolation. While we grow toward it, we need lesser embodiments. We need heroes we can understand to give content to the ideal. St. Paul fully recognized this and urged people to imitate him. In that imitation growth takes place. With that growth comes greater insight and the capacity, eventually, to recognize more truly who he is and learn to imitate him. But we never wholly "arrived." He was always ahead of us. A truly Christian community, therefore, was one that understood the Christian life as a pilgrimage. While "on the way" a disciple went through stages, levels of development that were defined for him by his "heroes." No doubt many of us remember some older sages in our communities who were heroes for us at various stages in our development. Really profound understandings of Jesus Christ depend upon this hierarchy of Christ-like embodiments. But what happened is that our "pop" culture does not recognize these saints to be heroes. With these higher approximations made invisible, two things happen.

In the first place, we lose any truly profound sense of who Jesus Christ is. We now imagine him in terms of the partial realizations possible to us at lower stages. Jesus becomes a "pop" hero, too. The second result is that the Christian ideal is debased to the easily attainable. Our evangelical heroes are "pop" heroes. At one level we idolize the newly converted, especially if their past is either sordid or if they are celebrities—that is another word for "pop" heroes. The "higher" models for evangelicals are evangelists, those whose own words and acts are geared to the production of babes. As such, they themselves seldom aim at, or even recognize, what a higher Christian maturity would be. With the loss of the vision of the Christian life as a lifelong growth toward sonship comes also an inability to recognize the need for those advanced saints with the gift of fostering this growth. We have no masters.

But we do have teachers. And we have techniques for quickly producing whatever lifestyle popular Christians are seeking. The result is a series of "ideals" that any half-bright youth can already fully comprehend. Since many can master the style, and since no higher styles are imaginable, the only way to reach toward superiority is to do what one does more vigorously. Energy, not wisdom or sanctity, has become the highest virtue. And youth has an abundance of energy.

The result is a Christianity that is a strange mixture of adults and youth, of faith-defending adults who set up methods to produce their highest ideal: energetic youth. American evangelicalism is Christianity reduced to its lowest common denominator. It is geared to reproduce itself in the image of its adolescents. So accurately does this spiritual state mirror the general culture that even the secular world can appreciate it. Billy Graham is the nation chaplain. American evangelicalism has gained its world.

The point of all of this, for us, is that is impossible to be a faith-affirming college in the sense defined above. The context that makes it all possible is gone. It is not one aspect of a maturational progress that goes on in the community until the end of its life. Indeed, in our setting, if a student catches the vision of what it would mean to become a higher type, whether religious or not, he specifically does not go back to his home community. That place is conceived of as a place for stagnating. What is expected of us by the incoming student and his church is that we are to give technical expertise, which the young need to "make it" in our sort of world, while protecting and nurturing that level of Christian becoming that can, if it has not, reach full term by age eighteen. Truly, we are meant to be a "finishing" school.

And so it is that if the hotshot Christian high-school student comes to Pacific College and catches a higher vision of what a Christian might be, we are more likely to be faulted than praised. For new stages of growth take time to work themselves out. Initially, there is the necessity of concentration upon oneself. There is spiritual confusion, and there is even a crisis of faith. Worst of all, there is a concomitant loss of outflowing energy. The irony is that we are seen as failing for doing precisely what the older faith-affirming college took to be in its mission. The tragedy is that such a person cannot easily go back to his own community. For the community cannot recognize anymore what constitutes higher approximations to what the community thinks is its ideal.

Another reason why we can no longer be faith-affirming in a true sense is that the loss of a coherent vision gives us nothing to affirm. So long as there was a "feel" for the unity of life, a "sense" of the coherence of things under God, and a hierarchy of approximations of that ideal, it was possible to carry on the task of helping the larger community to find words to express the meaning and shape of that shared worldview. Perhaps faith-affirming is an apt phrase only for this later stage. All we have left are "affirmations." We affirm that truth is one, that Christ is truth, and that integration of learning and of learning with life is the ideal. But the affirmation has no content. We point to Christ as the center of meaning and then quickly turn away lest we discover that we are pointing to the empty spaces that once contained him. Perhaps no question so quickly stirs the responses of fear and guilt as this: "But how does your teaching of this course differ from the way it is taught in a multiversity?" We affirm Christ as the center. But we do not know how to get back to the center from the loose ends that are our specialties.

Let us now take several specific areas and see whether this general analysis helps us to understand why we do what we do.

Faculty

I have already defined the character of the master-teacher of the original faith-affirming college. The typical teacher—that is not to say that anyone is wholly like the type—at a faith-defending institution is divided within himself. On one level he recognizes the modern malaise and is rightly horrified by it. He has recognized that Christ has come to save us from being lost and has accepted this by faith. He affirms that Christ is Lord, the key to history and the center of meaning. But he does not know how to integrate what he has learned at the multiversity with his experience. Nor can he live with this ambivalence. And so he retreats to an earlier formulation of the vision (a "systematics") that once had the power of expression of the felt wholeness. He insists that this formulation can state that wholeness, that it can integrate the whole body of knowledge. Of course, it no longer does so, and that is the problem. The felt wholeness cannot be restored by what expressed it. The long story of the evolution-versus-creation war illustrates the situation. Somehow, the new data that has risen since the older formulation was set down must be made to fit the older formulation. But one cannot either change the formulation or deny the data. This is a problem in all fields. Out of this dissonance comes the applauded virtue: energy. It is not power. That is what was possessed by the older masters. Power is what the Spirit can cause to flow from the man whose eye is single, whether he does much or little. What comes from dissonance is energy, not even the energy of youths, but the energy of neurosis. On the surface it looks very similar. But from it comes activity (vines and branches) rather than results (fruit). But schools with this kind of fervency have little trouble finding a constituency. They are where it is at for many, especially for the older many with money.

But what about us? I think that much that is puzzling can be understood once it is realized that most of us have our feet in both camps. On the one hand, we identify ourselves as evangelicals and even admit to being, or having been, fundamentalists. And we have a right to that title. At least we have the right to it after we get through defining what we know it should mean. Thus, when Hans gets through defining the word, it turns out to be equally well a definition of the Anabaptist Vision. And that is not simply dishonest. There is enough similarity to make it plausible. And even if it were not similar, our Mennonite churches in America have taken on a great deal of what it meant to be Bible-Belt Christianity. Whatever our theological pilgrimage, that remains at least one level of our own being.

But on the other hand, our own history is quite different from that of the great majority of people who call themselves evangelicals. Most of us come from Corn—I use "Corn" in what follows as the symbol for an idea. And Corn is more than the theology by which it defines its beliefs. In a real sense, American Mennonite Brethren existed before their theological formulations existed. We are a cultural entity, ethnics. We did not come into being in reaction against American theological liberalism as did American evangelicals. Blood is thicker even than baptismal water, that is, we have all sorts of reasons for staying in Mennonite Brethren churches that have little to do with theology.

Let me suggest one such reason. Our Corns had a coherent point of view. It was not an educated point of view. It was not a vision that was articulated. But it had evolved out of centuries of peasant experience with the land, with nature, and with God. In time, a wisdom developed, a folk wisdom that was handed down and that apprehended truth without being able to comprehend its structure. And hero-masters were developed. The actual Corn had a number of them. Some could speak and some could not, but they were, nonetheless, models for the growing youth. Ours may be the last generation that remembers a time when these sages were important, that is, when they were recognized as those who came closest to the image of Christ. From them we got a vision of what singleness of eye might mean. And we learned something about growth toward maturity that we cannot forget.

We have, however, been permitted to accept their worldview. They were, after all, rather ignorant of whole universes of discourse, the whole stock-in-trade of the multiversities. Nor did our younger leaders, the first ones to go to Bible schools and to preach in English, develop formulations to systemize the older wisdom. Those younger leaders, by and large, rejected the old ones as irrelevant to the new world. The formulations they brought back were borrowed from places like Moody and Dallas. The rhetoric did not really fit, though we worked hard to convince ourselves that it did.

But some of us cannot forget what we learned in the old setting. We hunger for primary community. We believe in saintly maturity. And we are in search of a worldview that is adequate to the knowledge we have learned. Most of us at Pacific College are here, in part, because of the pull of this older, ethnic-religious past. People like us, but without such a heritage, seldom feel strongly about returning to their church institutions after they outgrow the worldview of their childhood. Spiritually and psychologically we are different from faith-defending types, even though we often use faith-defending language to talk about our Christianity. Our conceptions of Christianity have been shaped more by our H. H. Flamings than by Carl F. H. Henrys.

Ironically, this creates misunderstandings even with our own brethren. Our churches, by and large, are conditioned by now to the rhetoric of American religiosity. Some of them have become so like their neighbors that the rhetoric fits. But for the ethnic among them, it does so only partially. The result is that what they say is not consonant with what they mean. They do, in part, still mean the kind of Christianity taught by their grandfathers. But they say that the kind of words taught by preachers influenced by the evangelical climate and by the radio preachers they listen to. The result for the intelligent and sensitive (namely, us) is that though we mean what they mean, we cannot easily say what they say. Granted education, there is one basic option left for our types. We cannot leave our churches. But we cannot comfortably worship and serve in them. And so we cluster together in church-peripheral institutions and commiserate with each other. We are Cornites who revere what it stands for but who cannot tolerate the place. On the whole, one can stipulate that Mennonite Brethren who are both educated and touched by the ethnic-spiritual wound end up in our conference offices and schools. Few of these, even pastors, survive long in the churches except, perhaps, if they are in settings where it is permitted to innovate. And so it is that our schools and seminary hold highest the Mennonite ideal. Deep down, we know A. H. Unruh is our guru. And to counter the prevailing rhetoric, we develop the Anabaptist Vision rhetoric. The irony is that many in the churches also mean what we mean while they use their rhetoric, but the rhetoric prevents us from realizing that what we both mean is Corn. Unfortunately, it seems to us that their number is diminishing.

Out of this conflict between our Mennonite Brethren past and the American present comes either shipwreck or superiority. One reason we stick with Pacific College is the joy we have in knowing each other. Seriously now, we are, even judged by the standard of other colleges, a superior lot. I mean it. There is no point in being hypocritically modest. But we have not yet learned how to speak about what we are. And so we are awkward even with each other, afraid to confront each other with feelings about each other, unwilling to let go of the sophisticated irony that masks deeper yearnings. (It seems that there was, once, a common vision and a language, that ideal that the Pacific College Idea tried to express, which made it possible to confront each other, to fight, to laugh, and to know that we were one.)

Administration

The growth of the multiversity has produced a new administrative style in American colleges. In the past, the president of a college was chosen because he symbolized the ideal of the constituency. He was a master, a hero. The people in the communities in which he developed could not necessarily understand his thoughts, though theological sophistication was sometimes astonishingly high, but they could recognize that he was a higher embodiment of what they also were. And they could trust their children to him. He, and the older teachers, had the authority of superiority, an authority that was paternal and avuncular at the same time and, therefore, did not need to be paternalistic.

But with the disintegration of the common vision, a new type of administrator has emerged. Like all others in the multiversity, he is a specialist. He has studied administration. He is an expert on personnel relations. And he is a politician. Among his vice-chancellors and department heads, he is first prima donna in a society of prima donnas. He does not last long.

A cross between this "ideal" and the older one is beginning to emerge on the campuses of small colleges. The new presidents are young, trained in administration, slightly "mod," and charismatic. They have the supreme virtue: energy. They are everywhere. They are up on what is happening anywhere. They are "creative." But they have no central vision what a society, or a college, is all about. The frantic way they flit from innovation to innovation is ample proof that though they know all about the inner workings of the ship, they have no idea of the destination and no charts to get them there. But they are exciting. In the absence of a single vision, dreams will have to do.

Deep down, constituencies sense the vacuum. They neither understand the colleges, nor do they recognize the new breed to be authentic heroes. Perhaps this is the heart of the financial problems faced by all American schools. But meanwhile the people are willing to be bemused. And so it is that the new breed brings its energy to bear on the public, and more and more they find themselves speaking and acting in terms of the "pop" heroes they really are. But still, deep down, the constituencies are not amused and the schools struggle for survival.

A note on the special problem of a growing "faculty-run" institution may be in order. When Pacific College was small, all faculty could know enough to participate in all major decisions. I do not believe this to be desirable anymore. But there is something more important in the concept that needs to be preserved. Faculty discussion, and consensus, should be reached on the basic philosophy of the school. We need to be hear each other out on the broad questions until we understand how each of us thinks and can, thus, trust him, in classes or in administration, to speak and make decisions for the rest of us. As it stands now, we have retained a monthly meeting that once made sense but is now neither decision-making nor philosophical. Nor will it become the latter until its structure is changed and considerable work is put into preparing for it. The best that can happen now is that catharsis occasionally takes place. But this catharsis, like yearly trips to the altar, does not lead to improvement. Granted this, I think it to be immoral even to attend.

Students and Their Recruitment

Our basic problem is that our natural constituency is too old and too small. They are people, like us, who still have the memory of the old wholeness. But our young people are entirely modern. They may still know some old sages, but they were never told that they were heroes. They have had only "pop" heroes held up for them.

We have, therefore, struggled to find a larger constituency. In this, our rhetoric has confused us. Because we also call ourselves "evangelical," we have turned to those who also call themselves by name. But they do not mean by it what we mean. If the students' testimonies are clear and they are able and energetic, then we assure them that Pacific College is for them. But we are dishonest in this. They are quite sure that they already understand Christianity and, in general terms, the nature of their mission in this world. What they expect from us is technical expertise and the reinforcement of their fervor. They do not expect to change their vision. But as soon as they arrive, we begin our subversive tasks. We do not accept their vision, even though we use their formulations. The older organic models we have learned in Corn begin to operate. We do not simply want to broaden their knowledge and stimulate their energy. What we really want to do is give them a new altitude. We want them to grow up to higher visions. Therefore, we fail precisely where we succeed. And we do often "succeed." Many of our students are led into the deep waters, suffering the collapse of their shallow worldviews and religious understandings. And of these, many find a profounder understanding of faith and life. In doing so, we alienate them from their own communities.

The truth is, had they known what was in store, they would not have come. Nor can they bring us their younger friends. One bunch comes, but seldom a second. The group from Judson College may be a good example. What happened to them at Pacific College may well be good as a very mixed blessing by those from where they came. I suspect that they see it as a tragedy. Insofar as they are faith-defenders, they would have to see it as unfortunate. The result is that our recruiters must constantly develop new sources of supply. One might even argue that "evangelicals," at least initially, are our unhappiest students. Those whose expectations are not shaped by our recruitment rhetoric suffer no such letdown. It may even be that among these we are finding a new constituency without realizing it. Our older worldview with its organic conception of progress is probably much more relevant to youth influenced by the (prophetic? reactionary?) newer movements. Indeed, we may be perceived to be more helpful to non-Mennonite ethnics than we are to neighboring Baptists. There is also the possibility that as modern evangelicals lose their defensiveness we will come to see them as carriers of a steadier vision than we had previously granted them. Unfortunately, that sort of insight may come only to people like professors at Fuller. The immediate prospect is disquieting.

Students and Their Teaching

It is interesting to me that the need for, and the nature of, teaching is probably the least problematic of the elements that make up Pacific College. Perhaps we look at it most because it is the least threatening. And yet, it is threatening enough.

We may, I think, posit that there will always be something like colleges, some method for imparting expertise. Unless barbarianism triumphs, the need for advanced knowledge will not diminish. Of course, the form within which it is carried on and the shape for doing it may have to change. There is already so much literature on this, and I have read so little of it, that I should not dare to say much.

I think it is fair to say, however, that the present search for new ways to teach is as much a sign of our confusion as it is a sign of hope. We have lost the context within that the old methods made sense and have not discovered a new context from which to justify new ones. The result is the test of one thing after another in the hope of finding something that works.

The problem is that two things are still confused. On the one hand is the imparting of an expertise. Here strides are being made. On the other is the inculcation of meaning. The multiversity has been embarrassed about this one. One reason is that it does not possess the central vision by which one can recognize it. Another is that the way we have come to do the first (teaching) makes impossible the doing of the second. The shape of what we are makes it impossible.

In the older setting, the two went together. The teacher was both teacher and master. Because the worldview was recognized by all, however imperfectly, the master function could take place largely by example. Perhaps that is the way it can best take place. In any case, they did not have to talk about this sort of thing very much to be doing it.

Because the dim outlines of the whole were already known, the imparting of pieces of knowledge did not create disintegration or boredom. The teacher could concentrate on telling what he knew. The lecture was appropriate. But when the coherence is gone, the special knowledge stands by itself. More and each segment of it became an end in itself. And the segments multiplied. The loss of a sense of an organic whole, thus, led naturally to the conceptualization of teaching as a mechanical process. Knowledge was broken down more and more into pieces. There is a proper sequence to learning the pieces, just as there is a proper sequence on an assembly line. The job of teachers is to break knowledge down properly. Then, so we are told, we can sit back; for students can pick up the pieces best if they do it by themselves. The end of this trend is that the teaching machine replaces the lecture.

Once, it was assumed that teaching was as much to give the student a new altitude as to impart knowledge. There was a rhythm to this process that demanded an appropriate time. In Europe the process was assumed to take an entire university career, and exams, philosophic in nature, took place at the end. In Canada each course could be assumed to have its own rhythm, but they still take a whole year. Here in the United States, the dividing went farther from semesters to quarters. Since knowledge is treated as more or less on the same level, one need not worry about the subconscious brooding that is required by those who would gain altitude. The logical result is the mini-quarter and the removal of the upper- and lower-level distinction.

But here the unexpected can happen. Teachers and students can play their machine roles for fifty minutes but not for two to three hours. Humanity, and even mastership, breaks through again. But one may well wonder about the results. Jesus' disciples were ready for a profound depth and height only after three years. The great masters through history spent years preparing their disciples for enlightenment. Perhaps what is possible in mini-quarters is a series of mini-insights. Well, it would suit our times to offer "pop" enlightenments built upon instant experience. (Is it really the case that most "T-groups" amount to much more than that?)[5]

All of this is not to say that the current experimentation is bad. There are different sorts of knowledge. We may be allowed to hope that in the end we will discover the appropriate method and rhythm for each sort of learning. It is not at all likely that a single rhythm and method is best for all. And so it is certainly necessary that we sit very loose to our traditional structures.

Students and Their Nurturing

The older faith-affirming colleges probably did not have to worry very much about rebellious sinners. Students went there, after all, because they assented to the kind of mental and spiritual discipline they received. One may assume that there were abundant hijinks, but this did not need to threaten anyone seriously. There is a rhythm to growth, and there are stages to maturity. Youth did not need to be prematurely perfect. Colleges then were, indeed, sodalities. But this is no longer the case. For one thing, nearly all youth are dragged into them at eighteen by the need for expertise and the lack of anything better to do. Moreover, they do not see us as masters. Regarding morality, they are fairly sure that they know as much as we do. On some matters, they are entirely sure that they know more. And since we are officially silent on moral subtleties, they are probably justified for thinking so. Disciplining at most colleges is, therefore, absent or is perceived as the perverse use of force. In neither case is it morally responsible. I will not go into this in greater detail since, with some modification, what I wrote last year in response to the dancing episode can be fit in here.

The amazing thing to me is that the guru-function survives at all in our schools. The structure appears to militate against it, and yet it is here. Surely, this is testimony to a great need. And we should remind ourselves how great is the modern quest for gurus, from true and fake swamis to Francis Schaeffers. We need to give much attention to this need. And we need to be deliberate about whom we invite on the staff. We should not

---

5. Delbert explains that "T-groups" was a buzzword in the early seventies that was used mostly for small-group brainstorming activities following a presentation and possible for therapy groups. Wiens, e-mail message to W. Marshall Johnston, December 22, 2014. –DJC.

all be aged saints. But some of us should be. Perhaps we should represent all the important stages of maturity.

I do have doubts about our ability to fill this function. In the faith-affirming college, it could be assumed that virtually all the students were going to be teachers, preachers, lawyers, or doctors. And all would be churchmen. They were the sort of people who would model themselves after their teachers. More than that, their own becoming would continue in their future relationships in the communities. But we cannot anymore assume this to be true. Modern professionals will find peer pressure to continue learning, but little community or church encouragement to keep on becoming.

Insofar as our students catch this vision for growth, graduation becomes almost an occasion for despair. Where are they going to find masters for continued becoming or a place to become masters themselves? They do not recognize any in their own communities. No wonder they return to school and become teachers themselves. This is the one community they have experienced that believes in growth. Here too the more we succeed, the sadder is the result. Becoming does not take place throughout life in our communities. One goes out of them to a special place for a few specified years. Then what? The latter condition of the student may well be worse than the first. There can be little chance of follow-through on the promise. It must be a very great temptation for our best graduates to be both our most nostalgic and cynical alumni. The problem is not simply ours, and so we cannot solve it. It is the problem of the larger society. What we do makes little sense except as a stage for something that goes on. If it does not go on, then as masters, we do not make sense either, however well we do it. Even multiversities are full of would-be gurus, but the context virtually forces us to be "pop" gurus. Are not the real ones more and more abandoning, or refusing to enter, the college system? One cannot administer growth to a group. Certainly, this cannot be done unless all are pretty much at the same stage in their own becoming. And the organic rhythms of the soul do not fit into the lockstep routines of a knowledge factory.

The Constituency

I have already said enough to indicate the shape of this problem. But I think it would be useful to analyze a specific incident in the light of what has so far been said.

On the night of February 16, 1970, three carloads of faculty went to Dinuba to answer questions and accusations that were current in that community and that had been written out so that they could be dealt with systematically.

We told them that Pacific teachers are expected to teach even mathematics from the "biblical point of view." With genuine humility, we acknowledged that it is difficult to do this in our disciplines since we know more about them in themselves than we do of their relation to "total truth." But, nevertheless, we left the impression that this is an ideal that is more or less attained. Now, we at least have some idea of what we are talking about when we say this even if we do not know what the necessary systematics are.

But what does this mean to the Dinuba brethren? Many of them are critical and defensive, even reactionary, because they are in the midst of actual social and economic crises that threaten the whole way of life that they have imagined as an ideal and have sought to build. They are constantly being forced to hear that their farming practices are obsolete and ruinous, that their church structures are out of date, and that the answers and loyalties by which they have lived are irrelevant to the world of their own children and grandchildren.

In the face of all these assaults, it is natural that defenses are thrown up that encircle the entire network of practices and beliefs by which they have lived and by which they have identified themselves. Never mind that these beliefs and practices are often a chaos of self-defeating contradictions. Though they are mostly a jumble of elements borrowed from here and there, they attain the status of a system by the mere fact that a wall must be built to surround them. This structure has many enemies: political liberals, leftist economists, neo-orthodox theologians, and radicals of all sorts. Whatever their words denote, their connotation is clear: they connote the denial of their worldview, of their "system," and therefore, the rejection of themselves. For them that is what these words mean.

Then we come in aggrieved that they believe so much about us that is not true. We are shocked that they would accept the rumor that an atheist had lectured on campus. To hear us tell it, they might be justified in thinking that any sort of liberal or new-orthodox thought might ever cross our minds. Of course, we first conveniently defined liberal as meaning "one who denies Jesus Christ" and neo-orthodox as "one who does not accept the scriptures." Fortunately, Pastor Baerg saw through that and gracefully laid those terms to rest for the evening.

So far we had said two things: "we accept and teach the biblical worldview," and "your enemies are our enemies." To them all this must mean that we accept their system. After all, they certainly believe that they are biblical, too. It is true that we do accept a very great deal that they accept. Much that we celebrate as authentically Christian and "Mennonite Brethren" is alive and perhaps even relatively well at Dinuba. From our point of view, we agree with them on the essentials. But we have not been honest and they know it. For we do not mean what they mean when they say the words we have so far said. And this becomes obvious when we begin to discuss certain symbolically significant issues.

For them the evolution issue is a significant sign. And they cited Theodore Epp and Vernon McGee to back up their position. But we come with a number of distinctions: the nature and limitations of scientific method; biology does not answer first and last questions; Genesis as a different sort of how-it-was-done details, etc. And so we say, "Yes, we accept the Genesis account," and, "Yes, evolutionary theory helps us explain the creative process." From their point of view, we are either deceiving ourselves or are deliberately trying to deceive them.

Then we were challenged on movies. But we were ready with another attack. To us, they cannot logically accept television within their walls while keeping movies out. For many of them, television and movies are different. One is within and the other is without. And that is enough. But we insisted that they are logically equivalent. We simply insisted that none of their children, and even neighboring pastors, accept their distinction. But we did not try to penetrate to the meaning behind their claim. This was not the time to help them to understand the issue. The argument is brought up to fill a different function.

As a matter of fact, the evening did achieve some positive results. Some people learned that the evolution issue is more complex than they realized. And I suspect that this was the occasion when the movie issue publically laid to rest in Dinuba. For our boldness made it possible for several of their brethren, and the pastor, to speak out on the issue with a freedom that was both responsible and, at least for one, emotional.

But these breakthroughs, if that is what they were, do not justify what we did. We did not handle the issues responsibly. We dealt with them only as a way to cow them. We had neither the time nor the intention to penetrate to the real issues. We discussed them only with sufficient detail to leave them with the forceful conviction that we know things that they do not know and that the best they can do is humbly to trust us. "I know I'm not educated like you are, but . . . ," and then the speaker trailed off, cowed but not convinced. Even on questions of evolution and movies, we did not educate. Rather, in an act of force, we helped some of them take two items that were inside the wall and thrust them outside.

It was in these terms that I had to judge my own contribution to the discussion. At the end of the evolution discussion, I rose to tell them that even evangelical scholars do not anymore interpret Genesis in the way they think. In fact, literal does not mean "literal" anymore. "Of course," I added, "some radio preachers educated a long time ago still do not know better." But by the next morning, I was convinced that I had done an immoral thing. I had no intention of showing how one should read Genesis. My para-message could only be: "Look, you not only know nothing about science, you are even ignorant of the real meaning of Scripture." I have studied Greek and Hebrew. I know something you do not know.

The actual effect of the evening was to do to them what they accuse us of doing to their youth: to knock down their systems. And that, it seems to me, is their final criticism. And many of them knew that they were right in this. Even our defense had proved it. But they were not allowed to enjoy even a pyrrhic victory. We pulled out test scores to prove that their children already have denied their system before they come to Pacific. They themselves have somehow done the things of which they accuse us. We even pretended to be shocked that freshmen should be so heretical.

That was perhaps the most dishonest of a whole string of dishonesties. Among ourselves we would probably agree that most of the "heresies" we cited were actually signs of growing Christian sophistication. From our point of view, the Dinuba faith-defending system is inadequate, and we have no intention of trying to defend it. It would be fatal to our mission with their children to attempt it. But we see ourselves as something more than destroyers of the faith. It is our intention to distinguish the peripheral from the central. We wish to promote maturity, elevation of view, a more soundly based apologetics. We think we are engaged in the noble mission of saving that which is present in our communities that is worth saving. We suspect that we are even the last bulwark preventing their children from abandoning entirely the faith of our fathers. How dare they be suspicious of us? We are quite sure that we deserve their profound gratitude. Yet they see us as destroying the faith.

And then, to myself, I even pretended to be shocked that these, my brothers who complain about our heterodoxy, do not come to admonish us personally, Matthew 18 firmly in mind. Why should they? What assurances do they have that we will not pull another "snow job." We are the ones who are supposed to be able to think these things through. Surely, it is up to us to go to them to help them understand why we both say what we say and what we really mean, pointing out and facing the deeper issue together. Only then do we have the right to ask their trust.

I think that we are really angry at each other, and we are angry because we so desperately need to understand each other, and yet cannot. We have an ideal image of what Corn should be and to a considerable extent was. We know that without the kind of community of becoming described above our own function is hopeless. And we perceive our Corns to be disintegrating socially and economically at the same time that they are becoming defensive and reactionary.

At the same time, they also know that they need us. They do not comprehend what is happening to them and cannot understand their own children. We seem to do so, at least up to a point. And they are really grateful for much that we do. But at the same time, we reinforce much of the critique that those children level against them. And we do so from an elevation that they do not understand and cannot recognize any longer as a higher approximation toward the ideal they also recognize. We both still name the name of Christ. But we are talking about different Christs.

Because we so tangibly need them, we are tempted to use their rhetoric. After all, understood our way, we can even use it honestly. In fact, we sometimes get very excited about it again (understood "profoundly" of course) and go back preaching it with the kind of self-righteousness that says, "Look, you say it but don't really believe it and do something about it as we do." But they understand that rhetoric their way, and so its use is either a self-deception first or is openly dishonest.

The miracle is that they are ambivalent at all. They and we have still a deep willingness to love each other. Deep down, they too are in search for what Corn and H. H. Flamings stood. There is a basis for a talking that can communicate. But it will take a context that is strong enough, and lasts long enough, that we can break through our mutual defenses.

But what sort of context can do that? We have floundered with that question for a long time. There are several problems. For one, most of us are more respected for our expertise than for our mastership. Or we are feared because of our brightness. For another, we are all losing the vision of what a pilgrimage of growth might be. Finally, we deeply suspect that our actual Corns are past saving and that our city churches cannot become communities. I often have the sinking feeling that what emotional and spiritual health I have has been the gift of my father and his setting. I can handle the world because Corn and he are still in me. I am living off that spiritual capital but am not replenishing it. And so I will not be able to reproduce it for my children. What they will know is Fresno, and Fresno is Babylon.

What we really need is a higher vision and a new site of Corn that can fit into Fresno. What we need is a church that is community. But we cannot, within the structure of a college, create the church. That is our dilemma. It is not the function of the sodality to remake the modality. Must we just wait? Well, we are also members of the whole, of churches. Perhaps it is from that stance that we must pray and speak. But we are too busy here to work at primary community elsewhere. I do not know how we are to break out of this vicious cycle.

A New Vision

One might even say that our whole civilization is living off its spiritual capital. The vision that shaped our worldview is being destroyed by the very sophistication that it made possible. That underlying assumption has the feel of truth. But I do not really know it to be so. I have suggested that it may be a trick of perspectives, but it is a feeling shared by a growing number of people.

I have also said that each culture shapes its institutions in the light of its vision. The structure of the modern college is itself a reflection of our civilization's soul. If that vision is not "played out," then the college structure, as we know it, may have a future. Of course, the vision may "played out" while the machine it has created grinds on. In that case, colleges can grind on too. But I see little reason then for a church to have one.

But a new question must be faced. What if a new culture is emerging? There are those who say that there is a greening of America, and they point to the counter-culture, the Jesus People etc., as the harbingers of a new thing. I do not know. It seems at least as likely that the whole movement is another example of the recurrent waves of American nativism.

In either case, we have been given something about which to think. If truly a new culture is emerging, then there is a kind of hope again. If it is a better vision that they have, then we may posit that it will make possible richer levels of becoming. And if the Holy Spirit is moving, then we had better discover how and where. But this may be no great comfort for us as an institution. For new visions require new forms. "Neither do men put new wine into old wine-skins. . . ."[6] If there is a new thing, then we must be prepared to die before we can be raised again.

The difficulty is that it will be hard to recognize when and if it comes. The way we see is also a structure that is, in considerable part, a function of the old ideal. It may well take a new sort of eye to see the new thing. And even when seen, it may not look like much. In its beginnings any vision must seem hopelessly naïve. It has not yet had time to unfold its potential. History may belong to it, but the past can only treat it scornfully, as pagan philosophers treated early Christianity. Those who have the new eye are, of course, equally scornful toward those of us who know so much, and yet are blind.

If what is happening is not so radically new a thing, we yet are faced with youth who think so. We can hardly, therefore, go on in our accepted routines. We must discover with the young what it is they think they know, just as we must rediscover this with Corn. And then, whether new or old, we can help each other to develop what is precious.

A First Tentative Conclusion

Every aspect of the foregoing has accentuated for me the smell of burning. There will always be teaching. One way or another, God will bring forth masters. But what has any college to do with this? The content of what we do is the smallest part of the problem. The really serious thing is that what colleges do has "succeeded" so well that the structure can no longer handle it. It is the whole form of it that seems obsolete. Our wineskins could once carry the wine. But the stuff we now buy cannot be handled by the goat hide. Nor has the brew retained its sacramental

---

6. Matt 9:17 ASV.

function. Society is drunk on it. The world must be remade. And scribes will not be those who do it.

Prophecy

I do not have the answers. The roaring in my bones is mostly an undifferentiated ache. About every third Thursday, I am convinced that there is no answer. How then is it possible for me to remain on the faculty of a college (any college) in conscience? I have not entirely settled that one, but two considerations keep me honest, so far. The first is that so many good things, profoundly good things, do happen in our setting despite all the odds. The disintegration I have described is not the whole story. The other is that I am very suspicious of the mind's ability to see the whole of anything. Some of us are too much in a hurry to abandon seemingly outmoded institutions. It often happens that they have functions we have not perceived. We must sometimes wait and let God kill them or remake them in his own good time, meanwhile serving in them patiently. While doing so, it is necessarily to do the best we can to understand and perfect what we are doing. And we must do this while being quite serene about the possibility that soon we may not be doing it in this way at all. What follows is a partial strategy for those who wait and pray until the true prophet emerges. Moreover, I am getting tired of working on this paper. Only at the end will I say a few words about the serious issues I have so far raised and that we should talk about. I too will go to the less threatening, curriculum reform.

In Lieu of a View

We must distinguish carefully between the sensed wholeness of things, the point of view with which a creature begins, and the scientific-philosophic-theological explications that are later developed to express it. (There is a mighty philosophical problem here. Is this beginning "feeling" learned or innate? But we rush on.)

The basic vision, once there, works itself out on a number of levels: political, economic, social, aesthetic, intellectual, spiritual, etc. Each of these modes are somehow expressions of an underlying "deep structure." Each does so in its own way, partially but truly. And those who "understand" the deep structure can sense the way in which the "message" of each partial mode somehow expresses the wholeness. In each case, an appropriate expression within a mode calls forth the deep "uh huh" that marks a certainty, a certainty that rises from the felt congruence of the part with the whole.

One of these modes is that of thought. And thought expressed in language can bring a culture to awareness of itself. Thinkers can even claim that a given structure of ideas can be the truth about that wholeness. From this it is a small step, and a step almost always taken, to the assumption that what one must think must be. And therefore, this systematics is the truth about reality. Its parts are not only elements of a coherence, but they are propositions that correspond to that which is. Thus, they are taken to be more than an aesthetics, though they are also that.

It seems to be the case that these systems are most highly developed during times of disintegration. The level of sophistication that is required cannot happen immediately. Indeed, part of the motivation for developing them is the hope that the "truth," thus, made explicit can be used as a prescription to halt that disintegration and restore the "Golden Age." Because the construction can express the old wholeness, it is easy to believe that it describes it, and it is then ready to become an ideology for "faith-defenders."

If only one such system arose, it would certainly be thought to be final. But at this point several systems are developed, each of which is about equally able to evoke the whole. And each appears to be a fundamental contradiction of the others. At this point, the same kind of skepticism afflicts the thinkers (except for the blind dogmatists) that is being expressed by the artists and prophets as well as by ordinary people who sense something amiss without being able to explain what. In time, forms of skepticism arise that eschew system-building at all and that are content to go at truth piecemeal. This is the spirit of the multiversity.

But the teaching of scattered pieces of knowledge developed by subspecialties is not an adequate reason for a college or even aspiring universities. And within the multiversities, too, there are those who are searching for some integrating idea. Where might we look for one for Pacific College?

1. The Right Systematics? But where would we find it? I do not know of one that is satisfactory. One or another might satisfy some of us, at least for a while. No doubt, we should perpetually search for one. I am, however, quite certain that we will not find more than that.

In fact, I do not think that a final systematics is or ever has been possible.

2. A Methodological Approach? Although there are many specialties, there are a limited number of methods that one may use in discovering and amassing knowledge. It has been suggested that integration around "method" would be most effective. Such an approach, it is held, would be especially appropriate for people who must forever be learning new contents to keep up with a changing world. I think it is very important to be aware of the methods we use, but I think the integration of a curriculum around them is a counsel of despair. Doing so implies a skepticism toward truth that has only its pragmatism to commend it.

3. What Else Is There? These first two are impossible for us. But even worse is a nihilistic skepticism. It seems to me that there is an approach that would be worth exploring together. To appreciate it, let us take another look at the making of systematics. I have said that a systematics, like any other artistic genre, is the expression of underlying structure. Would a comparative study of such genres reveal the shape of that structure? It has been, and is being, tried. Perhaps there is here some hope. But again, I am skeptical. Even if worked out, I do not see that this would give us anything more than an outline of the way that we must "express." But the chasm between what "must be thought" and "what is" would remain. Doubt would still be possible, even inevitable, and for a very simple reason. Man, as many have pointed out, is more than the sum of what he can think. The truth about himself is never fully caught by the thinker in the pigeonholes of the system he created. Nor would it ever be possible for man to comprehend the greater whole of which he is a part, to say nothing about the impossibility of getting God into those boxes.

How then do men go about constructing such a system? I think the case could be made that thinkers begin with that part of the whole that has most deeply impressed them as significant. There are some "uh huhs" that are so profound that the experience that elicits them is understood to be revelatory of the whole. The shape of the system is then determined by the character of that experience. These systematizations both help man to understand the character of these experiences and furnish an occasion for additional becoming. Once created, the thinker himself, and those who have entered into his thought, can step outside this objectification, consider it in relation to themselves and, thus, gain yet another vantage point that can serve to stimulate yet profounder reflection. The more such understandings he masters, the freer he becomes from the limitation of any of them. Here too is a route for fuller becoming, a strategy for a faculty of the "liberating arts."

But how should one teach such a series? One possibility is to take a historical approach. Here it would be most suitable to study a primitive worldview, then the Hebrew-Semitic, Greek, and medieval. Then one would close by giving some attention to the modern scene. This may well be pedagogically the best procedure.

But even if so, one could argue that this must be based on some way of comparing the "systematics" developed in all of these cultures. Otherwise the student may well assume that either the most recent is best or that they are all actually true and false. Can such expressions be classified and, even, judged and transcended?

Here also I am very tentative, even though I could cite others who have worked on this. Let us posit that in the Western world there have been two ways of ageing that have been complementary, the Greek and the Hebrew-Semitic. The revelatory experiences for the Hebrews were inter-relational: man with man and man with God. Knowledge was basically a "knowledge of something"; it was the result of a confrontation and was, therefore, inter-subjective. The primary metaphors for it were hearing and sexual intercourse. For the Greeks, knowledge was fundamentally a matter of observation, "knowledge about something." The basic metaphor was that of sight and was based on a subject-object relation. In the Hellenistic world, and especially in Christianity, the two streams mingled. The Christian reality was still largely Hebraic; the forms of expressing it were largely Greek. From this arises an enduring, and fruitful, tension in Christian theologizing.

Insofar as the Greek way of thinking prevails, thinkers tend to center their systems around one or two of the aspects of perceived reality: body, mind, soul (understood in the Greek, not the Christian sense). That is to say, a rough classification of types of systems can be made under the headings of materialisms, idealisms (rationalisms), vitalisms, or mixtures of these. Each of these (except materialisms?) can develop in either naturalistic or super-naturalistic directions. The latter sometimes end in full-blown mysticisms. One ought to mention also humanisms and skepticism.

But each of us is more that body, mind, and soul. Somehow the central self I never "observe" is a one that lies behind them. So also reality, though it reveals itself as matter, mind, and energy may be posited to be a one. By now it should be clear that we are thinking in terms of Trinitarian formulations: Father, Son (*logos*), and Holy Spirit. The Three are what we see when we look; the One lies in and behind the parts and is what we confront when we are being addressed. But the Three are related as persons. The Hebraic truth is also enshrined in the first principles of Christianity. Obviously, it is not possible to make this rationally coherent. It would be something like a categorical mistake to do so. For rationality is itself a partial mode, though one that expresses the whole, as do also the other modes, each in its own way.

The doctrine of the Trinity, then, is a way of thinking about this unsayable (as St. Augustine pointed out long ago). But it is also a mode of analysis, a way of holding systems alongside each other until the comprehensions are left behind in a transcending apprehension. And it does justice to the Hebraic categories as much as to the Greek. As to what each of these modes are (their ontology), the Christian can remain perfectly skeptical, just as he knows that the One is forever outside his powers of comprehension. Indeed, this may all be seen as an original skepticism. What is here given is not a systematics so much as it is a way of relativizing all systems. (Of course, theologians also are constantly tempted to take one or another aspect as a key for the building of a system. And there is in it an expressive validity.) But it is a skepticism that points beyond itself. And the revelation is also "relational." God sent Jesus Christ, not a set of propositions when he wished to reveal himself.

Somewhere in this is, I think, the "Christian point of view" for people who evolve beyond childhood dreams and a simplistic vision. From here I think it is possible to move even to our subspecialties. Of course, this does not give us the "truth" about evolution, history, matter, or mind. But I think it gives a way to handle the theories that have been evolved about such things. Well, we would have to work at it to see whether it works.

Finally, it could move us to an understanding of the self that opens us to a more profound understanding of Jesus Christ as the goal of our own becoming.

Back to Reality

I have used such an organizational principle for my own thinking and, sometimes, my teaching. But I would have to swallow very hard before I would publically defend it. We would have to look into it very carefully (and look at other options) before we could accept it for ourselves. But even if it is the best possible formulation, we would still have the job of deciding when and how to teach it. Some things are helpful only when discovered at the right time. If it takes us to middle age to come to it validly, by what stretch of the imagination are we to suppose that we are to unload it on teenagers?

Here again, the form of the modern college brings us to an apparent absurdity. The process we wish to initiate makes sense only if brought to its conclusion. And surely none of us is bold enough to claim that all are ready for it by age twenty-two.

Worse yet, it seems absurd to assume that most are ready even to begin it by then. Though all may need to learn some sort of practical expertise, it is unlikely that all are to be expected to do the head-trip thing posited above. Some saints are quite advanced (true heroes of the faith) even though they may be virtually incapable of expressing verbally to what they have come. They have "worked through" the kind of process I am recommending, but they have done so much more with their hearts than with their heads. Yet we assume that all who come to college are ready to work through it with their head.

Perhaps we can posit that modern Western culture has been on a massive head-trip. The university (and thinking) became the place for becoming rather than the village (working) or the monastery (praying). If there is a new stirring, then it appears that it is a return to soul. A sort of apprehension of power may be as valid a disclosure of reality as is the comprehension of concepts. After a lecture in a course last quarter, one of the members of the Church of the Living Word came to me and said, "Boy, you really blew it today." I asked where and how I had gone wrong. But he had not judged in terms of an intellectual's logic. He had done so in terms of my confused "vibes." Is it not possible that a logical critique and his would be equally true? They are, in fact, expressing a single reality perceived in different modes.

In fact, "liberal arts" may be almost wholly inappropriate for most eighteen-year-olds. The basic idea behind them is that they are the arts that liberate. But our youth may not need liberation in the old sense.

Once we came out of restrictive, but "whole" communities. We had a stability and needed freedom to transcend it. But those who come out of fragmentation may need structure before they can go on to freedom. In biblical terms, law is always needed as prelude to grace. But where do the young learn the law? Protestantism as a whole has failed to develop a rationale, and structures, for law. Perhaps our freshmen need old-fashioned Sunday school while we think of them as needing what we then needed: "graduate studies." But it is impossible to generalize. The diversity of our culture is so great that some students come as naïve as ever stepped off nearly virgin sod. Others have already done it all. Some have even denied it all. The rest are at every stage between. And yet we act as if they are all alike. How can one even lecture to so varied a group? The idea that rebuilds faith for one may destroy another.

If this is so, there is still need to be places where a student picks up practical expertise. But only a church that is a community can even become the locus of becoming and of the liberating arts. All members of the Trinity must receive their due for Christianity, and any person, to avoid heresy and to achieve full becoming. Power without meaning becomes demonic. Meaning without power is dead. If either does not become incarnated, they are nothing. But each person must work out his own rhythms in his distinctive way. Only in and for a continuing community can mastership be responsible. How can anything other than the involvement of the church as locus for growth be called "Anabaptist"? But college, as constituted, is elitist in basic intention.

But even for this, our buildings may not be wholly irrelevant. There is a necessary rhythm between retreat and action. Either we must periodically and seriously move out into the community or the community must periodically move in with us. Or God will raise up masters and real churches somewhere else. This, it seems to me, is the fundamental problem. If it is solved, all the others are solved. If it is not, then we may, by the mysterious working of the Spirit, lead others to faith, but we will ourselves be castaway.

17

The Sermon I Won't Preach Tomorrow (So Please Read It Today)

December 16, 1987

Introduction

I HAVE ASSERTED THAT THE "how" of what one believes might be almost as significant as the "what" and that "professional qualifications" might coincide with captivity to "the spirit of the age." I realize that my comments must often seem to be "off the wall," and so I would like to take this means to explain how I think about issues of this sort. And I invite your assistance. My thinking is very much "in process."

Since I catch myself moving between different points of view, I am also attuned to what I think are differences among us that are deeper than the verbal disagreements that occasionally surface. It seems to me that we pretty much assume that we share the same basic "turf" and that we are playing by the same set of rules, operating out of the same programming and sharing the same basic Christian presuppositions. I think that this assumption is partly wrong. Our discussions reveal that on some issues we do not share the same basic point of view, and so we misinterpret each other even when we think we are saying the same things.

For the sake of contrast, I will oversimplify two ways of thinking about these things that I recognize to be in myself. I will identify one of these as "modern" and the other as deriving, for me, from my "Mennonite" heritage. In effect, these "tags" point to two different worlds.

An Older World and the Modern World

For most of human history, and for me when I was young, the world was made up of small primary communities, each of which had its own "web" of expected responses and actions. "Growing up" was the process of internalizing the web so well that one's life was a reflection of the ethos of the whole. Over the whole, there is a "sacred canopy"[1] that invisibly sheltered and gave meaning to the physical and interpersonal and psychic spaces that it enclosed.

As "Believers Church" Mennonites, we knew that acculturation, though necessary, was not a sufficient condition of either personal fulfillment or godliness. Each of us would have to meet God outside this otherwise constrictive web so that we could freely reaffirm the community, either by becoming responsible for (and within) it or by transmitting its best qualities into other communities in other parts of the world. To stay at home meant that we built here the kingdom of God by incarnating God's care for the soil and God's rule over those of us who together prayed and worked to recreate Eden while awaiting its perfecting in a future time and place. To leave meant to accept the mission to incarnate the model elsewhere.

The basis for the model was Jesus Christ—"other foundation can no man lay."[2] His life and death was the original incarnation, and his abiding presence empowered and guided the reincarnations that were the concrete substance of God's rule among us. We were not good at expressing this in conceptual abstractions, but we knew that "theology" could also be expressed with our hands and our hearts.

---

1. "Sermon" was originally illustrated with numerous sketches of these "canopy"-related ideas; Josiah Muster has reproduced versions of some of them in this volume, and we will put others on the *Dangerous Mind* Facebook page.

2. 1 Cor 3:11 KJV. Fresno Pacific has a very interesting history with this passage, since we use it as our motto: Founded on Christ. The previous Latin translation, *Fundamentum Christus*, has been rescinded, for complex reasons that can be investigated in the FPU Wikipedia page. Several of us, at least Joshua Blagaila and I, would like to translate it *Conditor Christus*. –WMJ.

Most of my generation could not take it for granted that we could remain in any simple version of this older world of concrete primary communities. But the more far-sighted of our elders had built academies, and Tabor, to teach us sets of skills and concepts that would prepare us for the business and professional "secondary societies" outside the older sacred canopies that we would "choose" to join "as adults," new versions of a *secular* "Believers Church." Each of these organizations gathered similar sorts of people and focused their efforts on the production of some thing or service. Both the correlation of these efforts and the pattern of the product were shaped by "blueprints," and behind these blueprints was a set of axioms and postulates that were the foundation upon which all was rationalized. Many such secondary associations were springing up attracting individuals from *everywhere* to settle *anywhere* the work was going on: schools, businesses, factories, and clubs. In time, the old communities began to wither. As the new forms showed their power, even the work of the church began to be organized in the image of the secularized, rationalized associations.

In fact, the old sacred canopy has not entirely disappeared. Though it no longer encloses the whole of life, it is still celebrated in congregations with a collective memory of what it once meant. It is still supposed to shelter the nuclear family—that besieged remnant of larger communal concretions. But so ubiquitous is modernity that even church and home look more and more like voluntary associations. And even Presbyterians and Catholics and Lutherans and Episcopalians, whose "fathers" once persecuted the Baptists and Anabaptists for such heresies, now look more and more like "Believers Churches."

For many of us, some sort of recovery of the sense of the whole and of a sacred canopy seems essential, even if we are also quite sure that it cannot be based on the same kind of primary communities from a time when the great majority were farmers. The volume *Habits of the Heart*, by Bellah and others, shows that ethnics are not the only ones who recognize this need. And contemporary philosophers are busily at work deconstructing the rationalist assumptions underlying modernity. How are we now to be Christian? What does it mean to be a Christian college? And what really is the content of a "good news" for the coming generation? Are we appropriately living out a meaningful direction in our practice?

Two Visions from the "Personnel Selections Guidelines"

What we have tended not to notice is that the vocabulary we use to describe our life and task is taken from alternate visions. And so, many of our statements can be read in different ways, depending upon which point of view is dominant when we read. Depending upon the reader, we have two different documents before us. Or so I shall argue.

The preamble of the "Report to the Faculty—12.9.87"[3] stated that Fresno Pacific College belongs to "the confessional tradition of the Anabaptist (Believers Church) movement." I doubt that anyone knows what kind of Church the Anabaptists would have created had they not been persecuted—we do know that they reemerged as Mennonites—and I doubt that Mennonite Churches were secondary societies. For moderns, a Believers Church is constituted by those who have freely chosen (therefore, as adults) to covenant together ("contract" may now be more exact) and to carry on the public functions of the "spiritual" aspect of life, just as all our other secondary associations "meet the needs of" secular functions.

Like the nuclear family, the nuclear congregation retains a sense of the sacred canopy and claims the right to speak to how we live in the other settings of our lives. But more and more the ministries of the churches are channeled into specialized departments, and the really powerful agencies become the rationalized para-church secondary societies that are supported and joined by individuals. And so one's rootedness in a nuclear congregation is as tenuous as one's participation in a nuclear family, which one leaves when one has outgrown it. Loyalty to tradition and denomination grows more tenuous.

Mennonites, however, meant something different when they said "Believers Church." Though one must ultimately meet God "outside" the nurturing ethos, one is there called to incarnate the rule of God (kingdom ethics) in the same or in some other concrete community. For them, the sacred canopy was intact. It sheltered what God intended: a holy people that was more than the sum of its parts, for Jesus Christ was "the chief cornerstone" and its head. Those other communities that shared their larger history formed a larger body and provided a richer identity. From there, one could stretch "out" to other Christians by first stretching "up," transcending localism by keeping one's feet firmly in one's own tradition.

---

3. The actual birthdate of Daniel J. Crosby. –WMJ.

The Anabaptist Confessional Tradition

According to the preamble, the Anabaptist confessional tradition "provides the theological center for teaching and learning at the college." Again, there are very different ways to read these words. The modern reading assumes that a systematic set of literally true principles provides the foundation for rationalizing the efforts of all those who unite to serve a particular function. These are very like the axioms and postulates that underlie the geometry book and of which the whole book is an unfolding. For early moderns, these foundational principles were elaborately systematized theological statements and the creeds that lie behind them.

As in the sciences, there was an inherent drive within this worldview to reduce these statements to the most basic and most abstract principles from which the whole series derives. And so there was a transition, for example, from *The Institutes* of Calvin to the Thirty-Nine Articles. With the weakening of tradition and its loyalties, this modernity ends with "five fundamentals" or a deliberately vague "Jesus Christ is Lord" to make it possible for moderns to assume that the churches and agencies they join begin with the same like-mindedness.

For Mennonites (and others), "confessional tradition" implies more. Such churches can even sit loosely with "creedalized" formulas. They know that it is easy to assent to them. What is crucial is not merely saying, "Lord, Lord," but incarnating his Lordship in life. Therefore, as the descriptions appended to the guidelines reveal, something like ethics takes the place of creeds. But the lifestyle pointed to is more an ethos than an ethic, and the spirit out of which it emerges may sometimes degenerate.

All that is not to say that orthodox formulations are unimportant. This notion is difficult to understand for moderns who think that theological confessions are "foundational" axioms and postulates. But for Mennonites, as for an earlier Christian world, the foundations were laid in the acts of God—in events, and supremely in the event of Jesus Christ—that continued in the shaping of the lives of those who lived by his spirit. Doctrinal formulations were "confessions" that pointed truly to what could not literally be said. And they were regulative in the sense that they fenced ways of acting in the foundation that was Jesus Christ.[4]

What the Anabaptists added to these parameters was the insistence that all Christians could be "elect," living "in holy community" while

---

4. This expression is fascinatingly similar to the rabbinical ideal of fencing around the law. –WMJ.

pursuing normal vocations. This insistence necessarily resulted in different ecclesiological emphases. In contrast, modernity changed "confessions" into foundationalist rationalisms at the same time it reduced community to secondary associations. Modern apologists then legitimated the secularized structures by "baptizing" its initial assumptions ("all truths are God's truths"). And just as modern philosophers tried to ground foundational principles in either idealist rationalisms or empirical generalizations, so Christian apologists tried to ground the church's sets of principles in analogous rationalisms or "evidences."

The guidelines ask us to affirm the Apostles Creed, but it is not all clear whether it is meant to function as the almost most ancient "confession" or as a primitive (and therefore, a "least common denominator") rendering of foundational principles. The choice of this credo points to the first possibility, for it outlines a story, not the minimalist set of abstractions that always seem most appropriate to moderns.

The "Guide for Faith and Life."

There are also two possible interpretations in the affirmation that the Bible is "the infallible Word of God and the authoritative Guide for the faith and life of Christian discipleship." The second phrase points to a long tradition in which the Scriptures as a narrative whole embodies the structures that are to shape the people of God and that teaches by what they live and for what they hope. The first phrase is the one that derives from the modern view that makes Scriptures into the source of axioms and postulates and that hopes to validate the Scriptures as the source of these by showing it to be factually accurate. Words like "inerrant" and "infallible" are shibboleths for modernist conservatives.

"Professional Qualifications"

The fact that "professional" is the qualifier makes it clear that what follows will entirely reflect the modern functionalist perspective. What "credentials" communicates is the promise that a candidate has been thoroughly indoctrinated in the assumptions and subsequent procedures of that abstraction from a once-concrete reality that delineates her or his function as determined by the (equally brainwashed?) like-minded co-practiners who have also chosen that specialty. From the other perspective, this misses the most important point. For it, the spiritual insight that is the product and gift of a life shaped by obedience to Jesus Christ is a wisdom that knows how to fit the parts of life into a greater whole. And this is more important that mere aspectual competencies.

Ironically, the *Ph* in PhD originally made the same point. A "Master" could be counted on to be fully competent in a subject area. What merited the title of "Philosopher" was proof of the capacity to "see through" the subject matter, both in terms of the history of its development and how it was to be subordinated to larger purposes. By now, it too often means merely that the candidate is, however briefly, at some tiny point on a narrow front's leading edge.

The "Particular and Universal Mission" of the College

Modernity is embarrassed by particularity and by concreteness. Even in allowing Fresno Pacific College to equip the Mennonite Brethren "in particular," it assumes that we will be equipping them to be a Christian "presence" and a "missionary" in a secularized world while, on Sundays, they may "meet their spiritual needs" in Mennonite Brethren congregations. If they are trained for "full-time Christian work," it is assumed that this will take place in the context of churchly or para-churchly agencies that specialize in functional "ministries." In either case loyalty to particular traditions will be downplayed. From this point of view, the ideal Christian college will be nondenominational and serve the "universal" church.

One may note that there is an option that no reading of this section can yield. We have chosen not to be the kind of denominational college that exists "of, by, and for" its own particular tradition and that demands that all of its teachers adhere fully to that tradition. But it is possible to read "in particular" as the mandate to work at incarnating the kingdom in real communities. That is, it is our "particular" task to equip the Mennonite Brethren for a particular Mennonite Brethren peoplehood. And Fresno Pacific College's universal mission is to help Baptists and Pentecostals and Methodists and Catholics to return to their own particular traditions as disciples of Jesus Christ.[5]

Since any one historical tradition tends to become insular, we have asserted that it is good for us as Mennonite Brethren to have Catholics

---

5. This is the vision of page 2, paragraph 2 of the December 9, 1987, report, *supra*.

and Methodists and Pentecostals and Baptists as students and as staff. When all of us are faithful to our own historical traditions, then we can teach each other what our own particularities need to know but that we might not otherwise notice. Nor will we seek for a minimalist credo to define our like-mindedness. We will rather insist that each of us be active in our own churches and "confess" the rich and distinctive ways that we have built on the foundation of Jesus Christ. And, worshipping together, we testify to God's universal rule by both affirming our participation and being stretched beyond them.

Conclusions

I have lived with both points of view. Modernity has brought gifts that I cannot simply abandon. And my past has taught me that the promise of Godly concreteness *is* the good news, though I know that we cannot return to the rural condition that was the vessel for this treasure. Neither can I simply remain where modernity would have us. "Liberals" and "conservatives" who assume the inevitability of the modernist continuum urge us to move either to the right or to the left along it. But accepting that continuum is to be captive to the spirit of this age. What is now needed is to get off it. Modernity has ceased to be unalloyed good news. And I am sure that what is now needed is a more-than-modern way to accept what is good from modernity and the power to lift us to braver universalism. Anything less is not the gospel, and earlier forms of incarnation are essential to help us to understand what this will mean. In this way, our traditions will fulfill themselves on other levels. But they cannot help us if we deny that God continues to work with and through them. In asserting this ecumenicity, I align myself with many others from many traditions who are coming to the same conclusions. And I differentiate myself from many, even Mennonites and Evangelicals, who wish to abandon or "absolutize" particular pasts, even from those who wish to make "Anabaptist" or "orthodox" distinctives into universal recipes for secularized societies.

This differentiation also means that "percentages," however necessary, are inadequate in themselves to guarantee that Fresno Pacific College will continue to serve the Mennonite Brethren or any other churches. In the past, it was possible to assume that most "ethnic" Mennonite Brethren would have absorbed its ethos "into their bones," whether or not they had ever thought much about what it meant. "Good judgment" for how "whole" contexts worked and an instinct for when sternness or charity was appropriate "came with the territory." That can no longer be assumed. Of course a denominational church must insist that "its own" should represent them and shape the dominant tone of its own institutions, but it is no longer true that "its own" automatically understand the tradition. In fact, many a Swede or Presbyterian (etc.) understands the present sterility of modernity and the importance of concreteness better than do some of "us." Brilliantly accredited Mennonite Brethren may not automatically rate as "qualified." Choosing shepherds is a delicate task, especially for transitional times like these. We would do well to stop our searches until we are more sure than we are now what it is that counts as the qualities we require. It is all too possible that we could end with the hirelings that modernity prefers.

But I do not think that we are all that far from a basic consensus. The fruit of long wrestling with what it means to learn and to teach tends to move us beyond segregated contents and abstracted specialties. In our own spheres of competence, we are learning to move toward wholeness. But perhaps we have not yet generalized our own "breakthroughs" into a critique of the established patterns of modern higher education and presuppositions of our Western culture. Many of us have begun to speak of "story" as something far more central to "being" than is allowed for in the modernist reduction of narrative to "mere illustration." Elements of a "post-modern" view are all around us. We need to acknowledge this reality and to begin to pull them together. And I think that what I have tried to describe as a "Mennonite" sense of the quality of a holy community is also a description of the respect for truth and for each other that is at the heart of the educational process. The conditions of a liberating education turn out to converge with what is built upon the foundation of Jesus Christ, who in being the way and the life also turns out to be the truth.

18

My Saga: "In" and "Out"[1]

SEVERAL MONTHS AGO I realized that the historical context that I thought necessary might bore my grandchildren before they got to stories I was writing about my life. Then, one morning, I woke up thinking about In and Out, who were skunk twins in a joke that I read a very long time ago. Though I had never thought it to be a very clever joke, I decided that it should become my introduction.

The joke is built around a pun. Because In wanted so much to feel "in," he never went far from their hole unless he held his mommy's hand. One morning he was so bored with the same old skunk toys around the same old skunk hole that he decided to take a short walk into the forest. Of course, he quickly got lost. His mother was so worried that she asked Out, who loved to explore and who knew every trail, to go look for him. In a very short time, Out came back, leading his tired and scared brother. "How did you find In so quickly," asked his relieved mother? "Oh," said Out, "it was easy. In-stinkt."

I have only a few memories of the first time that I strayed sharply from the ethos of the Bessie Mennonite Brethren purity code that defined what was "in" and "out." My sin was not the result of rebellion or of bad ethics. At six years of age, I may have been capable of tantrums, but I was not rejecting parental authority, and I knew nothing about ethics. Yet there I was, stubbornly turning the corner with the rest of the first grade on the way to Cordell's small theater for a free movie. The teacher knew that my parents had instructed me to leave the class at that corner and

---

[1]. A version of this narrative was delivered to Senior Professionals on February 8, 2011.

to march alone across the street and home. What could she do when I insisted that it was alright?

My second memory is of a scene in the movie of pirates attacking a ship and of bodies falling out of the rigging, falling and twisting in the air, no doubt, right through the water and straight down all the way to hell. I had the sense that I too was falling with them.

Knowing that I fiercely wanted roller skates for Christmas, my parents offered two punishments for disobeying and going to the movies. I could choose a spanking or I could give up the hope of skates. I cherished those skates for a long time, but my *Schinka* paid for them with the spanking of its life.

My third memory is of crouching into a small closet under the stairs and nursing my conflicted feelings. On the one hand, I knew that I had been justly punished. I had broken my parents' command to come straight home. I had strayed outside the boundaries of the ethos of our small country church. I had "crossed over" to the other side. On the other hand, I was sure that there was something more. Somehow, it was not entirely my fault! And I did think that I had earned those skates!

It took years to figure out how I could be both the guilty sinner and the innocent victim. The Bessie MB community had inherited a code designed both to define good behavior and to set us apart from "the English," and I fully accepted its rightness and rejoiced in our holiness. Unfortunately, I lived in Cordell, surrounded by "*Englisha*" who had different ideas of what was proper. Every day when I walked to school, I left a home that was an honorary part of the geography of the Bessie MB holiness code and crossed the invisible boundary that marked the geography of the ethos that ruled Cordell's Jefferson Grade School.

At six years of age. I was happy to be defined by the MB code. I had wanted to fit securely within it. During my first two or three months in school, I had continued to do what the Bessie MB community taught me to do—to conform to its ethos. What else could I do? While turning that corner I had remained the good, conforming boy they wanted me to be. The devil did not make me do it. It was Mennonite Brethren training and my childish acceptance of its underlying logic that drove me around that corner. I do not think that I wanted to see the movie. I mostly wanted to belong, not to "stick out." Going around that corner, I was driven by fear, and at that moment, my fear of the dismay of absent Mennos was weaker than fear of the scorn of fellow students pressing around me.[2]

2. On the Sunday after typing this paragraph, I told this story to a young lady in

I have come to think that my fear of being "out" was strengthened by doubt that I had ever been fully "in." My father had met his South Dakota, Hutterish-speaking wife at Tabor College and brought her to his *Plautdietsch* German people. And so, while my church friends spoke Low German until they learned English in one-room country schools, my mother tongue was High German, the language of church and higher culture. While they went home from school to help with chores, I went home to read books.

When I was halfway through grade school, my father became principal of Corn Bible Academy. Though Bessie youth no longer had to invade Corn turf in convoy for protection, it was clear that Bessie lay "on the wrong side of the river." Worse yet, I was a short, chubby, bookish, pious "preacher's kid." My sister came home from school one day crying because she had been assaulted with the taunt, "Your brother reads the dictionary."

Not very many years ago, Bob Vogt grinned at me, "I didn't like you when we were growing up. You were the one my aunts always named when they scolded me, 'Why can't you be more like that nice little Wiens boy?'" During the year when I had gone back to Corn to teach at the academy, Bob's older brother John asked me to go to Gotebo, where he preached on Sunday mornings, to provide the community an evening's entertainment of slides and travel stories. On the way back, the wife of the couple whom he had invited along (one of my half-second cousins) came out of a reverie and began to giggle, progressed to laughing out loud, and ended with near hysterical shrieks, "To think! To think! That *Delbert Wiens* would ever do anything exciting."

What she would not have suspected is that my apparent piety had long masked guilt at not living up to "in" expectations. For example, "Personal Evangelism" was a required course when I was a freshman at Corn Bible Academy, and spiritually "in" students witnessed on street corners in neighboring towns. I might have been bold enough to sing with a group, but my voice had not yet changed. Though I had twice won the prize for "Timely Topics" at countywide 4-H contests, my soul curdled at the thought of delivering a testimony or sermonette to unknown sinners. Once, in desperation, I rolled some tracts in red cellophane, chucking them at Clinton pedestrians from the back seat of our car and ducking

---

our church who commented that growing up in College Community MB Church had taught her that she should feel guilty if she did not "stick out."

lest those targeted might try to see where they came from when I was fairly sure that my parents were distracted enough not to notice.

I had known what it was like to live "on the border" among the "English" in Cordell and later among the half-strangers of Corn. As a first year student at Corn Bible Academy, my bookishness was less of a social handicap. Students from up to a hundred miles away were housed at the academy, and some of them were also serious students, like Mary's brothers Malcolm and Vernon. In this setting, even some of my Corn Grade School classmates now seemed to be more like me than I had guessed. I did not want to leave Corn when my father agreed to become the principal of Immanuel Academy. I was beginning to belong, and dreaded to be again the outsider in communities owned by others.

To live in Corn had often been painful, but I now believe that it was a very good time for me to leave, and so I have decided to be grateful. I had lived in Corn long enough to have learned beginning steps of the intricate folk dance that every ethos creates while becoming concrete, and so, by age fifteen I had a hunger for the concrete and a desire to explore abstractions; however, I was not yet in rebellion against authority, nor was I an idealistic eighteen-year-old anxious to judge all flawed concretions against impossibly pure ideals.

I have also become grateful for Reedley, though I hated San Joaquin-style fieldwork. Asking for a job was almost as daunting for me as witnessing on a street corner and was exceeded only by mom's displeasure when I did not have one. One summer while between jobs, I found what seemed to me to be the perfect retort in a story I was reading. The hungry writer heard a knock at the door of his San Francisco garret. "I knew it wasn't opportunity knocking. Opportunity knocked once before, but I was out looking for a job."[3] I am still sure that Saroyan had uttered a profound half-truth, and I took it to heart, but my mother was not amused.

I have also been grateful for Immanuel, where I was greeted as an "Okie" whose relation to the principal made him suspect as a potential tattletale. By the end of the sophomore year, I had gone through a growth spurt that must have added nearly six inches to my height while I remained almost exactly the same weight. When I let my hair grow, my cowlick became a respectable wave, and I began to fantasize about becoming handsome. Unfortunately, my junior year was tormented by uncertainty whether my vocal cords would break or squeak during roll

---

3. This was Delbert's recollection of reading a short story by William Saroyan in his youth. We have been unable to identify the title of the piece. –DJC.

calls. Though I knew that I was not at the center of any of the important friendship groups in the school, I could count on their charity that accepted my presence along their porous boundaries.

It was the sensitivities of the teacher who taught psychology that threatened to undermine my hopes. He was the first to bring the marvels of "intelligence testing" to Immanuel High School. In a subsequent counseling session, he assured me that my score was at least a moderately "high average," but it was clear to him that it did not correspond to my grades. I was an "over-achiever," and it would be better for me to relax, to "accept myself," and to learn to get more fun out of life.

He must have pitied my lack of social graces, but his "liberal" assurance of my need to "adjust" to what I feared was mediocrity depressed me for weeks and was remembered during later discouragements. We students admired Arthur Wiebe, and so I clung to the hope that he offered a group of us one day during a sidewalk discussion about college. Responding to a question about "what it took," he insisted that anyone with an IQ of 110 can earn a PhD. Of my teachers there, he and the psychologist reached that degree.

I think I was five years old when I knew that I would attend Tabor College. Since I always had high aspirations, it is hard to explain why I arrived in Hillsboro with no clear notions to what I should aspire, and so I was shocked that the first official stop along the registration line was a faculty member sitting behind a desk and asking each of us in turn what would be our major. To make things worse, it became clear from the confident answers of those ahead of me that I was the only one there who had not run away from opportunity by looking for a future. Two lads in front of me had given identical answers, and I realized, after passing the desk, that I also had said "premed."

After two years, I transferred to Fresno State College so that I could quietly change my major and save money by living at home. Now cold sober, I took a catalog and methodically plowed through descriptions of all the courses offered in each field while asking, "Can I endure taking the required number of courses in this major?" When I got to the last page, and every answer had been "No!" I turned over the catalog and began again at the beginning, now asking, "Which 'no' was the weakest?" I had become an English literature major. When I was forced to specify what I would do with it, I became a would-be teacher of high-school English and had periodically to confront a puzzled advisor who asked if I was still intending to teach secondary-school English. I would admit it, and she would respond, "But, Mister Wiens, you aren't taking some of the required courses." "I know that," I would say. "Why aren't you taking them?" she would ask, and I would miserably respond, "I don't like them."

By my senior year I realized that I could become a mere English major and enjoy elegantly expressed ideas in essays, kibitz on the relationships described in fiction, and appreciate the power of poetry to stimulate the imagination and excite insight. I also decided to choose professors with a reputation for being interesting and then pick from among their courses the ones that suited my schedule. Like my Immanuel teacher, a psychology professor seemed to be far more sure than I what should be my future, and he called me to his office to explain at length why I should become a fireman.

I also chose to take an ethnology course from an Army Reserve officer. I do not think I had heard of his profane scorn of Christian missionaries who messed up the "happy heathen." Though some of his gibes were aimed at me, I felt most sorry for Henry Krahn, who was taking the course as part of his PBI program to become a missionary. After one snide harangue, the professor huffed, "Well, I guess I shouldn't talk like this. Ha! Ha! Ha! There may be someone in this room who plans to be a missionary."

I got my reward while walking to the stands for the graduation ceremonies. He spoke first, "Damn you, Wiens. I was *not* going to give you an A, but your final exam was so good I had to!" Perhaps it was literature courses, like the one on Chaucer taught by Earl Lyons, who could link obscure medieval tales to unexpected ranges of human experience that had helped me to learn how to turn even desperate guesses into cogent paragraphs under the pressure of essay exams.

I graduated, but I was still so wholly "at sea" what I should make of my life that I was grateful that the need for soldiers in Korea gave me cover for not having to choose. I had applied to Mennonite Central Committee and had been accepted to a Voluntary Service orientation at Akron. The Fresno County Draft Board had not yet fully worked out how to handle conscientious objectors, and I forced their hand when I volunteered to be drafted into alternative service.

Akron was wonderful for me. There were perhaps a handful of us MBs among the dominant OMs and GCs, but even that was an advantage. The term "Affirmative Action" had probably not yet been invented, but it partly applied to me. My father had begun a long string of terms on the MB Board of Reference and Counsel, and I assumed that there were two reasons why I was given some attention. P. C. Hiebert, who had been a guest in our home, was the chairman of the board of MCC, but they needed to groom some more to stand between the dominant Mennonite groups and to represent the many smaller ones. They were also anxious to help convert MBs to the Anabaptist Vision, and I was, and remain, a willing student.

I was asked, therefore, to remain in Akron after orientation to Voluntary Service and was assigned to be the most junior member of the office of I-W services, where I was put to the task of trying to help conscientious objectors to organize into units that fostered educational and spiritual aspirations, especially for those from conservative Mennonite communities so traditional that few of their youth had attended college or even high school and who often took advantage of their temporary escape from the home ethos to explore "worldly pleasures," or at least to ignore taken-for-granted expectations.

My "inside" but "back-row" seat at important meetings with officials like General Hershey and with leading churchmen sometimes led to disillusion. At what may have been the last of a series of important national conferences on the nature of Christian pacifism, I was deeply troubled at what I considered the use of sneaky parliamentary procedures by which leading Mennonite advocates of "biblical" Anabaptism squelched the waning voices of the "old line" liberal pacifists after having assured them earlier of their right to include a statement of their views in the final report. That was not the only source of doubts about the adequacy of the concept of "nonresistance" to identify the Jesus-way of handling conflict or to serve as the organizing center of discipleship.

I had even been troubled by very important Mennonites who seemed to be very sure that they were ordained to declare the will of God for those who were being taught nonresistance. Thus, Orie O. Miller abruptly announced, "Delbert, God wants you to go to Vietnam." I had been hoping that God wanted me in Germany, and I wished devoutly that it had been God who had spoken to me instead of Orie because, as I muttered to myself, "With God it would be possible to argue." On one flight, Orie did confide in me some personal perplexities, and I continue to honor the incredible accomplishments and insights of men like Miller and Bender. Without their wider Christian vision, my life might have been very different.

We MBs centered discipleship around evangelism, but a conference with the head of the Mission Board that had a near monopoly of the evangelical Protestant presence in Vietnam left me marveling at the logic of heavenly bookkeeping to which that emphasis could lead. The heavy and monotonous rhetoric with which it was expounded during the hasty meeting that Miller and William Snyder had arranged in New York did not help. "We of the Christian Missionary Alliance have not engaged in institutional work since we have discovered that the cost per soul of institutional evangelism is greater than the cost per soul of direct evangelism." He must have been very uncomfortable. North Vietnamese members of their churches were also fleeing south, and he had to welcome our desire to work with their missionaries and their churches to assist them.

With a few quiet words to important people, Miller could move even mountains of Washington bureaucracy. I barely had time to figure out the location and importance of Vietnam before a passport and visa arrived, and I was on a plane going west and then farther west after a five-day stop in Reedley. One purpose of the growing up stories I have told is to help you to believe that I was both blessed and cursed with the reality of being always both "in" and "out" and with the habit of sniffing out ironies.[4]

In August of 1954, I was far too young (barely twenty-three) and inexperienced to organize an appropriate niche for MCC's assistance to the hundreds of thousands of refugees to the southern part of a country that had experienced a long war of liberation from French control and which had been divided into a "communist" North and a "democratic" South scarcely two months prior to my arrival.

French bureaucrats were frantically handing over governance to their Vietnamese staff and arriving American bureaucrats were figuring out how to cloak their growing superintendence of a "democracy" presided over by a member of an important, aristocratic Vietnamese family from central Vietnam whom J. Foster Dulles had plucked from a New Jersey monastery a month before I arrived. I soon learned that only a small minority of the refugees had any clear idea why their lives were being torn apart. Most of them were village peasants whose parish priests had heeded the order of higher-ups to bring their flock to a northern port so that the US Navy could transport them south. They

---

4. My bedroom in Corn was also the guest room, and I was moved to the couch while visiting church leaders would sit around the dining room table. I learned that if I shifted around restlessly before turning over, relaxing, and changing my rate of breathing, the conversations moved swiftly to the reasons for the meeting and might include churchly and ministerial scandal. What I later remembered was the seriousness of their efforts to work at reconciliation, not any of the details.

were pawns of the international and religious politics of the Cold War. In that context, relief agencies, even MCC, were treated by the powers that be as the "enablers" who would help the refugees to reestablish their lives and to symbolize the humanitarian face of the free world in a huge propaganda campaign to counter communism. I was once again a minor participant-observer, this time watching how the sausage of international politics was ground out.

Since intact villages of northern peasants could quickly be fitted onto newly available, productive land in the south, it made sense for MCC and Church World Service to focus on the individuals, whether or not Christians, who had better understood the dangers they would face under the communistic, nationalistic zealots who were taking over North Vietnam. "In the name of Christ," MCC was responding to genuine human need, and it was probably better to be naïve than sophisticated about all the tangled motives that were coming into play in the chaos that was South Vietnam. I did not then know about things like culture shock or worldview shifts. I merely stumbled into them.

I almost did not survive the first chaotic months. The senior missionary with whom I lived was the field treasurer, and he was still shaken by his arrest, a month or two before I arrived, when he was "caught" exchanging the mission's funds on the black market. When I later expressed my judgmental shock at this to a Mennonite "old-China hand," he merely smiled and asked me how I thought the MB Mission Board had financed our China fields. Indeed, I learned that official money markets mostly expressed a different kind of immorality.

I also endured the shock of dangers to my life and comfort. The first night I was there, a gun battle erupted around the house, and the next morning we admired splintered woodwork with embedded shells inside the house and the casings that littered the yard. I knew that my "heretical" Mennonite presence added to my host's traumas, and I was not surprised that I was given an ultimatum to depart before two months had passed. Unfortunately, I could find no place to live. I enlisted Americans in the Embassy, French agents, missionaries, and locals to help me, and one person finally suggested a hotel in neighboring Cholon. I wandered down its hall trying to figure out the strange reception I got until I finally realized that I had been sent to what was, essentially, a whorehouse. When I told them, the missionaries relented and let me stay a bit longer. Later, I was very near sleeping on the street when someone relayed a tip that a half-crazy old French colonial was desperate enough to rent out a room in his small house.

About eight months after arriving, the South Vietnamese Army attacked, and defeated, the Saigon police, whose "warlord" general and priest had created a religion, a government, and a substantial army for his river bandits who had been actively helped by the French and the Americans so long as they fought nationalist and communist rebels. Several years earlier they had bought the police, customs, and Saigon post office, "concessions" from the emperor who was enjoying life on the French Riviera. In addition to listening to bullets winging overhead while rescuing families of the translator for Church World Service, I went to sleep a night or two watching tracer bullets streaking above the house.

I quickly overcame one minor Corn/Bessie, and MCC taboo. It seemed entirely presumptuous for someone so "small beer" as I either to make a righteous scene by requesting a soft drink when a champagne toast was called for by the ethos of international diplomacy or merely to pretend to take a sip when the president's health and welfare was being wished. When seated directly across from the president and next to the Italian ambassador's wife at an official dinner, I was worried about making a more serious *faux pas*.

Though I could fudge on minor issues when there were good reasons, I was a stickler on major ones. I was so sure that I should avoid "corruption" that I was mostly successful at avoiding even the thought that a long-awaited signature could have been expedited. But when is "bribery" wrong? I had to do a lot of rationalizing while keeping formally pure. I learned to send my wonderfully wise, competent, and very Christian Vietnamese assistant to secure important permissions and assistance, and I carefully declined to ask how he succeeded when I had not.

One example of a genuine crisis emerged when I became the point of contact for the Geneva office of the World Council of Churches, and they responded to the plea of a Swiss Brethren missionary to alleviate starvation in an outlying section of southern Laos. I was sent a significant amount of money to buy rice for them.

My meetings with the local governor in south Laos to negotiate the purchase of low-cost rice available in government warehouses moved from cordiality to threats when I made it clear that I could not just give him the money and let him oversee the distribution. When I finally suggested that it would be unfortunate to have to pay a much higher price for black market Thailand rice piled high on the bank of the Mekong River (halfway between visible police and custom posts), he angrily threatened to send his army and police to stop me if I persisted.

I was both exhilarated and scared, but that is what we did, using a truck so far as it could manage bad roads, shuttling the one hundred kilo bags of rice to the banks of a river in Jeeps, and loading them into a fleet of dugout canoes so loaded that I amused myself pretending that I needed to breathe evenly in both nostrils lest we tip into the river.

The missionary later mentioned that such officials got no salary. He may even have paid for the privilege, or the necessity, of skimming off enough to secure a living and to "serve his country"—and himself. Of course, I had to rationalize the probability that I had "inadvertently" made possible his percentage on the black market rice I had bought.

I have finally learned that many cultures believe that the concrete logic of relationships undergirds a morality of assistance to those with whom there are special ties and that this supersedes the logic of abstract justice that governs our own condemnation of the way they "misuse" our aid. And so I was amused at the irony that the first outright "bribe" I paid was five dollars to get my scooter across fifty feet of bare land between the freighter on which I had traveled to Sri Lanka on my way home and the shed in which its presence would miraculously become legal. After all, it would have been immoral to trouble the captain with an unwanted scooter.

Besides the anxieties involved in mere survival were the greater anxieties of responsibility for others. My greatest sin in this confession is to be unable to do justice to the wonderful MCCers who did the real work in the distributions and who built a jungle hospital in the face of apparently insuperable obstacles. I frequently had to cope with my resentment at MCC's willingness to send people when they did not have the resources needed to sustain our morale and ministry.

When I took over Church World Service projects, I also became the chief of a resettlement project in the jungle alongside the road to Dalat that their initial short-term director had begun for Protestant and other refugees who did not have the organizational advantages of Catholic villagers led by parish priests. The clash of cultural expectations became acute as my "wards" waited to ascertain what I "really" wanted while I tried desperately to convince them that I wanted them to govern themselves in the way that made sense to them. But it was not simple. What was I to do when the most competent of my elders grabbed a large kitchen knife and chased another through the village?

Also troubling were the shocks to my spiritual sensibilities. There were missionaries in Vietnam who were wonderful, especially those in the plateau and mountains in the part of the country that had become the center of our efforts. I wished that my profane teacher of ethnology could have accompanied a trek into the deeper jungle that had just become sufficiently cleared of communist guerillas that missionaries could visit Christian villages that had been off limits for years. It was the time of year after the harvest that the surplus grain was adequate to keep entire villages drunk for up to a month. In striking contrast, the Christian villages were clean, the children were being taught to read, and the citizens stood cheerfully upright.

But I mostly had to deal with some older leaders in the Delta who had learned too much from French colonialists. At an early "underground" meeting with perhaps two dozen native pastors, J. Lawrence Burkholder and I were given a history of the Evangelical Church that so emphasized their deep ambivalence about missionaries that I began to wonder whether I could have told the MB Mission Board that a sufficient guarantee of support might have handed them a substantial ready-made "MB" constituency.

Later, I had several occasions to hone a sermon urging the unity of the body of Christ based on John 17. It hurt that some leading missionaries were trying to undermine us by spreading rumors that American Mennonites were liberal heretics and that I was urging their converts to remain faithful to their church. I also had to face the mysteries of Christian pluralism. For political reasons, I attended the American Congregation led by a missionary whose sermons and style seemed to me to be adequately symbolized by the strawberry Kool-Aid sipped at communion. To receive the spiritual nourishment I desperately needed, I attended the small French Reformed congregation in Saigon served by Pasteur DeLuze who, with his wife, turned out to be Huguenots more spiritual and even more lovingly sacrificial than I could be. They were saints, and they "adopted" me.

Somehow this Bessie/Corn/Reedley MB with Anabaptist polish had become a representative of all American Mennonites, the director of Church World Service's program in South Vietnam (supported by mostly mainline denominations), and a sometime, informal agent for the World Council of Churches. When it was insisted that I should join the elderly French lady who was a schoolteacher, a rubber plantation manager, and a French army colonel on the governing board of the

Saigon French Reformed Church, my resistance was overridden with the pastor's cheerful, "Oh, it does not matter; I run the church like a fascist anyway." Like the song in *Oklahoma!*, "Kansas City," I "had gone about as fur as I could go."

Until I landed in Vietnam, I had little occasion to stray from the MB ethos. My parents were not the sort of legalists who heightened the attractiveness of "wild oats." I also was not tempted by the hypocrisy of the merely "naughty" boys who continued to believe in the rightness of the rules they deliberately broke, though they did have one advantage over me. They could more easily prove that conversion had reformed them when seeking baptism.

I had never heard of "culture shock" or of "worldview shifts," but I did know that I was worn out. I had awakened too early and too often on sheets soaked deeply with my perspiration. Near the end, a Vietnamese layman came to thank me for having honored them by eating what they ate. I had tried to avoid tainted water and uncooked food when I could, but the cost of trying to live with a "missionary stomach" had been frequent bouts of intestinal distress and a nearly five-foot tapeworm. Though one of the leading pastors wept while recounting how our efforts and testimony had deepened their understanding of the gospel, I knew that I was physically and spiritually empty.

I had early come to terms with the fact that "muddling" was inevitable in such a desperate time and place, and I had decided that I would "muddle forward" instead of simply in circles. I knew that our efforts were being applauded; I also knew, with St. Paul, that it was possible to save others while becoming oneself a "castaway." During the last months, I would sometimes stop at the USIS Library and read a month of comic strips in the Paris edition of the *New York Herald Tribune* so that I could face going to the office.

I was grateful that I was "finishing the row," and I knew that I could not stay. I also knew that I could not yet face returning home. I had seen too much. What if churches asked me to give glowing reports on what had been done "in the name of Christ"?

My solution was to take a long time getting home. For a month, I wandered around the decks and lounge of a Danish freighter, reading *From Here to Eternity* and staring over the rail at the flying fishes. I almost got left behind in Djakarta and was very lucky that a guard, who was not there when I wandered out of a small port on Sumatra, did not pursue when I streaked for the boat, ignoring his order to stop.

After getting off the boat in Colombo, I drove my Lambretta scooter north and crossed to Danushkodi, India: "Like entering the United States by parachuting into Death Valley," I read later in a lurid travelogue. After stops in Madaura and Kodaikanal, I had gone up the Malabar Coast on a canal boat and angled up the middle of India toward Hyderabad. Two things were reasonably clear. I was headed home; and I did not want to get there quickly. Yet, I was detouring to Gadwal to visit the MB missionaries in Andhra Pradesh.

I tried not to think about Vietnam and about my ambivalence toward home communities and America. But I could not shut out another fear. For the last week or two, I had begun to be taken for an Indian. My complexion was burned by sun and wind, and at first it amused me that the first response to my requests was the demand, "What caste are you?"

A Mennonite Christian in Gadwal welcomed me generously. He took me into his two-room home and offered a pot of water and a tin can so that I could take a bath. He asked if I was hungry, but I thought I detected a catch in his voice and, thinking of the cucumber, tangerine, piece of stale bread, and old cheese that had been my food for the day, I assured him that I had eaten. The hot coffee he brought was delicious. He had come to this village as an evangelist, supporting himself and his new bride as a tailor.

His cot was moved into the open square for me, and I started to decline since I saw that it was shorter than I, but I remembered in time that I would have to accept. And so twenty or more villagers and several dogs rearranged themselves around the cot and I laid down. For a while, I looked up at a brilliant full moon, and knew that in this strange place I had truly "come home." I smiled back at God and went to sleep.

This event gave me a revelatory metaphor for thinking about my reality, and I later linked it to Matthew 14. Like Peter, I have been placed into the "boat" that is my churchly ethos and into the boats of my natural contexts. Though it is the more or less fixed structure that provides passage across the "chaos" that is life, there are storms that it cannot survive. When all seemed lost, Jesus appeared and Peter realizes that only one who is Lord of both the chaos and of the boat can provide salvation. And so he walks to Jesus on the water. Of course, only very great saints can walk on water for long, and he has to be returned to the boat. Though necessary, the boat cannot save and cannot itself escape the lake to enter Gennesaret, the "Valley of Princes." Only those who have stepped outside it can fully discern the difference between "earthen vessels" and "transcendent treasures" and become, like Peter, its responsible crew.

I quickly learned that the delegation sent a few months earlier by the Mennonite Brethren Board of Foreign Missions to "indigenize" the churches in India had left deep wounds. The missionaries generally understood that "foreigners" could not long continue to exercise formal responsibility for churches becoming numerous and possessing capable leaders. But they also knew that radically renovating old boats while sailing through troubled waters would be traumatic. And I was happy that several of the older missionaries I visited sufficiently trusted my own "crash course" in the ironies involved in building vessels with strange materials for foreign waters that they could share the affronts to their identities that they had suffered.

Four-and-a-half months after leaving Saigon, on January 1, 1958, I boarded a passenger ship in Karachi that also carried much freight below the main deck for a nine- or ten-day trip up the Persian Gulf to Basrah, Iraq. Along with about four hundred Muslim pilgrims and oil field workers, I slept on the deck or, when it rained, with the freight below. Then I shared a very large, empty lower floor breathing foul, smoky air with hundreds of often coughing people crowded together along with the cackling chickens that they barbecued enroute. I am grateful for those who watched over me.

I got home, I think, sometime in March. Perhaps a month later, I went to San Francisco, collected my scooter from another Maersk freighter, and drove it to Reedley. I had my very first flat at the corner of old 99 and Manning. That September, I enrolled at Yale Divinity School. Among my reasons were two alumni in Asia whom I had met and admired and who encouraged me to apply. I also had learned that poor boys should attend rich, expensive schools. I visited the campus after landing in New York and realized that its campus had the monastic serenity that I knew I needed and that its reputation could help me to become a teacher should other ministries among Mennonites be impossible.

I also knew that I had seen too much ecclesiastical "sausage making" among some "evangelicals" and that my nose for irony might help me become more "conservative" than would Dallas or the still brand-new seminary in Fresno. The more I look back over my life, the more I have realized that I have been guided along my haphazard journeying without ever having chosen crucial turns for the "right" reasons. As it turned out, I discovered that I had even been wrong about Yale Divinity

School. The professors could not be confused with Fundamentalists, but there was a deep commitment to the Christian church and a profound respect for its historic doctrinal tradition. Hans Frei and Brevard Childs had just arrived to join others who were seeking to recover the meaning of Scripture and tradition in the context of the very different world—and worlds—from which, and through which Christianity had moved.

I selected the program called "Teaching and Research in Religion" because it allowed me to keep open the most options. As a good MB, I mostly took courses centered in specific biblical books, but I increasingly did so with an interest in how they would be read by their original Hebrew and Gentile readers. I could not forget Paul Minear's advice, "Delbert, remember that reading an epistle is like listening to one end of a telephone conversation. The better you know the person whom you cannot hear, the better you will be able to understand what is being communicated by the one you hear."

Each summer I returned home to work at Kings View Hospital, where I learned that insanity was as likely to manifest itself in hyper-rationalism as in sheer incoherence. Those paranoid enough to believe that everyone intended to destroy them seldom lacked perfectly rational reasons to maintain their delusion. Their logical abilities were not the problem; it was the too-narrow compass of their initial assumptions that betrayed them.

After graduating I returned for a final summer and to await a "call," despite knowing well that I had been too long gone, had attended the wrong school, and was a bachelor. Two weeks before the beginning of the school year, I had a call from an uncomfortable Corn leader. Would I be willing to teach freshman, sophomore, and junior English courses for a year? The pastor at the church had resigned, and their English teacher had agreed to become a one-year interim pastor while the church sought a replacement. He would continue to teach two courses at the academy, and I would fill out my assignment by assisting him. It was very clear that they had not been able to find anyone to teach English at so late a date and that I was not to think of myself as an assistant pastor, or an associate pastor. I would be a part-time assistant to a one-year interim pastor and would received $3,100 for a nine-month appointment. I accepted.

A month or two later, while passing the superintendent in the hall, he abruptly stopped, smiled at me, and asked, "Have you ever wondered why we hired you?" "Constantly," I answered. He grinned, "Come with me." In the office, he handed me the letter of recommendation that had been persuasive. It read, "Dear brethren at Corn. This is to bring Delbert Wiens to your attention. He has just graduated from Yale Divinity School, and we don't know if he's worth a hill of beans anymore; but he is H. R.'s son, and we owe it to him to find out."

The next year I was hired by Tabor College to write publicity pieces and to teach several sections of freshman English. About two weeks before school started, Waldo Hiebert's twin brother, Lando, was killed in an auto accident, and I was informed that I would teach his course in Introduction to Philosophy. "I can't," I insisted. "I've never had a course in it in my life." Wes Prieb was unshaken, "You have taken theology courses, and it is pretty much the same thing." Over three years, I taught more and more philosophy, even for one year teaching half time at Bethel College to cover their philosophy professor's sabbatical. I was still trying to think about MB churches from the standpoint of the older tradition that I had discovered at Corn, and I worked out a sermon at Ebenfeld based on Peter's call to walk on the water. I knew that I had found my purpose when a very bright student who belonged to the early-sixties generation accosted me a couple of day's later. "Wiens," he announced, "now I know why we put up with your attempts to push us back into the church boats. It's because we know that you are telling our parents that it is time for them to step out of them."

Appendices
Bibliography of Delbert L. Wiens' Works

Wiens, Delbert L. "Getting an Education or Becoming Educated." *Christian Leader*, September 4, 1962.
———. "Letter to the Editor." *Christian Leader*, November 11, 1964.
———. "Imitate Their Faith." *Christian Leader*, June 8, 1965.
———. "New Wineskins for Old Wine: A Study of the Mennonite Brethren Church." *Christian Leader*, October 12, 1965.
———. "Light in the Darkness." *Christian Leader*, December 20, 1966.
———. "Darkness in the Light." *Christian Leader*, January 17, 1967.
———. "The Old Wine: Will It Sour? One Man's View of the Future of the Mennonite Church." *Canadian Mennonite*, April 18, 1967.
———. "Brotherhood Must Grow in Maturity." *Mennonite Weekly Review*, June 22, 1967.
———. "A Book Review." *Christian Leader*, September 26, 1967.
———. "An Open Letter to Our Missionaries." *Christian Leader*, July 2, 1968.
———. "Open Letter /2." *Christian Leader*, November 5, 1968.
———. "Exegesis of Romans 5:12-21." *Journal of Church and Society* 5, no. 2 (Fall 1969) 42-54.
———. "Mutual Aid in a Culture of Abundance." *Missionary Messenger*, October 1969.
———. "A Fable for Mennonites." *Christian Leader*, February 10, 1970.
———. "Musonius Rufus and Genuine Education." PhD diss., University of Chicago, 1970.
———. "That I May Know Him: A Meditation of Philippians 3." *Journal of Church and Society* 7, no. 1 (Spring 1971) 46-51.
———. "Work and Worship: The Becoming of the Sons of God." *Direction* 1, no. 4 (October 1972) 122-26.
———. "On Building Towers." *Mennonite Brethren Herald*, December 1, 1972.
———"From the Village to the City: A Grammar for the Languages We Are." *Direction* 2, no. 4 (October 1973-January 1974) 98-149.
———. "The Making of Sages, Philosophers, and Theologians." In *The Seminary Story: Twenty Years of Education in Ministry, 1955-1975*, edited by A. J. Klassen, 99-102. Fresno: Mennonite Brethren Biblical Seminary, 1975.

———. "Window on the Bible: Acts 2:1–13: Introduction." *Christian Leader*, March 16, 1976.

———. "Window on the Bible: Acts 2:1–13: First Question." *Christian Leader*, March 30, 1976.

———. "Window on the Bible: Acts 2:1–13: Second Question." *Christian Leader*, April 13, 1976.

———. "A 'Review of Reviews.'" *Christian Leader*, December 21, 1976.

———. "Window on the Bible: Was the Steward 'Unjust' or 'Clever'?" *Christian Leader*, December 21, 1976.

———. "Window on the Bible: Mirrors: Reflection and Glory." *Christian Leader*, January 4, 1977.

———. "Response to Erwin Penner." *Direction* 6, no. 3 (July 1977) 48–49.

———. "Memories Revived: A Review of *Come Let Us Stand United: A History of Corn Bible Academy, 1902–1977* by Vernon R. Wiebe." *Christian Leader*, August 16, 1977.

———. "Incarnation and Ideal: The Story of a Truth Becoming Heresy." In *Pilgrims and Strangers: Essays in Mennonite Brethren History*, edited by Paul Toews, 28–51. Fresno: Center for Mennonite Brethren Studies, 1977.

———. "Window on the Bible: Ancient Cosmologies." *Christian Leader*, April 11, 1978.

———. "Window on the Bible: The Greek Globe." *Christian Leader*, April 25, 1978.

———. "Contexts for Education." *Direction* 7, no. 4 (October 1978) 44–49.

———. "The Church and the 'Liberal Arts' after Denver." *Christian Leader*, April 10, 1979.

———. "Review of *Beyond Our Tribal Gods: The Maturing of Faith*, by Ronald Martin." *Mission Focus* 8, no. 1 (March 1980) 17–18.

———. "Mores, Morals, Morale, and Hard Cases or 'Whatever Happened to Consensus.'" *Direction* 9, no. 2 (April 1980) 3–17.

———. "The Author's Reply: Achieving Clarity." *Direction* 9, no. 2 (April 1980) 21–22.

———. "On Not Going Under: Immersion and the Mennonite Brethren Identity Crisis." *Direction* 14, no. 1 (Spring 1985) 14–25.

———. "Perspectives and Interpretations: Cultural Change." *Direction* 14, no. 2 (Fall 1985) 43–49.

———. "The Moralities of the Mennonite Brethren." *Direction* 16, no. 2 (Fall 1987) 29–44.

———. "Philosophy and Mennonite Self-Understanding." In *Mennonite Identity: Historical and Contemporary Responses*, edited by Calvin W. Redekop and Samuel Steiner, 117–35. Lanham: University Press of America, 1988.

———. "Ethos, Ethoi, and Ethics: The Moralities of the Mennonite Brethren." *Conrad Grebel Review* 6, no. 1 (Winter 1988) 45–64.

———. "Theological Response to Ethnicity in the Modern World." *Direction* 17, no. 1 (Spring 1988) 103–17.

———. "Mennonite Brethren: Neither Liberal nor Evangelical." *Direction* 20, no. 1 (Spring 1991) 38–63.

———. "Luke on Pluralism: Flex with History." *Direction* 23, no. 1 (Spring 1994) 44–53.

———. "The 'Christian College' as Heresy." In *Mennonite Idealism and Higher Education: The History of the Fresno Pacific College Idea*, edited by Paul Toews, 43–65. Fresno: Center for Mennonite Brethren Studies, 1995.

———. *Communities: Abstract and Concrete*. VHS. 1996.
———. *Video Recordings of History 120 Lectures at Fresno Pacific University*. 20 VHSs. 1996.
———. "The Questions We Face." *Direction* 26, no. 1 (Spring 1997) 9–15.
———. *Stephen's Sermon and the Structure of Luke-Acts*. North Richland Hills, TX: Scott, 1998.
———. "Deconstructing the Draft Revision of the MB Confession of Faith." *Direction* 27, no. 1 (Spring 1998) 4–13.
———. "Propriety, Purity, and Partnership." *Other Side* 34, no. 3 (May–June 1998) 14–17.
———. "A Confusing Statement." *Christian Leader*, September 1998.
———. "To Politic—or Not." *Christian Leader*, October 1999.

Delbert, So Far: A Chronology

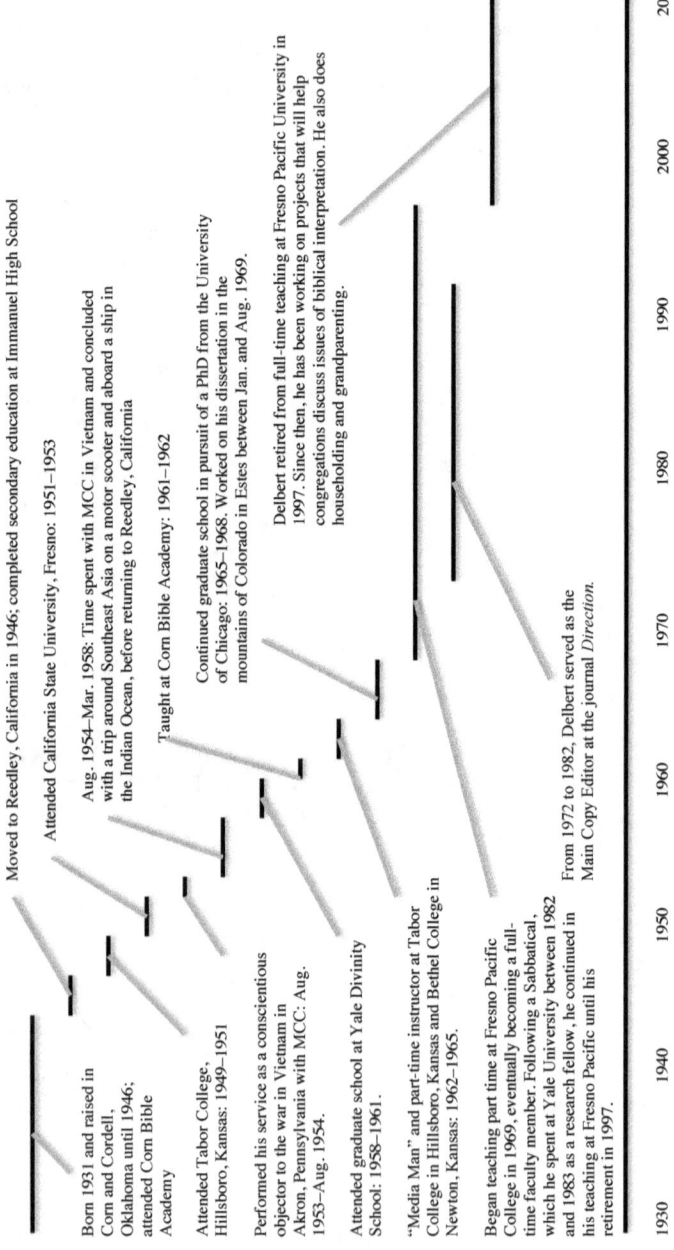

Moved to Reedley, California in 1946; completed secondary education at Immanuel High School

Attended California State University, Fresno: 1951–1953

Aug. 1954–Mar. 1958: Time spent with MCC in Vietnam and concluded with a trip around Southeast Asia on a motor scooter and aboard a ship in the Indian Ocean, before returning to Reedley, California

Taught at Corn Bible Academy: 1961–1962

Continued graduate school in pursuit of a PhD from the University of Chicago: 1965–1968. Worked on his dissertation in the mountains of Colorado in Estes between Jan. and Aug. 1969.

Delbert retired from full-time teaching at Fresno Pacific University in 1997. Since then, he has been working on projects that will help congregations discuss issues of biblical interpretation. He also does householding and grandparenting.

Born 1931 and raised in Corn and Cordell, Oklahoma until 1946; attended Corn Bible Academy

Attended Tabor College, Hillsboro, Kansas: 1949–1951

Performed his service as a conscientious objector to the war in Vietnam in Akron, Pennsylvania with MCC: Aug. 1953–Aug. 1954.

Attended graduate school at Yale Divinity School: 1958–1961.

"Media Man" and part-time instructor at Tabor College in Hillsboro, Kansas and Bethel College in Newton, Kansas: 1962–1965.

Began teaching part time at Fresno Pacific College in 1969, eventually becoming a full-time faculty member. Following a Sabbatical, which he spent at Yale University between 1982 and 1983 as a research fellow, he continued in his teaching at Fresno Pacific until his retirement in 1997.

From 1972 to 1982, Delbert served as the Main Copy Editor at the journal *Direction*.

www.ingramcontent.com/pod-product-compliance
Lightning Source LLC
Chambersburg PA
CBHW050436240426
43661CB00055B/2398